French

Phrasebook

LAROUSSE

Editors
Marie Chochon, Sinda López, Donald Watt

with
Christy Johnson, Val McNulty

Supplement on French language and culture
Valerie Grundy

Publishing manager
Janice McNeillie

Design and typesetting
Sharon McTeir

© Larousse 2006
21, rue du Montparnasse
75283 Paris Cedex 06

ISBN: 2-03-542150-0

Sales: Houghton Mifflin Company, Boston

Achevé d'imprimer en Mai 2006 sur les presses de « La Tipografica Varese S.p.A. » à Varese (Italie)

Introduction

This phrasebook is the ideal companion for your trip. It gets straight to the point, helping you to understand and make yourself understood so that you don't miss a thing. Use it like a dictionary to find the exact word you're looking for right away. And at each word we've provided a selection of key phrases that will help you in any situation, no matter how tricky things may have gotten.

The English–French section contains all those essential expressions that you'll need to get by in France. And because you need to be able to pronounce the words you see on the page properly, we've provided a simple and straightforward phonetic transcription that will enable you to make yourself understood with ease.

The French–English section provides all the most important words and expressions that you might read or hear while on vacation.

And that's not all: we've added practical and cultural tips for getting by, a supplement on French language, life and culture – everything, in fact, to make your trip go as smoothly as possible.

Bon voyage!

Pronunciation

So that you can say what you want to say in French without running any risk of being misunderstood, we have devised a simple and straightforward phonetic transcription to show how every French word or phrase used in this phrasebook is pronounced. This phonetic transcription is shown in brackets after each French word or phrase.

One of the most distinctive things about the way French is pronounced is how some sounds are made through the nose rather than the mouth. In this book we have represented such sounds using the following two symbols:

ON – this is used to show the pronunciation of **on, om, en, em, an** and **am**, plus a few less common combinations. It is similar to the English sound *ong* as in the word *song* but pronounced more through your nose.

> Examples: **pont** [pON], **nombre** [nONbr], **enveloppe** [ONvlop], **temps** [tON], **plan** [plON], **ampoule** [ONpool]

AN – this is used to show the pronunciation of **un, um, in, im, ain, aim** and **ein**, plus a few less common combinations. It is similar to the English sound *ang* as in the word *bang* but pronounced more through your nose.

> Examples: **commun** [komAN], **parfum** [parfAN], **matin** [matAN], **timbre** [tANbr], **main** [mAN], **faim** [fAN], **plein** [plAN]

Another tricky sound is the French **u** sound, which we represent in this guide by:

U – to make the French *u* sound, you move your mouth into the shape you use to say *oo* in English, but say *ee* instead while your mouth is still in that shape. Note that the sound in French that corresponds to the English *oo* is **ou**.

> Examples: **occupé** [okU-pay] – as opposed to – **ouvert** [oover]

Other unusual sounds for English speakers are:

ey – this is used to represent the pronunciation of -**eil** and -**eille**. It is similar to the English sound *ey* as in *hey* with a short *ee* sound added to the end.

Examples: **appareil** [apa-rey], **oreille** [orey]

eey – this is used to represent the pronunciation of -**ille**. It is similar to the English sound *ee* as in *bee* with a short *y* sound added to the end.

Example: **pastille** [pasteey]

oy – this is used to represent the pronunciation of **euil**. It is similar to the English sound *oy* as in *toy* with a short *y* sound added to the end.

Example: **fauteuil** [fautoy]

uh – this is used to represent the pronunciation of **e**, **eu** and **œ**, plus a few less common combinations. It is similar to the English sound *uh* as in *huh*.

Examples: **le** [luh], **peu** [puh], **cœr** [kuhr]

r – to make the French *r* sound, you move your mouth into the shape you use to say *r* in English, but make your tongue vibrate towards the back of the roof of your mouth.

In devising the phonetic transcription we have used as many standard English sounds as possible, so that the transcription is easy to understand and use. The following list provides further clarification:

> [ay] as in w**ay**
>
> [ee] as in f**ee**
>
> [eh] as in g**e**t
>
> [o] as in h**o**t
>
> [oh] as in c**oa**t
>
> [oo] as in p**oo**l
>
> [sh] as in **sh**op
>
> [tsh] as in ca**tch**
>
> [zh] as in plea**s**ure

Abbreviations

abbr	abbreviation
adj	adjective
adv	adverb
art	article
conj	conjunction
excl	exclamation
f	feminine
m	masculine
n	noun
num	numeral
pl	plural
prep	preposition
pron	pronoun
v	verb

English–French phrasebook

a

able
- to be able to... pouvoir... [poovwar]
- I'm not able to come tonight je ne pourrai pas venir ce soir [zhuh nuh pooray pa vuhneer suh swar]

about environ [ONvee-rON]
- I think I'll stay for about an hour je pense rester une heure environ [zhuh pONs restay Un uhr Onvee-rON]

abroad *(live, travel)* à l'étranger [a laytrON-zhay]
- I've never been abroad before je ne suis jamais parti à l'étranger [zhuh nuh swee zhameh partee a laytrON-zhay]

absolutely tout à fait [toot a fay]
- you're absolutely right vous avez tout à fait raison [vooz avay toot a fay rayzON]

accept accepter [aksep-tay]
- do you accept traveler's checks? est-ce que vous acceptez les travellers ? [eskuh vooz aksep-tay lay travluhr]

access l'accès *m* [akseh]
- is there disabled access? y a-t-il un accès pour handicapés ? [ee ateel AN akseh poor ONdee-kapay]

accident l'accident *m* [aksee-dON]
- there's been an accident il y a eu un accident [eel ya U AN aksee-dON]

according to selon [suhlON]
- it's well worth seeing, according to the guidebook ça vaut vraiment le coup d'être vu, d'après le guide [sa voh vraymON luh koo detr vU dapreh luh geed]

acquaintance la connaissance [koneh-sONs]
- delighted to make your acquaintance ravi de faire votre connaissance ! [ravee duh fehr votr koneh-sONs]

address *(details of place)* l'adresse *f* [adres] ♦ *(speak to)* s'adresser à [sadre-say a]
- could you write down the address for me? est-ce que vous pouvez m'écrire l'adresse ? [es-kuh voo poovay maykreer ladres]
- here is my address and phone number, if you're ever in the United States voilà mes coordonnées aux États-Unis, si vous passez un jour [vwala may koh-ordo-nay ohz aytaz-Unee see voo pasay AN zhoor] ▶ see box on p. 2

adult l'adulte *mf* [adUlt]
- two adults and one student, please deux adultes, un étudiant, s'il vous plaît [duhz adUlt AN aytU-dyON seel voo play]

addressing people

When you're meeting another adult for the first time, you should use the *vous* form instead of the *tu* form, even though you are talking to only one person, e.g. *comment allez-vous ?* (how are you?). You should use this form when you speak to older people, strangers, in professional situations, etc. The *tu* form is only to be used with your family and close friends (people you call by their first name), e.g. *qu'est-ce que tu fais ce soir ?* (what are you doing tonight?). If in doubt, use the *vous* form, to be on the safe side.

advance *(money)* l'avance *f* [avONs] ✦ **in advance** *(pay, reserve)* à l'avance [a lavONs]
▸ do you have to book in advance? **est-ce qu'il faut réserver à l'avance ?** [es-keel foh rayzer-vay a lavONs]

after après [apreh]
▸ it's twenty after eight **il est huit heures vingt** [eel eh weet uhr vAN]
▸ the stadium is just after the traffic lights **le stade est juste après le feu** [luh stad eh zhUst apreh luh fuh]

afternoon l'après-midi *m* [apreh-meedee]
▸ the museum is open in the afternoons **le musée est ouvert l'après-midi** [luh mUzay eht oover lapreh-meedee]

aftershave l'après-rasage *m* [apreh-razazh]
▸ a bottle of aftershave **un flacon d'après-rasage** [AN flakON dapreh-razazh]

afterwards après [apreh]
▸ join us afterwards **rejoins-nous après** [ruh-zhwAN-nooz apreh]

again encore [ONkor], à nouveau [a noovoh]
▸ the train is late again **le train est à nouveau retardé** [luh trAN eht a noovoh ruhtar-day]

age l'âge *m* [azh] ✦ **ages** l'éternité *f* [aytehr-neetay]
▸ we've been waiting for ages! **ça fait une éternité qu'on attend !** [sa feht Un aytehr-neetay kON atON]
▸ what ages are your children? **quel âge ont vos enfants ?** [kel azh ON vohs ONfON]

agency l'agence *f* [azhONs]
▸ contact the agency if there's a problem **contactez l'agence en cas de problème** [kONtak-tay lazhONs ON kah duh problem]

ago
▸ I've been before, several years ago **je suis déjà venu il y a plusieurs années** [zhuh swee dayzha vuhnU eel ya plUzyuhr zanay]

agreement l'accord *m* [akor]
▸ we need to come to some agreement about where we're going next **il faut**

agreement/disagreement

▶ absolutely! absolument ! [abso-lUmON]
▶ that's fine by me pas de problème [pah duh problem]
▶ you're right vous avez raison [vooz avay rayzON]
▶ go on, then bon, d'accord [bON dakor]
▶ I'm not at all convinced je ne suis pas convaincu [zhuh nuh swee pah kONvAN-kU]
▶ I disagree je ne suis pas d'accord [zhuh nuh swee pa dakor]

qu'on se mette d'accord sur notre destination d'après [eel foh kON suh met dakor sUr notr destee-nasyON dapreh]

ahead devant [duhvON]
▶ is the road ahead clear? est-ce que la route est dégagée devant nous ? [eskuh la root eh dayga-zhay duhvON noo]

air *(wind)* l'air *m* [ehr]
▶ the air is much fresher in the mountains l'air est beaucoup plus frais en montagne [lehr eh bohkoo plU fray ON mONtan-yuh]

air-conditioning la climatisation [kleema-teeza-syON]
▶ do you have air-conditioning? y a-t-il l'air conditionné ? [ee a-teel lehr kONdee-syonay]

airline la compagnie d'aviation [kONpan-yee davya-syON]
▶ which airline are you traveling with? vous voyagez sur quelle compagnie ? [voo vwa-yazhay sUr kel kONpan-yee]

airmail [par avyON]
▶ I'd like to send it airmail je voudrais l'envoyer par avion [zuh voodreh lONvwa-yay par avyON]

airport l'aéroport *m* [a-ayro-por]
▶ how long does it take to get to the airport? combien de temps faut-il pour aller à l'aéroport ? [kONbyAN duh tON foh-teel poor alay a la-ayro-por]

at the airport

▶ where is gate number 2? où se trouve la porte deux ? [oo suh troov la port duh]
▶ where is the check-in desk? où dois-je enregistrer mes bagages ? [oo dwahzh ONruh-zheestray may bagazh]
▶ I'd like an aisle seat je voudrais une place côté couloir [zhuh voodreh Un plas kohtay koolwar]
▶ where is the baggage claim? où dois-je aller récupérer mes bagages ? [oo dwazh alay raykU-payray may bagazh]

airport shuttle la navette pour l'aéroport [navet poor la-ayro-por]
  ▸ is there an airport shuttle? est-ce qu'il y a une navette pour l'aéroport ? [es-keel ya Un navet poor la-ayro-por]

air pressure la pression (de l'air) [presyON (duh lehr)]
  ▸ could you check the air pressure in the tires? pourriez-vous vérifier la pression des pneus ? [pooryay-voo vayree-fyay la presyON day pnuh]

airsick malade en avion [malad on avyON]
  ▸ she's airsick elle a le mal de l'air [el a luh mal duh lehr]

aisle *(on plane)* le couloir [koolwar]
  ▸ two seats, please: one window and one aisle deux places, s'il vous plaît : une fenêtre et une couloir [duh plas seel voo play Un fuhnetr ay Un koolwar]

aisle seat la place côté couloir [plas kohtay koolwar]
  ▸ I'd like an aisle seat je voudrais une place côté couloir [zhuh voodreh Un plas kohtay koolwar]

alarm (clock) le réveil [rayvey]
  ▸ I set the alarm for nine o'clock j'ai mis le réveil à neuf heures [zhay mee luh rayvey a nuhv uhr]

alcohol l'alcool *m* [alkol]
  ▸ I don't drink alcohol je ne bois pas d'alcool [zhuh nuh bwah pa dalkol]

alcohol-free sans alcool [sONz alkol]
  ▸ what kind of alcohol-free drinks do you have? qu'est-ce que vous avez comme boissons sans alcool ? [kes-kuh vooz avay kom bwasON sONz alkol]

all *(the whole amount)* tout [too]; *(everybody)* tous [too]
  ▸ all the time tout le temps [too luh tON]
  ▸ all English people tous les Anglais [toolayz ONglay]
  ▸ will that be all? ce sera tout ? [suh suhra too]

allergic allergique [aler-zheek]
  ▸ I'm allergic to aspirin/nuts/wheat/dairy products je suis allergique à l'aspirine/ aux noix/au blé/aux produits laitiers [zhuh sweez aler-zheek a laspee-reen/oh nwah/ oh prodwee laytyay]

allow autoriser [ohto-reezay]
  ▸ how much luggage are you allowed? combien de bagages sont autorisés ? [kONbyAN duh bagazh sONt ohto-reezay]
  ▸ are you allowed to smoke here? c'est autorisé de fumer ici ? [set ohto-reezay duh fUmay eesee]

almost presque [presk]
  ▸ it's almost 1 p.m. il est presque une heure [eel eh presk Un uhr]

alone seul(e) [suhl]
  ▸ leave us alone! laissez-nous tranquilles ! [laysay-noo trONkeel]

along le long de [luh ION duh]
 ▸ along the river le long de la rivière [luh ION duh la reevyehr]

altogether *(in total)* en tout [ON too], tout compris [too kONpree]
 ▸ how much does it cost altogether? combien ça coûte tout compris ? [kONbyAN sa koot too kONpree]

always toujours [toozhoor]
 ▸ it's always the same thing c'est toujours la même chose [seh toozhoor la mem shohz]

ambulance l'ambulance *f* [ONbU-IONs]
 ▸ could you send an ambulance right away to...? pouvez-vous envoyer d'urgence une ambulance au... ? [poovay-vooz ONvwa-yay dUrzhONs Un ONbU-IONs oh]

ambulance service le SAMU [samU]
 ▸ what's the number for the ambulance service? quel est le numéro du SAMU ? [kel eh luh nUmay-roh dU samU]

America Amérique [amay-reek]
 ▸ I'm from America je viens d'Amérique [zhuh vyAN damay-reek]
 ▸ I live in America j'habite en Amérique [zhabeet ON amay-reek]
 ▸ have you ever been to America? es-tu déjà allé en Amérique ? [ehtU dayzha alay ON amay-reek]

American américain(e) [amay-reekAN(-reeken)] ◆ Américain(e) [amay-reekAN (-reeken)]
 ▸ I'm American je suis américain/américaine [zhuh sweez amay-reekAN/amay-reeken]
 ▸ we're Americans nous sommes des Américains/Américaines [noo som dayz amay-reekAN/amay-reeken]

ankle la cheville [shuhveey]
 ▸ I've sprained my ankle je me suis tordu la cheville [zhuh muh swee tordU la shuhveey]

announcement l'annonce *f* [anONs]
 ▸ was that an announcement about the London train? ce message concernait-il le train de Londres ? [suh mesazh kONser-neht-eel luh trAN duh IONdr]

another un(e) autre [an(Un) ohtr]
 ▸ another coffee, please un autre café, s'il vous plaît [an ohtr kafay seel voo play]
 ▸ (would you like) another drink? (voulez-vous) un autre verre ? [(voolay-vooz) an ohtr vehr]

answer la réponse [raypONs] ◆ répondre [raypONdr]
 ▸ I didn't understand your answer: could you repeat that please? je n'ai pas compris votre réponse, pourriez-vous répéter ? [zhuh nay pah kONpree votr raypONs pooryay-voo raypay-tay]
 ▸ there's no answer ça ne répond pas [sa nuh raypON pah]
 ▸ I phoned earlier but nobody answered j'ai appelé plus tôt mais personne n'a répondu [zhay aplay plU toh may pehrson na raypON-dU]

answering machine le répondeur (téléphonique) [raypON-duhr (taylay-foneek)]
- I left a message on your answering machine je t'ai laissé un message sur ton répondeur [zhuh tay laysay AN mesazh sUr tON raypON-duhr]

anti-dandruff shampoo le shampooing anti-pelliculaire [shONpwAN Ontee-pelee-kUlehr]
- do you have an anti-dandruff shampoo? auriez-vous un shampooing anti-pelliculaire ? [ohryay-vooz UN shONpwAN Ontee-pelee-kUlehr]

anybody, anyone quelqu'un [kelkAN]
- is there anybody there? il y a quelqu'un ? [eel ya kelkAN]

anything quelque chose [kelkuh shohz]
- is there anything I can do? est-ce que je peux faire quelque chose ? [eskuh zhuh puh fehr kelkuh shohz]

anywhere quelque part [kelkuh par], nulle part [nUl par], partout [partoo]
- I can't find my room key anywhere je ne retrouve nulle part ma clé de chambre [zhuh nuh ruhtroov nUl par ma klay duh shONbr]
- do you live anywhere near here? tu habites dans le coin ? [tU abeet dON luh kwAN]

apartment l'appartement m [apar-tuhmON]
- we'd like to rent an apartment for one week nous voudrions louer un appartement pour une semaine [noo voodree-ON lway AN apar-tuhmON poor Un suhmen]

apologize demander pardon [duhmON-day pardON], s'excuser [sekskU-zay]
- there's no need to apologize ne vous excusez pas [nuh vooz ekskU-zay pa]

appetizer l'entrée f [ONtray]
- which of the appetizers would you recommend? quelle entrée recommendez-vous ? [kel ONtray ruhko-mONday-voo]

apple la pomme [pom]
- could I have a kilo of apples, please? puis-je avoir un kilo de pommes, s'il vous plaît ? [pweezh avwar AN keeloh duh pom seel voo play]

---

apologizing

- excuse me! *(to get past)* excusez-moi ! [ekskU-zay-mwa]
- I'm sorry, I can't come on Saturday je regrette de ne pas pouvoir venir samedi [zhuh ruhgret duh nuh pa poovwar vuhneer samdee]
- that's OK ce n'est pas grave [suh neh pa grav]
- it doesn't matter ça ne fait rien [sa nuh feh ryAN]
- don't mention it je vous en prie [zhuh vooz ON pree]

apple juice le jus de pomme [zhU duh pom]
- I'd like an apple juice j'aimerais un jus de pomme [zhemuh-reh AN zhU duh pom]

appointment le rendez-vous [rONday-voo]
- could I get an appointment for tomorrow morning? pourrais-je avoir un rendez-vous demain matin ? [poorehzh avwar AN rONday-voo duhmAN matAN]
- I have an appointment with Doctor... j'ai rendez-vous avec le Docteur... [zhay rONday-voo avek luh doktuhr]

April avril [avreel]
- April 6th le six avril [luh sees avreel]

area (region) la région [rayzh-yON]; (small) la zone [zon]; (sector) le secteur [sektuhr]; (locality) les environs [ONvee-rON]; (of town) le quartier [kartyay]
- I'm visiting the area je visite la région [zhuh veezeet la rayzh-yON]
- what walks can you recommend in the area? qu'est-ce que vous nous conseillez comme marche dans les environs ? [kes-kuh voo noo kON-seyay kom marsh dON layz ONvee-rON]

area code (for telephoning) l'indicatif m [ANdee-kateef]
- what's the area code for Paris? quel est l'indicatif pour Paris ? [kel eh lANdee-kateef poor paree]

arm le bras [brah]
- I can't move my arm je ne peux pas bouger mon bras [zhuh nuh puh pa boozhay mON brah]

around (in all directions) autour [ohtoor]; (nearby) dans le coin [dON luh kwAN]
+ (encircling) autour de [ohtoor duh]; (through) à travers [a travehr]; (approximately) autour de [ohtoor duh], vers [vehr]
- we're traveling around together on voyage ensemble [ON vwa-yazh ONsONbl]
- we've been traveling around Europe nous faisons un tour d'Europe [noo fezONz AN toor duhrop]
- I don't know my way around yet je ne me repère pas encore [zhuh nuh muh ruhpehr paz ONkor]
- I arrived around two o'clock je suis arrivé vers deux heures [zhuh sweez aree-vay vehr duhz uhr]
- I'd like something for around 15 euros je voudrais quelque chose autour de quinze euros [zhuh voodreh qelkuh shohz ohtoor duh kANz uhroh]

arrive arriver [aree-vay]
- my luggage hasn't arrived mes bagages ne sont pas arrivés [may bagazh nuh sON paz aree-vay]
- we arrived late nous sommes arrivés en retard [noo somz aree-vay ON ruhtar]
- we've just arrived nous venons d'arriver [noo vuhnON daree-vay]

art l'art m [ar]
- I'm not really interested in art je ne suis pas un passioné d'art [zhuh nuh swee paz AN pasyo-nay dar]

as *(while)* au moment où [oh momON oo]; *(like)* comme [kom]; *(since)* puisque [pweesk] ♦ *(in comparisons)* aussi [ohsee], autant [ohtON]

- the lights went out just as we were about to eat la lumière s'est éteinte juste au moment où nous allions manger [la lUmyehr seht aytANt zhUst oh momON oo nooz alyON mONzhay]
- as I said before comme je l'ai déjà dit [kom zhuh lay dayzha dee]
- leave it as it is laisse-le comme c'est [les-luh kom seh]
- as much as autant que/autant de... que [ohtON kuh/ohtON duh... kuh]
- as many... as autant de... que [ohtON duh... kuh]

ashtray le cendrier [sONdree-yay]

- could you bring us an ashtray? est-ce que vous pourriez nous apporter un cendrier ? [es-kuh voo pooryay nooz apor-tay AN sONdree-yay]

ask *(question)* poser [pozay]; *(time)* demander [duhmON-day]

- can I ask you a question? puis-je vous poser une question ? [pweezh voo pozay Un kestyON]

aspirin l'aspirine *f* [aspee-reen]

- I'd like some aspirin je voudrais de l'aspirine [zhuh voodreh duh laspee-reen]

asthma l'asthme *m* [asm]

- I have asthma j'ai de l'asthme [zhay duh lasm]

at *(indicating place, position, time)* à [a]

- our bags are still at the airport nos bagages sont encore à l'aéroport [noh bagazh sONt ONkor a la-ayro-por]
- we arrive at midnight nous arrivons à minuit [nooz aree-vONz a meenwee]

ATM le distributeur automatique (de billets) [deestree-bUtuhr ohtoh-mateek (duh beeyeh)]

- I'm looking for an ATM je cherche un distributeur automatique [zhuh shersh AN deestree-bUtuhr ohtoh-mateek]

asking questions

- is this seat free? est-ce que cette place est libre ? [es-kuh set plas eh leebr]
- where is the station? où se trouve la gare ? [oo suh troov la gar]
- could you help me get my case down, please? pouvez-vous m'aider à attraper ma valise, s'il vous plaît ? [poovay-voo mayday a atra-pay ma valeez seel voo play]
- could you give me a hand? pouvez-vous me donner un coup de main ? [poovay-voo muh donay AN koo du mAN]
- could you lend me ten euros? tu ne pourrais pas me prêter dix euros ? [tU nuh pooreh pa muh prehtay deez uhroh]

ATMs

These are very common now at French banks and provide instructions in both French and English on how to withdraw cash using a debit or credit card.

▸ the ATM has swallowed my card le distributeur de billets a avalé ma carte [luh deestree-bUtuhr duh beeyeh a ava-lay ma kart]

attack *(of illness)* l'attaque *f* [atak] ◆ *(person)* agresser [agreh-say]

▸ he had an attack il a eu une attaque [eel a U Un atak]
▸ I've been attacked j'ai été agressé [zhay aytay agreh-say]

attention l'attention *f* [atON-syON]

▸ may I have your attention for a moment? pouvez-vous m'accorder votre attention un instant ? [poovay-voo makor-day votr atON-syON AN ANstON]

attractive beau [boh], belle [bel]

▸ I find you very attractive je te trouve très belle [zhuh tuh troov treh bel]

August août [oot]

▸ we're arriving on August 29th nous arrivons le vingt-neuf août [nooz aree-vON luh vANt-nuhf oot]

automatic automatique [ohtoh-mateek] ◆ *(car)* la voiture à boîte de vitesse automatique [vwatUr a bwat duh veetes ohtoh-mateek]

▸ I want a car with automatic transmission je veux une voiture à boîte automatique [zhuh vuhz Un vwatUr a bwat ohtoh-mateek]
▸ is it a manual or an automatic? c'est une boîte manuelle ou automatique ? [seht Un bwat manUel oo ohtoh-mateek]

available disponible [deespo-neebl]

▸ you don't have a table available before that? vous n'avez pas de table libre plus tôt ? [voo navay pa duh tabl leebr plU toh]

average moyen(ne) [mwa-yAN(yen)]

▸ what's the average price of a meal there? quel est le prix moyen d'un repas là-bas ? [kel eh luh pree mwa-yAN dAN ruhpa la-ba]

avoid éviter [ayvee-tay]

▸ is there a route that would enable us to avoid the traffic? y a-t-il une route qui permettrait d'éviter la circulation ? [ee-ateel Un root kee perme-treh dayvee-tay la seerkU-lasyON]

away *(indicating position)* à (… d'ici) [a (… deesee)] ◆ **away from** loin de [lwAN duh], éloigné de [aylwan-yay duh]

▸ the village is twenty kilometers away le village est à 20 kilomètres (d'ici) [luh veelazh eht a vAN keelo-metr (deesee)]

- we're looking for a cottage well away from the town nous cherchons une maison très éloignée de la ville [noo shershONz Un mayzON trez aylwan-yay duh la veel]
- do you have any rooms away from the main road? avez-vous des chambres qui ne donnent pas sur la rue principale ? [avay-voo day shONbr kee nuh don pa sUr la rU prANsee-pal]

b

back de retour [duh ruhtoor] ◆ *(part of body)* le dos [doh]; *(of room)* le fond [fON]
- I'll be back in 5 minutes je reviens dans cinq minutes [zhuh ruhvyAN dON sANk meenUt]
- we will be back around Christmas nous serons de retour aux environs de Noël [noo suhrON duh ruhtoor ohz ONvee-rON duh no-el]
- I've got a bad back j'ai le dos fragile [zhay luh doh frazheel]
- I prefer to sit at the back je préfère m'asseoir au fond [zhuh prayfehr maswar oh fON]

backache le mal au dos [mal oh doh]
- I've got a backache j'ai mal au dos [zhay mal oh doh]

backpack le sac à dos [sak a doh]
- my passport's in my backpack mon passeport est dans mon sac à dos [mON paspor eh dON mON sak a doh]
- can you watch my backpack for a minute, please? pouvez-vous surveiller mon sac à dos une minute, s'il vous plaît ? [poovay-voo sUr-veyay mON sak a doh Un meenUt seel voo play]

back up reculer [ruhkU-lay]
- I think we have to back up and turn right il me semble qu'il faut reculer et prendre à droite [eel muh sOMbl keel foh ruhkU-lay ay prONdr a drwat]

bad mauvais(e) [moh-vay(-vez)]
- the weather's bad today il fait mauvais aujourd'hui [eel fay mohvay ohzhoor-dwee]
- it's a bad line la ligne est mauvaise [la leen-yuh eh mohvez]

bag le sac [sak]; *(suitcase)* le bagage [bagazh]; *(purse)* le sac (à mains) [sak (a mAN)]
- are these the bags from flight 502? s'agit-il des bagages du vol cinq cent deux ? [sazheet-eel day bagazh dU vol sANk sON duh]
- can someone take our bags up to the room, please? on peut nous monter les bagages dans la chambre ? [ON puh noo mONtay lay bagazh dON la shONbr]
- can we leave our bags in reception? peut-on laisser nos valises à la réception ? [puht-ON laysay noh valeez a la raysep-syON]
- my bag's just been stolen on vient de me voler mon sac (à mains) [ON vyAN duh muh volay mON sak (a mAN)]

baggage les bagages *m* [bagazh]

> ▸ my baggage hasn't arrived mes bagages ne sont pas arrivés [may bagazh nuh sON paz aree-vay]

> ▸ I'd like to report the loss of my baggage je voudrais faire une déclaration de perte pour mes bagages [zhuh voodreh fehr Un daykla-rasyON duh pert poor may bagazh]

baggage cart le chariot [sharyoh]

> ▸ I'm looking for a baggage cart je cherche un chariot pour mes bagages [zhuh shersh AN sharyoh poor may bagazh]

bakery la boulangerie [boolONzh-ree]

> ▸ is there a bakery nearby? y a-t-il une boulangerie dans le coin ? [ee ateel Un boolONzh-ree dON luh kwAN]

balcony le balcon [balkON]

> ▸ do you have any rooms with a balcony? avez-vous des chambres avec balcon ? [avay-voo day shONbr avek balkON]

banana la banane [banan]

> ▸ a kilo of bananas, please un kilo de bananes, s'il vous plaît [AN keeloh duh banan seel voo play]

bandage la bande [bONd], le pansement [pONsmON]

> ▸ I need a bandage for my ankle j'ai besoin d'une bande pour ma cheville [zhay buhzwAN dUn bONd poor ma shuhveey]

Band-Aid® le sparadrap [spara-drah], le pansement [pONsmON]

> ▸ I'll put a *Band-Aid* on your cut je vais mettre un pansement sur ta coupure [zhuh veh metr AN pONsmON sUr ta koopUr]

bank *(finance)* la banque [bONk]

> ▸ is there a bank nearby? y a-t-il une banque près d'ici ? [ee ateel Un bONk preh deesee]

---

at the bank

> ▸ I'd like to change 100 dollars into euros je voudrais changer cent dollars en euros [zhuh voodreh shONzhay sON dolar ON uhroh]

> ▸ in small bills, please en petites coupures, s'il vous plaît [ON puhteet koopUr seel voo play]

> ▸ what is the rate for the euro? à combien est l'euro ? [a kONbyAN eh luhroh]

> ▸ how much is that in dollars? en dollars cela fait combien ? [ON dolar suhla feh kONbyAN]

> ▸ do you take traveler's checks? acceptez-vous les chèques de voyage ? [aksep-tay-voo lay shek duh vwa-yazh]

> ▸ do you charge a commission? vous prenez une commission ? [voo pruhnay Un komee-syON]

▸ are banks open on Saturdays? les banques sont-elles ouvertes le samedi ? [lay bONk sONt-el oovert luh samdee]

bank card la carte bancaire [kart bONkehr]

▸ I've lost my bank card j'ai perdu ma carte bancaire [zhay perdU ma kart bONkehr]

bar *(establishment serving alcohol)* le bar [bar]; *(of chocolate)* la tablette [tablet]

▸ are there any good bars around here? est-ce qu'il y a des bars sympas dans le coin ? [es-keel ya day bar sANpa dON luh kwAN]

base la base [baz], le point de départ [pwAN duh daypar]

▸ the base of the lamp got broken le pied de la lampe est cassé [luh pyay duh la lONp eh kasay]

▸ we're going to use the village as our base to explore the area le village va être notre point de départ pour découvrir la région [luh veelazh va etr notr pwAN duh daypar poor daykoov-reer la rayzh-yON]

basic de base [duh baz] ◆ **basics** les bases *f* [baz]

▸ the staff all have a basic knowledge of English tout le personnel se débrouille en anglais [too luh perso-nel suh daybrweey ON ONglay]

▸ I just know basic French je ne connais que le français de base [zhuh nuh konay kuh luh frONsay duh baz]

▸ I know the basics, but no more than that je connais les bases mais pas plus [zhuh konay lay baz may pa plUs]

basis la base [baz]

▸ the price per night is on the basis of two persons sharing le prix de la nuitée est sur une base de deux personnes [luh pree duh la nweetay eh sUr Un baz duh duh person]

bat *(for table tennis)* la raquette de ping-pong [raket duh peeng-pONg]

▸ can you rent bats? peut-on louer des raquettes de ping-pong ? [puh-tON lway day raket duh peeng-pONg]

bath le bain [bAN]

▸ to take a bath prendre un bain [prONdr AN bAN]

bathroom *(with toilet and bathtub or shower)* la salle de bains [sal duh bAN]; *(with toilet)* les toilettes *f* [twalet]

▸ where's the bathroom? où sont les toilettes ? [oo sON lay twalet]

bathtub la baignoire [benyuh-war]

▸ there's no plug for the bathtub il n'y a pas de bonde pour la baignoire [eel neeya pa duh bONd poor la benyuh-war]

battery *(for radio, flashlight)* la batterie [batree], la pile [peel]; *(in car)* la batterie [batree]

▸ the battery needs to be recharged il faudrait recharger la batterie [eel fohdreh ruhshar-zhay la batree]

▸ the battery's dead la batterie est à plat [la batree eht a plah]

be *(with adj, n)* être [etr]; *(referring to health, movement)* aller [alay]; *(referring to age)* avoir [avwar]; *(referring to weather, prices, measurements)* faire [fehr]

▸ where are you from? d'où êtes-vous ? [doo et-voo]
▸ I'm a teacher je suis prof [zhuh swee prof]
▸ I'm happy je suis content [zhuh swee kONtON]
▸ what day is it? quel jour sommes-nous ? [kel zhoor som-noo]
▸ it's eight o'clock il est huit heures [eel eh weet uhr]
▸ how are you? comment allez-vous ? [komONt alay-voo]
▸ I'm fine je vais bien [zhuh veh byAN]
▸ where is terminal 1? où se trouve le terminal un ? [oo suh troov luh termee-nal AN]
▸ could you show me where I am on the map? pourriez-vous m'indiquer où je me trouve sur la carte ? [pooryay-voo mANdee-kay oo zhuh muh troov sUr la kart]
▸ have you ever been to the United States? êtes-vous déjà allé aux États-Unis ? [et-voo dayzha alay ohz aytaz-Unee]
▸ it's the first time I've been here c'est la première fois que je viens [seh la pruhmyehr fwah kuh zhuh vyAN]
▸ how old are you? quel âge as-tu ? [kel azh a-tU]
▸ I'm 18 (years old) j'ai dix-huit ans [zhay deez-weet ON]
▸ it was over thirty-five degrees il a fait plus de trente-cinq degrés [eel a feh plUs duh trONt-sANk duhgray]
▸ it's cold in the evenings il fait froid le soir [eel feh frwah luh swar]
▸ how much is it? ça fait combien ? [sa feh kONbyAN]
▸ I'm 1.68 meters tall je fais un mètre soixante huit [zhuh fehz AN metr swasONt-weet]

beach la plage [plazh]
▸ it's a sandy beach c'est une plage de sable [seht Un plazh duh sabl]
▸ is it a quiet beach? c'est une plage tranquille ? [seht Un plazh trONkeel]

beach umbrella le parasol [para-sol]
▸ can you rent beach umbrellas? est-ce que l'on peut louer des parasols ? [eskuh lON puh lway day para-sol]

beautiful beau [boh], belle [bel]
▸ isn't the weather beautiful today? quel temps superbe, aujourd'hui ! [kel tON sUperb ohzhoor-dwee]

bed le lit [lee]
▸ is it possible to add an extra bed? c'est possible d'ajouter un lit supplémentaire ? [seh poseebl dazhoo-tay AN lee sUplay-mONtehr]
▸ do you have a children's bed? est-ce que vous avez un lit pour enfant ? [es-kuh vooz avay AN lee poor ONfON]
▸ to go to bed se coucher [suh kooshay]
▸ I went to bed late je me suis couché tard [zhuh muh swee kooshay tar]
▸ could you put the children to bed? tu peux coucher les enfants ? [tU puh kooshay layz ONfON]

bedroom la chambre (à coucher) [shONbr (a kooshay)]
- how many bedrooms does the apartment have? l'appartement comporte combien de chambres ? [lapar-tuhmON kONport kONbyAN duh shONbr]

bedside lamp la lampe de chevet [lONp duh shuhveh]
- the bedside lamp doesn't work la lampe de chevet ne fonctionne pas [la lONp duh shuhveh nuh fONksyon pa]

beef le bœuf [buhf]
- I don't eat beef je ne mange pas de bœuf [zhuh nuh mONzh pa duh buhf]
- do you only have beef? I would have preferred white meat vous n'avez que du bœuf ? j'aurais préféré une viande blanche [voo navay kuh dU buhf? zhohreh prayfay-ray Un vyONd blONsh]

beer la bière [byehr]
- two beers, please deux bières, s'il vous plaît [duh byehr seel voo play]

begin (start) commencer [komON-say]
- when does the performance begin? à quelle heure commence le spectacle ? [a kel uhr komONs luh spektakl]

beginner le débutant [daybU-tON], la débutante [daybU-tONt]
- I'm a complete beginner je suis un parfait débutant [zhuh sweez AN parfeh daybU-tON]

behind derrière [deryehr]
- from behind de dos [duh doh]
- the rest of our party is in the car behind les autres sont dans la voiture de derrière [layz ohtr sON dON la vwatUr duh deryehr]

Belgium la Belgique [belzheek]
- are you from Belgium? tu viens de Belgique ? [tU vyAN duh belzheek]
- do you live in Belgium? tu habites en Belgique ? [tU abeet ON belzheek]
- I've not been to Belgium before je ne suis jamais allé en Belgique [zhuh nuh swee zhamehz alay ON belzheek]

berth (on ship) la couchette [kooshet]
- I'd prefer the upper berth je préférerais la couchette du haut [zhuh prayfay-ruhreh la kooshet dU oh]

beside à côté de [a kohtay duh]
- is there anyone beside you? y a-t-il quelqu'un à côté de vous ? [ee ateel kelkAN a kohtay duh voo]

best le meilleur [me-yuhr], la meilleure [me-yuhr]
- what's the best restaurant in town? quel est le meilleur restaurant de la ville ? [kel eh luh me-yuhr resto-rON duh la veel]

better meilleur(e) [me-yuhr] ◆ mieux [myuh]
- I've been on antibiotics for a week and I'm not any better je suis sous antibiotiques depuis une semaine et ça ne va pas mieux [zhuh swee sooz ONtee-byoteek duhpweez Un suhmen ay sa nuh va pa myuh]

▸ the better situated of the two hotels **le mieux situé des deux hôtels** [luh myuh seetUay day duhz ohtel]

between entre [ONtr]

▸ a bus runs between the airport and the hotel **il y a un bus entre l'aéroport et l'hôtel** [eel ya AN bUs ONtr la-ayro-por ay lohtel]

bicycle le vélo [vayloh]

▸ is there a place to leave bicycles? **avez-vous un endroit où laisser les vélos ?** [avay-vooz AN ONdrwah oo laysay lay vayloh]

bicycle lane la piste cyclable [peest seeklabl]

▸ are there any bicycle lanes? **y a-t-il des pistes cyclables ?** [ee ateel day peest seeklabl]

bicycle pump la pompe à vélo [pONp a vayloh]

▸ do you have a bicycle pump? **vous avez une pompe à vélo ?** [vooz avay Un pONp a vayloh]

big *(town, difference)* grand(e) [grON(d)]; *(box, crowd)* gros(se) [groh(s)]; *(piece of clothing)* large [larzh]

▸ do you have it in a bigger size? **vous l'avez en plus large ?** [voo lavay ON plU larzh]

▸ it's too big **c'est trop grand** [seh troh grON]

bike le vélo [vayloh]

▸ I'd like to rent a bike for an hour **je voudrais louer un vélo pour une heure** [zhuh voodreh lway AN vayloh poor Un uhr]

bill *(in hotel)* la note [not]; *(for goods)* la facture [faktUr]; *(paper money)* le billet [bee-yeh]

▸ I think there's a mistake with the bill **je crois qu'il y a une erreur dans l'addition** [zhuh krwa keel ya Un eruhr dON ladee-syON]

▸ put it on my bill **mettez-le sur ma note** [metay-luh sUr ma not]

▸ can you make up my bill, please? **vous pouvez préparer ma note, s'il vous plaît ?** [voo poovay praypa-ray ma not seel voo play]

▸ it's not the right bill **ce n'est pas la bonne facture** [suh neh pa la bon faktUr]

▸ I only have a 100 euro bill **je n'ai qu'un billet de cent euros** [zhuh nay kAN bee-yeh duh sONt uhroh]

birthday l'anniversaire *m* [anee-versehr]

▸ Happy Birthday! **joyeux anniversaire !** [jwa-yuhz anee-versehr]

bite *(of animal)* la morsure *f* [morsUr]; *(of insect)* la piqûre *f* [peekUr] ◆ *(animal)* mordre [mordr]; *(insect)* piquer [peekay]

▸ I've been bitten by a dog **je me suis fait mordre par un chien** [zhuh muh swee feh mordr par AN shyAN]

▸ do you have a cream for mosquito bites? **est-ce que vous avez une crème contre les piqûres de moustique ?** [es-kuh vooz avay Un krem kONtr lay peekUr duh moosteek]

black noir(e) [nwar]
- I'm looking for a little black dress je cherche une petite robe noire [zhuh shersh Un puhteet rob nwar]

black-and-white noir et blanc [nwar ay blON], noire et blanche [nwar ay blONsh]
- I'd like a black-and-white film je voudrais une pellicule noir et blanc [zhuh voodreh Un pelee-kUl nwar ay blON]

black ice le verglas *m* [verglah]
- there's black ice il y a du verglas [eel ya dU verglah]

blanket la couverture [koover-tUr]
- I'd like an extra blanket je voudrais une couverture supplémentaire [zhuh voodreh Un koover-tUr sUplay-mONtehr]

bleed saigner [sayn-yay]
- it won't stop bleeding cela n'arrête pas de saigner [suhla naret pa duh sayn-yay]

blind *(on window)* le store [stor]
- can we pull down the blinds? peut-on baisser les stores ? [puht-ON besay lay stor]

blister l'ampoule *f* [ONpool]
- I got a blister je me suis fait une ampoule [zhuh muh swee feht Un ONpool]

block *(pipe, sink)* bloquer [blokay]; *(road)* boucher [booshay]
- the toilet's blocked les toilettes sont bouchées [lay twalet sON booshay]
- my ears are completely blocked mes oreilles sont complètement bouchées [mayz orey sON kONplet-mON booshay]

blond blond(e) [blON(blONd)]
- I have blond hair j'ai les cheveux blonds [zhay lay shuhvuh blON]

blood le sang [sON]
- traces of blood des traces de sang [day tras duh sON]

blood pressure la tension [tONsyON]
- I have high blood pressure j'ai de la tension [zhay duh la tONsyON]

blood type le groupe sanguin [groop sONgAN]
- my blood type is A positive mon groupe sanguin est A plus [mON groop sONgAN eh ah plUs]

blue bleu(e) [bluh]
- the blue one le bleu [luh bluh], la bleue [la bluh]

board *(plane)* monter à bord (de) [mONtay a bor (duh)]
- what time will the plane be boarding? quelle est l'heure d'embarquement ? [kel eh luhr dONbark-mON]
- where is the flight to Nice boarding? où se fait l'embarquement du vol pour Nice ? [oo suh feh lONbark-mON dU vol poor nees]

boarding pass la carte d'embarquement [kart dONbark-mON]
- I can't find my boarding pass je ne trouve plus ma carte d'embarquement [zhuh nuh troov plU ma kart dOMbark-mON]

boat le bateau [batoh]
- can we get there by boat? est-ce accessible en bateau ? [es akse-seebl ON batoh]

boat trip la promenade en bateau [promnad ON batoh]
- are there boat trips on the river? y a-t-il des promenades en bateau sur le fleuve ? [ee ateel day promnad ON batoh sUr luh fluhv]

boiled egg l'œuf *m* (à la) coque [uhf (a la) kok]
- I'd like two boiled eggs and toast je voudrais deux œufs coque avec un toast [zhuh voodreh duhz uh kok avek AN tost]

book *(for reading)* le livre [leevr]; *(of tickets, stamps)* le carnet [karneh]; *(of matches)* la pochette [poshet] ◆ réserver [rayzer-vay]
- do you sell English books? est-ce que vous vendez des livres en anglais ? [es-kuh voo vONday day leevr ON ONglay]
- is it more economical if you buy a book of tickets? est-ce que cela coûte moins cher si on achète les billets par carnet ? [es-kuh suhla koot mwAN shehr see ON ashet lay bee-yeh par karneh]
- I'd like to book a ticket je voudrais réserver un billet [zhuh voodreh rayzer-vay AN bee-yeh]
- do you need to book? est-ce qu'il faut réserver ? [es-keel foh rayzer-vay]

born
- to be born naître [nehtr]
- I was born on March 3rd 1985 je suis né le trois mars mille neuf cent quatre-vingt cinq [zhuh swee nay luh trwah mars meel nuhf sON katr-vAN sANk]

bottle la bouteille [bootey]
- a bottle of red wine, please servez-nous une bouteille de vin rouge [sehrvay-nooz Un bootey duh vAN roozh]

bottle opener le décapsuleur [daykap-sUluhr]
- can you pass me the bottle opener? tu peux me passer le décapsuleur ? [tU puh muh pasay luh daykap-sUluhr]

bottom *(of a well, of a box)* le fond [fON]
- my passport's in the bottom of my suitcase mon passeport est au fond de ma valise [mON paspor eht oh fON duh ma valeez]

box la boîte [bwat]
- could I have a box of matches, please? pourrais-je avoir une boîte d'allumettes, s'il vous plaît ? [poorehzh avwar Un bwat dalU-met seel voo play]

boy le garçon [garsON]
- he seems a nice boy il a l'air d'un garçon gentil [eel a lehr dAN garsOn zhONtee]
- she has two boys elle a deux garçons [el a duh garsON]

boyfriend le copain [kopAN], le (petit) ami [(puhteet) amee]
- I'm with my boyfriend je suis avec mon copain [zhuh sweez avek mON kopAN]

bread

French bread comes in all shapes and sizes (more than thirty), not just the *baguette* that we all know and love. The three main types are *pains de campagne* (country loaves), *pains fantaisie* (fancy breads) and *pains spéciaux* (specialty breads). You never need to go very far to find a *boulangerie* – just follow your nose...

brake le frein [frAN]
- ▸ the brakes aren't working properly les freins ne marchent pas bien [lay frAN nuh marsh pa byAN]

brake fluid le liquide de frein [leekeed duh frAN]
- ▸ I've checked the brake fluid j'ai vérifié le liquide de frein [zhay vayreef-yay luh leekeed duh frAN]

branch *(of bank)* l'agence f [azhONs]
- ▸ you can collect your traveler's checks from any of our branches vous pouvez récupérer vos chèques de voyage dans chacune de nos agences [voo poovay raykU-payray voh shek duh vwa-yazh dON shakUn duh noz azhONs]

bread le pain [pAN]
- ▸ do you have any bread? avez-vous du pain ? [avay-voo dU pAN]
- ▸ could we have some more bread? pourrions-nous avoir plus de pain ? [pooryON-nooz avvar plU duh pAN]

break *(pause)* la pause [pohz] ◆ casser [kasay]
- ▸ shall we take a break? on fait une pause ? [ON feh Un pohz]
- ▸ be careful you don't break it attention à ne pas le/la casser [atON-syON a nuh pa luh/la kasay]
- ▸ I think I've broken my ankle Je crois que je me suis cassé la cheville [zhuh krwa kuh zhuh zhuh muh swee kasay la shuhveey]

break down tomber en panne [tONbay ON pan]
- ▸ my car has broken down ma voiture est (tombée) en panne [ma vwatUr eh (tONbay) ON pan]

breakdown la panne [pan]
- ▸ we had a breakdown on the freeway nous avons eu une panne sur l'autoroute [nooz avONz U Un pan sUr lohtoh-root]

breakfast le (petit) déjeuner [(puhtee) dayzhuh-nay]
- ▸ to have breakfast prendre son petit déjeuner [prONdr sON puhtee dayzhuh-nay]
- ▸ what time is breakfast served? le petit déjeuner est servi à quelle heure ? [luh puhtee dayzhuh-nay eh servee a kel uhr]

breakfast

Surprisingly, most French people don't eat *croissants* for breakfast every day, but have them as a snack later in the day if they eat them at all. If they eat breakfast, it's likely to be bread, toast or *biscottes*, which are crisp, brittle cookies, and a cup of coffee. Nowadays, however, more and more people skip breakfast altogether. In hotels, you'll probably be served *croissants*, fresh bread or *brioches*, along with breakfast cereals, fresh fruit, etc.

bridge le pont [pON]
- do you have to pay a toll to use the bridge? est-ce que c'est un pont à péage ? [es-kuh seht AN pOn a peyazh]

bring apporter [apor-tay]
- what should we bring to drink? que faut-il apporter à boire ? [kuh foht-eel apor-tay a bwar]

bring down *(bags, luggage)* descendre [desONdr]
- could you get someone to bring down our luggage, please? pouvez-vous demander à quelqu'un de descendre nos bagages, s'il vous plaît ? [poovay-voo duhmON-day a kelkAN duh desONdr noh bagazh seel voo play]

bring in *(bags, luggage)* rentrer [rONtray]
- can you bring in my bags, please? pouvez-vous porter mes bagages à l'intérieur, s'il vous plaît ? [poovay-voo portay may bagazh a lANtayr-yuhr seel voo play]

broken cassé(e) [kasay]
- the lock is broken la serrure est cassée [la serUr eh kasay]
- I think I've got a broken leg je crois que j'ai la jambe cassée [zhuh krwa kuh zhay la zhONb kasay]

bronchitis la bronchite [brONsheet]
- do you have anything for bronchitis? vous avez quelque chose contre la bronchite ? [vooz avay kelkuh shohz kONtr la brONsheet]

brother le frère [frehr]
- I don't have any brothers and sisters je n'ai pas de frères et sœurs [zhuh nay pa duh frehr ay suhr]

brown brun(e) [brAN(brUn)], marron [marON]
- he has brown hair il a les cheveux bruns [eel a lay shuhvuh brAN]
- I'm looking for a brown leather belt je cherche une ceinture en cuir marron [zhuh shersh Un sANtUr ON kweer marON]

brush *(for hair, clothes)* la brosse [bros]; *(broom)* le balai [baleh]; *(with short handle)* la balayette [bala-yet] ♦ *(hair)* brosser [brosay]

▶ can I borrow a brush? je peux vous emprunter une brosse ? [zhuh puh vooz ONprAN-tay Un bros]

▶ where's the dustpan and brush? où sont la pelle et la balayette ? [oo sON la pel ay la bala-yet]

▶ to brush one's teeth se laver les dents [suh lavay lay dON]

bulb *(light)* l'ampoule *f* [ONpool]

▶ the bulb's gone in the bathroom l'ampoule de la salle de bain est grillée [lONpool duh la sal duh bAN eh greeyay]

bunk beds les lits *m* superposés [lee sUper-pohzay]

▶ there are bunk beds for the children il y a des lits superposés pour les enfants [eel ya day lee sUper-pohzay poor layz ONfON]

burn brûler [brUlay]

▶ the food's completely burned le plat est complètement brûlé [luh plah eh kONplet-mON brUlay]

▶ I've burned my hand je me suis brûlé la main [zhuh muh swee brUlay la mAN]

burst crever [kruhvay], éclater [aykla-tay]

▶ one of my tires burst j'ai un pneu crevé [zhay AN pnuh kruhvay]

bus le bus [bUs]

▶ does this bus go to the station? est-ce que ce bus va à la gare ? [es-kuh suh bUs va a la gar]

▶ which bus do I have to take to go to...? quel bus faut-il prendre pour aller à... ? [kel bUs foht-eel prONdr poor alay a...]

▶ what time does the last bus go? à quelle heure passe le dernier bus ? [a kel uhr pas luh dernyay bUs]

bus driver le chauffeur de bus [shohfuhr duh bUs]

▶ can you buy tickets from the bus driver? peut-on acheter les billets au chauffeur du bus ? [puht-ON ashtay lay beeyeh oh shohfuhr dU bUs]

business *(commerce)* les affaires *f* [afehr]; *(company)* l'entreprise *f* [ONtr-preez]; *(concern)* l'affaire *f* [afehr]; *(affair, matter)* la tâche [tash], l'histoire *f* [eestwar]

▶ it's none of your business ça ne te regarde pas [sa nuh tuh ruhgard pa]

▶ I run my own business j'ai ma propre entreprise [zhay ma propr ONtr-preez]

business card la carte de visite [kart duh veezeet]

▶ here's my business card voici ma carte de visite [vwasee ma kart duh veezeet]

business class la classe affaires [klas afehr]

▶ are there any seats in business class? est-ce qu'il y a des places en classe affaires ? [es-keel ya day plas ON klas afehr]

▶ I prefer to travel business class je préfère voyager en classe affaires [zhuh prayfehr vwa-yazhay ON klas afehr]

business hours les heures *f* d'ouverture [uhr doovehr-tUr]

▶ what are the bank's business hours? quelles sont les heures d'ouverture de la banque ? [kel sON layz uhr doovehr-tUr duh la bONk]

bus station la gare routière [gar rootyehr]

- I'm looking for the bus station je cherche la gare routière [zhuh shersh la gar rootyehr]

bus stop l'arrêt *m* de bus [areh duh bUs]

- where's the nearest bus stop? où se trouve l'arrêt de bus le plus proche ? [oo suh troov lareh duh bUs luh plU prosh]

busy *(person, phone line)* occupé(e) [okU-pay]; *(town, beach, street)* animé(e) [anee-may], très fréquenté(e) [treh fraykON-tay]; *(period)* chargé(e) [sharzhay], plein(e) [plAN(plen)]

- the line's busy ça sonne occupé [sa son okU-pay]
- I'm afraid I'm busy tomorrow je crains d'être pris demain [zhuh krAN detr pree duhmAN]

butter le beurre [buhr]

- could you pass the butter please? pouvez-vous me passer le beurre, s'il vous plaît ? [poovay-voo muh pasay luh buhr seel voo play]

buy acheter [ashtay]

- where can I buy tickets? où achète-t-on les billets ? [oo ashet-tON lay beeyeh]
- can I buy you a drink? je vous offre un verre ? [zhuh vooz ofr AN vehr]

bye salut ! [salU]

- bye, see you tomorrow! salut, à demain ! [salU a duhmAN]

C

cab le taxi [taksee]

- can you order me a cab to take me to the airport? pouvez-vous me commander un taxi pour m'emmener à l'aéroport ? [poovay-voo muh komON-day AN taksee poor mONmuh-nay a la-ayro-por]

cab driver le chauffeur de taxi [shohfuhr duh taksee]

- does the cab driver speak English? est-ce que le chauffeur de taxi parle anglais ? [eskuh luh shohfuhr duh taksee parl ONglay]

cabin *(on plane, boat)* la cabine [kabeen]

- can I have breakfast in my cabin? puis-je avoir mon petit-déjeuner dans la cabine ? [pweezh avwar mON puhtee-dayzhuh-nay dON la kabeen]

cable le câble [kabl]

- does the hotel have cable? y a-t-il le câble à l'hôtel ? [ee ateel luh kabl a lotel]

cafés

The French love their *cafés*, whether they are sitting at a table outside, watching the world go by, or inside, with the newspapers and a cup of coffee. If you want to have a drink at the counter, you order there. Otherwise, sit down and a waiter will take your order. Prices are sometimes higher if you sit outside. Remember that *cafés* usually serve sandwiches and light meals, with perhaps a couple of hot dishes at lunchtime. Sometimes the waiter will leave your check on the table and make a small tear in it when you pay (to keep track of who's paid!). Otherwise, you can pay when you leave.

café le café [kafay]
  ▸ is there a café near here? y a-t-il un café dans les environs ? [ee ateel AN kafay dON layz ONvee-rON]

cake le gâteau [gatoh]
  ▸ a piece of that cake, please une part de ce gâteau, s'il vous plaît [Un par duh suh gatoh seel voo play]

call *(on phone)* l'appel *m* [apel], le coup de fil [koo duh feel] ◆ appeler [aplay]
  ▸ I have to make a call je dois passer un coup de fil [zhuh dwah pasay AN koo duh feel]
  ▸ what is this called? comment cela s'appelle-t-il ? [komON suhla sapel-teel]
  ▸ who's calling? c'est de la part de qui ? [seh duh la par duh kee]

call back rappeler [raplay]
  ▸ could you ask her to call me back? vous pouvez lui demander de me rappeler ? [voo poovay lwee duhmON-day duh muh raplay]
  ▸ I'll call back (later) je rappellerai (plus tard) [zhuh rapel-uhray (plU tar)]

calm calme [kalm]
  ▸ keep calm! restez calmes ! [restay kalm]

camera *(for taking photos)* l'appareil *m* photo [apa-rey fotoh]; *(for filming)* la caméra [kamay-ra]
  ▸ can I film with my camera here? je peux filmer avec ma caméra ici ? [zhuh puh feelmay avek ma kamay-ra eesee]

in a café

  ▸ is this table/seat free? cette table/place est-elle libre ? [set tabl/plas et-el leebr]
  ▸ excuse me! s'il vous plaît ! [seel voo play]
  ▸ two black coffees/white coffees, please deux cafés noirs/cafés crème, s'il vous plaît [duh kafay nwar/kafay krem seel voo play]
  ▸ can I have another beer, please? une autre bière, s'il vous plaît [Un ohtr byehr seel voo play]

camper le camping-car [kONpeeng-kar]

> do you have a space left for a camper? est-ce qu'il vous reste un emplacement pour camping-car ? [eskeel voo rest AN ONplas-mON poor kONpeeng-kar]

campground le camping [kONpeeng]

> I'm looking for a campground je cherche un camping [zhuh shersh AN kONpeeng]

camping le camping [kONpeeng]

> I love going camping j'adore faire du camping [zhador fehr dU kONpeeng]

can *(of food, drink)* la boîte de conserve [bwat duh kONserv]; *(of oil)* le bidon [beedON]; *(of paint)* le pot [poh] ♦ *(be able to)* pouvoir [poovwar]; *(know how to)* savoir [savwar]

> can I help you? je peux vous aider ? [zhuh puh vooz ehday]
> can you speak English? savez-vous parler anglais ? [savay-voo parlay ONglay]

Canada le Canada [kana-da]

> I'm from Canada je viens du Canada [zhuh vyAN dU kana-da]
> I live in Canada j'habite au Canada [zhabeet oh kana-da]
> have you ever been to Canada? êtes-vous déjà allé au Canada ? [et-voo dayzha alay oh kana-da]

Canadian canadien(ne) [kana-dyAN(-yen)] ♦ Canadien(ne) [kana-dyAN(-yen)]

> I'm Canadian je suis canadien/canadienne [zhuh swee kana-dyAN/kana-dyen]
> we're Canadians nous sommes des Canadiens/Canadiennes [noo som day kana-dyAN/kana-dyen]

cancel annuler [anU-lay]

> is it possible to cancel a booking? est-il possible d'annuler la réservation ? [eteel poseebl danU-lay la rayzer-vasyON]

canoeing le kayak [ka-yak]

> I was told we could go canoeing on m'a dit qu'on pouvait faire du kayak [ON ma dee kON pooveh fehr dU ka-yak]

car *(automobile)* la voiture [vwatUr]; *(on train)* le wagon [vagON], la voiture [vwatUr]

> I'd like to rent a car for a week je voudrais louer une voiture pour une semaine [zhuh voodreh lway Un vwatUr poor Un suhmen]

---

renting a car

> with comprehensive insurance avec une assurance tous risques [avek Un asU-rONs too-reesk]
> can I leave the car at the airport? pourrais-je rendre la voiture à l'aéroport ? [poorehzh rONdr la vwatUr a la-ayro-por]
> here's my driver's license voici mon permis de conduire [vwasee mON permee duh kONdweer]

- I've just crashed my car je viens d'avoir un accident de voiture [zhuh vyAN davwar AN aksee-dON duh vwatUr]
- can you help us to push the car? pouvez-vous nous aider à pousser la voiture ? [poovay-voo nooz ayday a poosay la vwatUr]
- my car's been towed away ma voiture a été emmenée à la fourrière [ma vwatUr a aytay ONmuh-nay a la fooryehr]
- my car's broken down ma voiture est en panne [ma vwatUr et ON pan]

carafe *(of water)* la carafe [karaf] *(of wine)* le pichet [peesheh]

- a carafe of water, please apportez-nous une carafe d'eau, s'il vous plaît [apo-tay-nooz Un karaf doh seel voo play]
- a carafe of house wine un pichet de la cuvée du patron [AN peesheh duh la kUvay dU patrON]

car crash l'accident *m* de voiture [aksee-dON duh vwatUr]

- he's been killed in a car crash il est mort d'un accident de la route [eel eh mor dan aksee-dON duh la root]

card la carte [kart]

- the waiter hasn't brought my card back le serveur ne m'a pas rendu ma carte [luh servuhr nuh ma pa rONdU ma kart]
- I need to get a card for my sister's birthday il faut que je trouve une carte pour l'anniversaire de ma soeur [eel foh kuh zhuh troov Un kart poor lanee-versehr duh ma suhr]
- can I give you my card? puis-je vous laisser ma carte ? [pweezh voo laysay ma kart]

cardigan le gilet [zheeleh]

- should I take a cardigan for the evening? est-ce qu'il faut que je prenne un gilet pour le soir ? [eskeel foh kuh zhuh pren AN zheeleh poor luh swar]

carpet le tapis [tapee], la moquette [moket]

- the carpet hasn't been vacuumed l'aspirateur n'a pas été passé [laspee-ratuhr na paz aytay pasay]

car rental la location de voitures [loka-syON duh vwatUr]

- is car rental expensive? ça revient cher, de louer une voiture ? [sa ruhvyAN shehr duh lway Un vwatUr]

car rental agency l'agence *f* de location de voitures [azhONs duh loka-syON duh vwatUr]

- do you know any car rental agencies? tu connais une agence de location de voitures ? [tU koneh Un azhONs duh loka-syON duh vwatUr]

carry porter [portay]

- can I carry something for you? est-ce que je peux vous porter quelque chose ? [eskuh zhuh puh voo portay kelkuh shohz]

carry-on bag les bagages *m* à main [bagazh a mAN]

- do you have any carry-on bags? avez-vous des bagages à main ? [avay-voo day bagazh a mAN]

cart *(for luggage, in supermarket)* le chariot [sharyoh]
- where do you get the carts? où puis-je trouver un chariot ? [oo pweezh troovay AN sharyoh]

carton *(of cigarettes)* la cartouche [kartoosh]
- I'd like a carton of cigarettes je voudrais une cartouche de cigarettes [zhuh voodreh Un kartoosh duh seega-ret]

case
- in case au cas où [oh kah oo]
- just in case à tout hasard [a toot azar]

cash *(notes and coins)* les espèces *f* [espes], (l'argent *m*) liquide [arzhON leekeed]
♦ *(check)* encaisser [ONkay-say]
- I'll pay cash je vais payer en liquide [zhuh veh peyay ON leekeed]
- I want to cash this traveler's check je désire encaisser ce chèque de voyage [zhuh dayzeer ONkay-say suh shek duh vwa-yazh]

castle le château [shatoh]
- is the castle open to the public? le château est-il ouvert au public ? [luh shatoh et-eel oovehr oh pUbleek]

catalog le catalogue [kata-log]
- do you have a catalog? avez-vous un catalogue ? [avay-vooz AN kata-log]

catch attraper [atra-pay]; *(hear clearly)* saisir [sayzeer]
- I've caught a cold j'ai attrapé un rhume [zhay atra-pay AN rUm]
- I'm sorry, I didn't quite catch your name excusez-moi, je n'ai pas bien saisi votre nom [ekskU-zay-mwa zhuh nay pa byAN sayzee votr nON]

Catholic catholique [kato-leek]
- where is there a Catholic church? où peut-on trouver une église catholique ? [oo puht-ON troovay Un aygleez kato-leek]

CD le CD [sayday]
- how much do CDs usually cost? combien coûte un CD, en général ? [kONbyAN koot AN sayday On zhaynay-ral]

cellphone le (téléphone) portable [(taylay-fon) portabl]
- what's your cellphone number? tu as un numéro de portable ? [tU a AN nUmay-roh duh portabl]

center le centre [sONtr]
- we want to be based near the center of the region nous aimerions être plutôt au centre de la région [nooz ehmuh-ryONz etr plUtoh oh sONtr duh la rayzh-yON]

chair la chaise [shehz]
- could we have another chair in our room? pourrions-nous avoir une autre chaise dans la chambre ? [pooryON-nooz avwar Un ohtr shehz dON la shONbr]

change le changement [shONzhmON]; *(money)* la monnaie [moneh] ♦ changer [shONzhay]

- there's been a change of plan il y a eu un changement de programme [eel ya U AN shONzhmON duh program]
- do you have any change? avez-vous de la monnaie ? [avay-voo duh la moneh]
- keep the change gardez la monnaie [garday la moneh]
- I don't have the exact change je n'ai pas l'appoint [zhuh nay pa lapwAN]
- is it possible to change a booking? est-il possible de modifier la réservation ? [et-eel poseebl du modee-fyay la rayzer-vasyON]
- I'd like to change 200 dollars into euros j'aimerais changer deux cents dollars en euros [zhehmuh-reh shONzhay duh sON dolar ON uhroh]
- I'd like to change these traveler's checks je voudrais changer ces chèques de voyage [zhuh voodreh shONzhay say shek duh vwa-yazh]
- can I change radio station? je peux changer de radio ? [zhuh puh shONzhay duh radyoh]
- can you help me to change the wheel? vous pouvez m'aider à changer la roue ? [voo povay mayday a shONzhay la roo]
- the oil needs to be changed il faut faire la vidange [eel foh fehr la veedONzh]
- where do I change for Nice? où dois-je changer pour Nice ? [oo dwazh shONzhay poor nees]

changing table la table à langer [tabl a lONzhay]

- is there a changing table? y a-t-il une table à langer ? [ee ateel Un tabl a lONzhay]

charge *(cost)* le coût [koo], les frais *m* [freh]

- is there a charge for the car park? est-ce que le parking est payant ? [eskuh luh parkeeng eh peyON]
- is there a charge for using the facilities? faut-il payer pour utiliser les équipements ? [foht-eel peyay poor Utee-leezay layz aykeep-mON]
- is there a charge for cancellations? doit-on payer des frais pour annuler une réservation ? [dwat-ON peyay day freh poor anU-lay Un rayzer-vasyON]
- I'd like to speak to the person in charge je voudrais parler au responsable de l'établissement [zhuh voodreh parlay oh respON-sabl duh laytab-leesmON]

charter flight le vol charter [vol shartehr]

- we're on a charter flight nous voyageons en charter [noo vwa-yazhONz ON shartehr]

cheap *(goods)* bon marché [bON marshay]; *(ticket)* à tarif réduit [a tareef raydwee]

- I'm trying to find a cheap flight home je cherche un vol à tarif réduit pour mon retour [zhuh shersh AN vol a tareef raydwee poor mON ruhtoor]

check *(in restaurant)* l'addition *f* [adee-syON]; *(for paying)* le chèque [shek]
♦ *(test, verify)* vérifier [vayree-fyay]

- the check, please! l'addition s'il vous plaît ! [ladee-syON seel voo play]
- can I pay by check? acceptez-vous les chèques de voyage ? [aksep-tay-voo lay shek duh vwa-yazh]
- can you check the oil? pouvez-vous vérifier le niveau d'huile ? [poovay-voo vayree-fyay luh neevoh dweel]

checkbook le chéquier [shaykyay], le carnet de chèques [karneh duh shek]

▸ my checkbook's been stolen on m'a volé mon chéquier [ON ma volay mON shaykyay]

check in *(airport)* enregistrer [ONruh-zheestray]; *(hotel)* arriver à l'hôtel [aree-vay a lotel], s'inscrire [sANskreer]

▸ I'd like to check in both these bags, please je voudrais faire enregistrer ces deux sacs, s'il vous plaît [zhu voodreh fehr ONruh-zheestray say duh sak seel voo play]

▸ what time do you have to be at the airport to check in? à quelle heure doit-on arriver à l'aéroport pour l'enregistrement des bagages ? [a kel uhr dwat-ON aree-vay a la-ayro-por poor lONruh-zheestruh-mON day bagazh]

check-in desk *(at airport)* le comptoir d'enregistrement (des bagages) [kONtwar dONruh-zheestruh-mON (day bagazh)]

▸ where is the United Airlines check-in desk? où est le comptoir d'enregistrement de United Airlines ? [oo eh luh kONtwar dONruh-zheestruh-mON duh United Airlines]

check out *(from hotel)* quitter l'hôtel [keetay lotel]

▸ what time do you have to check out by? à quelle heure faut-il quitter l'hôtel ? [a kel uhr foht-eel keetay lotel]

cheers! (à ta) santé ! [(a ta) sONtay]

▸ cheers and all the best! à ta/votre santé ! [a ta/votr sONtay]

cheese le fromage [fromazh]

▸ what are the best local cheeses? quels sont les meilleurs fromages de la région ? [kel sON lay mey-yuhr fromazh duh la rayzh-yON]

chicken le poulet [pooleh]

▸ half a roast chicken, please un demi-poulet rôti, s'il vous plaît [AN duhmee-pooleh rohtee seel voo play]

▸ chicken and fries un poulet-frites [AN pooleh-freet]

---

checking

▸ is it right and then left? c'est bien à droite, puis à gauche ? [seh byAN a drwat pweez a gohsh]

▸ is this the train for Marseilles? ce train va bien à Marseille ? [suh trAN va byAN a marsey]

▸ could you tell me where to get off, please? pourriez-vous me dire quand il faut descendre, s'il vous plaît ? [pooryay-voo muh deer kONt eel foh desONdr seel voo play]

▸ is this the right stop for...? c'est bien l'arrêt pour... ? [seh byAN lareh poor]

▸ are you sure that he'll be able to come? tu es sûr qu'il pourra venir ? [tU eh sUr keel poora vuhneer]

child l'enfant [ONfON]
- do you have children? as-tu des enfants ? [a-tU dayz ONfON]
- two adults and two children, please deux adultes et deux enfants, s'il vous plaît [duhz adUlt ay duhz ONfON seel voo play]
- do you do reductions for children? faites-vous des réductions pour les enfants ? [fet-voo day raydUk-syON poor layz ONfON]

children's menu le menu enfant [muhnU ONfON]
- do you have a children's menu? avez-vous un menu enfant ? [avay-vooz AN muhnU ONfON]

chilled (wine) frais [freh], fraîche [fresh]
- this wine isn't chilled enough ce vin n'est pas assez frais [suh vAN neh paz asay freh]

chocolate le chocolat [shoko-lah]
- I'd like a bar of chocolate je voudrais une tablette de chocolat [zhuh voodreh Un tablet duh shoko-lah]

choose choisir [shwazeer]
- I don't know which one to choose je ne sais pas lequel choisir [zhuh nuh seh pa luhkel shwazeer]

Christmas Noël [no-el]
- Merry Christmas! joyeux Noël ! [zhwa-yuh no-el]
- I wish you a very merry Christmas je vous souhaite de très bonnes fêtes de fin d'année [zhuh voo swet duh treh bon fet duh fAN danay]

Christmas Day le jour de Noël [zhoor duh no-el]
- is it closed on Christmas Day? c'est fermé le jour de Noël ? [seh fermay luh zhoor duh no-el]

church (Catholic) l'église f [aygleez]; (Protestant) le temple [tONpl]
- how old is the church? de quand date l'église ? [duh kON dat laygleez]
- where is there a Catholic church? où peut-on trouver une église catholique ? [oo puht-ON troovay Un aygleez kato-leek]
- where can we find a Protestant church? où peut-on trouver un temple protestant ? [oo puht-ON troovay AN tONpl protes-tON]

cigarette la cigarette [seega-ret]
- can I ask you for a cigarette? je peux vous demander une cigarette ? [zhuh puh voo duhmON-day Un seega-ret]
- where can I buy cigarettes? où est-ce que je peux acheter des cigarettes ? [oo eskuh zhuh puh ashtay day seega-ret]

cigarette lighter le briquet [breekeh]
- do you have a cigarette lighter? avez-vous un briquet ? [avay-vooz AN breekeh]

city la ville [veel]
- what's the nearest big city? quelle est la grande ville la plus proche ? [kel eh la grONd veel la plU prosh]

class *(on train, plane)* la classe [klas]
- which class are your seats in? vos places sont en quelle classe ? [voh plas sONt ON kel klas]

clean propre [propr] ♦ nettoyer [netwa-yay]
- the sheets aren't clean les draps ne sont pas propres [lay drah nuh sON pa propr]
- do we have to clean the apartment before leaving? est-ce qu'il faut nettoyer l'appartement avant de partir ? [eskeel foh netwa-yay lapar-tuhmON avON duh parteer]
- could you clean the windshield? pourriez-vous nettoyer le pare-brise ? [pooryay-voo netwa-yay luh par-breez]

cleaning le ménage [maynazh]
- who does the cleaning? qui fait le ménage ? [kee feh luh maynazh]

clear *(easily understood)* clair(e) [klehr]; *(way)* libre [leebr] ♦ *(road, path)* dégager [dayga-zhay]
- is that clear? est-ce que c'est clair ? [eskuh seh klehr]
- is the road ahead clear? est-ce que la route est dégagée ? [eskuh la root eh dayga-zhay]
- when will the road be cleared? quand est-ce que la route sera dégagée ? [kONd eskuh la root suh-ra dayga-zhay]

climb monter [mONtay]
- the road climbs steadily after you leave the village la route monte progressivement après le village [la root mON progreh-seevmON apreh luh veelazh]

climbing l'escalade *f* [eska-lad]
- can you go climbing here? est-ce que l'on peut faire de l'escalade ici ? [eskuh lON puh fehr duh leska-lad eesee]

cloakroom *(in a museum, a theater)* vestiaire [vest-yehr]
- is there a charge for the cloakroom? le vestiaire est payant ? [luh vest-yehr eh peyON]
- I'd like to leave my things in the cloakroom j'aimerais déposer mes affaires au vestiaire [zhemuh-reh daypo-zay mayz afehr oh vest-yehr]

close *(weather)* lourd(e) [loor(loord)] ♦ fermer [fermay]
- it's close il fait lourd [eel feh loor]
- what time do the stores close? à quelle heure ferment les magasins ? [a kel uhr ferm lay maga-zAN]
- what time do you close? à quelle heure vous fermez ? [a kel uhr voo fermay]
- it won't close ça ne ferme pas [sa nuh ferm pa]

closed fermé(e) [fermay]
- are the stores closed on Sundays? est-ce que les magasins sont fermés le dimanche ? [eskuh lay maga-zAN sON fermay luh deemONsh]

clothes les vêtements *m* [vetmON]
- where can we wash our clothes? où peut-on laver ses vêtements ? [oo puht-ON lavay say vetmON]

ordering a coffee

In French *cafés*, if you want a small cup of strong black coffee ask for *un (petit) café*, *un express* or *un petit noir*. If you want it extra-strong, ask for *un café serré*; for weak, say *un café léger*; and if you want it diluted with some hot water, ask for *un café allongé*. If you'd like an espresso with a dash of milk, it's *une noisette*. A large cup of black coffee is *un grand café* or *un grand noir*. Coffee with frothy, steam-heated milk is called *un (grand/petit) crème*. People never ask for *café au lait* in cafés.

club *(nightclub)* la boîte (de nuit) [bwat (duh nwee)]
▸ we could go to a club afterwards on pourrait aller en boîte après [ON pooreht alay ON bwat apreh]

coach le car [kar]
▸ what time does the coach leave? à quelle heure part le car ? [a kel uhr par luh kar]

coast la côte [koht]
▸ I'd like to go to the Atlantic coast j'aimerais aller sur la côte atlantique [zhemuh-rheh allay sUr la koht atlON-teek]

coffee *(drink, beans)* le café [kafay]
▸ white coffee café crème/au lait [kafay krem/oh leh]
▸ black coffee café noir [kafay nwar]
▸ I'd like a coffee je voudrais un café [zhuh voodreh AN kafay]
▸ would you like a coffee? tu veux un café ? [tU vuh AN kafay]

coin la pièce [pyes]
▸ the machine only takes coins la machine n'accepte que les pièces [la masheen naksept kuh lay pyes]

cold froid(e) [frwah(frwad)] ◆ *(illness)* le rhume [rUm]; *(low temperature)* le froid [frwah]
▸ it's cold today il fait froid aujourd'hui [eel feh frwah ohzhoor-dwee]
▸ I'm very cold j'ai très froid [zhay treh frwah]
▸ to have a cold avoir un rhume [avwar ANrUm]
▸ I've caught a cold j'ai attrapé un rhume [zhay atra-pay AN rUm]

collect *(person)* aller chercher [alay shershay]; *(ticket, package, luggage)* retirer [ruhtee-ray] ◆ *(call)* en PCV [ON paysay-vay]
▸ I've come to collect the tickets I booked by phone je viens retirer les billets que j'ai réservés par téléphone [zhuh vyAN ruhtee-ray lay beeyeh kuh zhay rayzer-vay par taylay-fon]
▸ where do we collect our luggage? où est-ce que l'on retire les bagages ? [oo eskuh ION ruhteer lay bagazh]
▸ I can call my parents collect je peux appeler mes parents en PCV [zhuh puh aplay may parON ON paysay-vay]

collect call l'appel *m* en PCV [apel ON paysay-vay]
- to make a collect call appeler en PCV [aplay ON paysay-vay]

color la couleur [kooluhr]
- do you have it in another color? avez-vous une autre couleur ? [avay-vooz Un ohtr kooluhr]

color film la pellicule couleur [pelee-kUl kooluhr]
- I'd like a color film je voudrais une pellicule couleur [zhuh voodreh Un pelee-kUl kooluhr]

come venir [vuhneer]; *(pass by)* passer [pasay]
- come here! viens ici ! [vyAN eesee]
- coming! j'arrive ! [zhareev]
- when does the bus come? quand passe le bus ? [kON pas luh bUs]
- the motorbike was coming from the right la moto venait de la droite [la motoh vuhneh duh la drwat]

come from venir de [vuhneer duh]
- where do you come from? d'où venez-vous ? [doo vuhnay-voo]

come in *(enter)* entrer [ONtray]; *(train)* arriver [aree-vay]; *(tide)* monter [mONtay]
- may I come in? puis-je entrer ? [pweezh ONtray]
- come in! entrez ! [ONtray]
- the tide's coming in la mer est en train de monter [la mehr et ON trAN duh mONtay]

come on *(light, heating)* s'allumer [salU-may], se mettre en marche [suh metr ON marsh]
- the heating hasn't come on le chauffage ne s'allume pas [luh shohfazh nuh salUm pa]
- come on! allez ! [alay]

come with *(go with)* accompagner [akON-panyay]; *(be served with)* être servi avec [etr servee avek]
- could you come with me to...? pourriez-vous m'accompagner jusqu'à... ? [poor-yay-voo makON-panyay zhUska]
- what does it come with? avec quoi ce plat est-il servi ? [avek kwa suh plah et-eel servee]

comfortable *(person)* bien [byAN]
- we're very comfortable here on est vraiment bien, ici [ON eh vrehmON byAN eesee]

commission la commission [komee-syON]
- what commission do you charge? qu'est-ce que vous prenez comme commission ? [keskuh voo pruhnay kom komee-syON]

company *(firm)* l'entreprise *f* [ONtr-preez]
- is it a big company? c'est une grande entreprise ? [seht Un grONd ONtr-preez]

compartment le compartiment [kONpar-teemON]

▸ which compartment are our seats in? dans quel compartiment se trouvent nos places ? [dON kel kONpar-teemON suh troov noh plas]

complain se plaindre [suh plANdr]
▸ I will be writing to your head office to complain je vais écrire au siège de votre société pour me plaindre [zhuh vehz aykreer oh syezh duh votr sosyay-tay poor muh plANdr]

complaint *(protest)* la plainte [plANt]; *(in store)* la réclamation [raykla-masyON]
▸ I'd like to make a complaint *(protest)* j'aimerais porter plainte [zhemuh-reh portay plANt]; *(in store)* j'aimerais faire une réclamation [zhemuh-reh fehr Un raykla-masyON]

complete *(form)* remplir [rONpleer]
▸ here's the completed form voici le formulaire rempli [vwasee luh formU-lehr rONplee]

comprehensive insurance l'assurance *f* tous risques [asU-rONs too reesk]
▸ how much extra is the comprehensive insurance coverage? combien coûte le supplément pour une assurance tous risques ? [kONbyAN koot luh sUplay-mON poor Un asU-rONs too reesk]

computer l'ordinateur *m* [ordee-natuhr]
▸ is there a computer I could use? pourrais-je utiliser un ordinateur ? [poorehzh Utee-leezay AN ordee-natuhr]

concert le concert [kONsehr]
▸ did you like the concert? ce concert vous a-t-il plu ? [suh kONsehr vooz ateel plU]

condom le préservatif [prayzer-vateef]
▸ do you have any condoms? as-tu des préservatifs ? [a-tU day prayzer-vateef]

confirm confirmer [kONfeer-may]
▸ I confirmed my reservation by phone j'ai confirmé ma réservation par

---

complaints

▸ I'd like to see the manager, please je voudrais voir le directeur, s'il vous plaît [zhuh voodreh vwar luh deerek-tuhr seel voo play]
▸ I have a complaint j'ai une réclamation à faire [zhay Un raykla-masyON a fehr]
▸ there's a problem with the heating il y a un problème avec le chauffage [eel ya AN problem avek luh shohfazh]
▸ I am relying on you to sort this problem out je compte sur vous pour régler ce problème [zhuh kONt sUr voo poor rayglay suh problem]
▸ I expect the cost of the camera to be fully reimbursed j'exige le remboursement intégral de l'appareil photo [zhegzeezh luh rONboor-suhmON ANtaygral duh lapa-rey fotoh]

téléphone [zhay kONfeer-may ma rayzer-vasyON par taylay-fon]

▸ I'd like to confirm my return flight je voudrais confirmer mon vol de retour [zhuh voodreh kONfeer-may mON vol duh ruhtoor]

congratulations les félicitations f [faylee-seeta-syON]

▸ congratulations! (toutes mes) félicitations ! [(toot may) faylee-seeta-syON]

connecting flight la correspondance [kores-pONdONs]

▸ does the connecting flight leave from the same terminal? la correspondance part-elle du même terminal ? [la kores-pONdONs part-el dU mem termee-nal]

connection *(on phone)* la communication [komU-neeka-syON]; *(transportation)* la correspondance [kores-pONdONs]

▸ the connection is very bad: I can't hear very well la communication est très mauvaise, je t'entends mal [la komU-neeka-syON eh treh mohvez zhuh tONtON mal]

▸ I've missed my connection j'ai raté ma correspondance [zhay ratay ma kores-pONdONs]

consulate le consulat [kONsU-lah]

▸ where is the American consulate? où est le consulat américain ? [oo eh luh kONsU-laht amay-reekAN]

contact *(communication)* le contact [kONtakt] ◆ contacter [kONtak-tay]

▸ I need to contact my family in the States je dois contacter ma famille aux États-Unis [zhuh dwah kONtak-tay ma famee ohz aytaz-Unee]

▸ do you know how to get in contact with him? savez-vous comment le contacter ? [savay-voo komON luh kONtak-tay]

contact lens la lentille [lONteey], le verre de contact [vehr duh kONtakt]

▸ I've lost a contact lens j'ai perdu une lentille [zhay perdU Un lONteey]

cookie *(food)* le biscuit [beeskwee], le gâteau sec [gatoh sek]

▸ a box of cookies, please un paquet de biscuits, s'il vous plaît [AN pakeh duh beeskwee seel voo play]

cooking la cuisine [kweezeen]

▸ we prefer to do our own cooking on préfère faire notre propre cuisine [ON prayfehr fehr notr propr kweezeen]

▸ do you like French cooking? tu aimes la cuisine française ? [tU em la kweezeen frONsez]

cork *(for a bottle)* le bouchon [booshON]

▸ where's the cork for the bottle? où est le bouchon de la bouteille ? [oo eh luh booshON duh la bootey]

corked bouchonné(e) [boosho-nay]

▸ this wine is corked ce vin est bouchonné [suh vAN eh boosho-nay]

corner le coin [kwAN]

▸ stop at the corner arrêtez-vous au coin de la rue [areh-tay-vooz oh kwAN duh la rU]

coronary l'infarctus *m* [ANfark-tUs]

> he's had a coronary il a fait un infarctus [eel a fet AN ANfark-tUs]

correct *(check)* juste [zhUst]

> that's correct c'est juste [seh zhUst]

cost coûter [kootay]

> how much will it cost to go to the airport? combien ça va me coûter pour aller à l'aéroport ? [kONbyAN sa va muh kootay poor alay a la-ayro-por]

> it cost us 150 euros ça nous est revenu à cent cinquante euros [sa nooz a ruhvuh-nU a sON sANkONt uhroh]

cot le lit de camp [lee duh kON]

> we can put a cot in the room for you on peut mettre un lit de camp dans la chambre pour toi [ON puh metr AN lee duh kON dON la shONbr poor twa]

cough la toux [too] ◆ tousser [toosay]

> I have a cough je tousse [zhuh toos]

> I need something for a cough j'aurais besoin de quelque chose contre la toux [zhohreh buhzwAN duh kelkuh shohz kONtr la too]

could pouvoir [poovwar]

> could you help me? pourriez-vous m'aider ? [pooryay-voo mayday]

counter *(in store)* le comptoir [kONtwar]; *(in bank)* le guichet [geesheh]

> which counter do I have to go to? à quel guichet dois-je m'adresser ? [a kel geesheh dwazh madreh-say]

> do you sell this medication over the counter? vendez-vous ce médicament sans ordonnance ? [vONday-voo suh maydee-kamON sONz ordo-nONs]

country le pays [peyee]

> what country do you come from? de quel pays viens-tu ? [duh kel peyee vyAN-tU]

couple le couple [koopl]

> it's for a couple and two children c'est pour un couple et deux enfants [seh poor AN koopl ay duhz ONfON]

course *(of a meal)* le plat [plah]; *(of a ship, a plane)* la route [root]; *(for a race)* le champ de courses [shON duh koors]; *(in yoga, sailing)* le stage [stazh] ◆ **of course** bien sûr [byAN sUr]

> is the set meal three courses? il y a trois plats dans le menu ? [eel ya trwah plah dON luh muhnU]

> how much does the sailing course cost? combien coûte le stage de voile [kONbyAN koot luh stazh duh vwal]

> of course he'll come bien sûr qu'il va venir [byAN sUr keel va vuhneer]

cream *(for the skin)* la crème [krem]

> do you have a cream for a sunburn? vous avez de la crème contre les coups de soleil ? [vooz avay duh la krem koNtr lay koo duh soley]

credit cards

Carte Bleue® is the name given to all debit cards in France, although only one of them is actually blue. It's used to withdraw cash from ATMs, to pay for goods and services, or to make payments online. Most stores, hotels and restaurants will accept payment with a credit card such as Visa®.

credit card la carte de crédit [kart duh kraydee]
▶ do you take credit cards? acceptez-vous les cartes de crédit ? [aksep-tay-voo lay kart duh kraydee]

cross *(street, river)* traverser [traver-say]; *(border)* passer [pasay]
▶ how do we cross? comment on traverse ? [komOnt ON travers]

cross-country skiing le ski de fond [skee duh fON]
▶ where can we go cross-country skiing around here? où peut-on faire du ski de fond par ici ? [oo puht-ON fehr dU skee duh fON par eesee]

crosswalk le passage clouté [pasazh klootay]
▶ always cross at the crosswalk traversez toujours dans les passages cloutés [traver-say toozhoor dON lay pasazh klootay]

cruise la croisière [krwazyehr]
▶ how much does a cruise on the Seine cost? combien coûte une croisière sur la Seine ? [kONbyAN koot Un krwazyehr sUr la sehn]

cry pleurer [pluhray]
▶ don't cry ne pleure pas [nuh pluhr pah]

cup la tasse [tas]
▶ I'd like a cup of tea je voudrais une tasse de thé [zhuh voodreh Un tas duh tay]
▶ a coffee cup une tasse à café [Un tas a kafay]

currency *(money)* la monnaie [moneh]
▶ how much local currency do you have? combien avez-vous en monnaie locale ? [kONbyAN avay-vooz ON moneh lokal]

currency exchange le bureau de change [bUroh duh shONzh]
▶ is there a currency exchange around here? est-ce qu'il y a un bureau de change près d'ici ? [es-keel ya AN bUroh duh shONzh preh deesee]

cut couper [koopay]
▶ I've cut my finger je me suis coupé le doigt [zhuh muh swee koopay luh dwah]

d

daily quotidien(ne) [kotee-dyAN(-dyen)]
▸ what's the name of the local daily newspaper? comment s'appelle le quotidien local ? [komON sapel luh kotee-dyAN lokal]

damage abîmer [abee-may]
▸ my suitcase was damaged in transit ma valise a été abîmée pendant le voyage [ma valeez a aytay abee-may pONdON luh vwa-yazh]

damp humide [Umeed]
▸ it's damp today il fait humide aujourd'hui [eel feht Umeed ohzhoor-dwee]

dance danser [dONsay]
▸ shall we dance? on danse ? [ON dONs]
▸ I can't dance je ne sais pas danser [zhuh nuh seh pa dONsay]

dancing la danse [dONs]
▸ will there be dancing? est-ce qu'on dansera ? [eskON dONsuh-ra]
▸ where can we go dancing? où peut-on aller danser ? [oo puht-ON alay dONsay]

dandruff les pellicules *f* [pelee-kUl]
▸ I suffer from dandruff j'ai des pellicules [zhay day pelee-kUl]

danger le danger [dONzhay]
▸ hurry! someone's in danger! venez vite, quelqu'un est en danger ! [vuhnay veet kelkAN eht ON dONzhay]

dangerous dangereux [dONzh-ruh], dangereuse [dONzh-ruhz]
▸ this stretch of the river is quite dangerous cette partie du fleuve est assez dangereuse [set partee dU fluhv eht asay dONzh-ruhz]

dark *(room, night)* sombre [sONbr], noir(e) [nwar]; *(hair)* brun(e) [brAN(brUn)]
▸ it's dark il fait noir [eel feh nwar]
▸ she has dark hair elle a les cheveux bruns [el a lay shuhvuh brAN]

dark chocolate le chocolat noir [shoko-lah nwar]
▸ I prefer dark chocolate je préfère le chocolat noir [zhuh prayfehr luh shoko-lah nwar]

date *(in time)* la date [dat]; *(appointment)* le rendez-vous [rONday-voo]
▸ I've got a date tonight je sors avec quelqu'un ce soir [zhuh sor avek kelkAN suh swar]

date-stamp composter [kONpos-tay]
▸ do I have to date-stamp this ticket? est-ce qu'il faut composter le billet ? [eskeel foh kONpos-tay luh beeyeh]

daughter la fille [feey]
- this is my daughter voici ma fille [vwasee ma feey]

day le jour [zhoor]; *(expressing duration)* la journée [zhoornay]
- what day is it? quel jour sommes-nous ? [kel zhoor som-noo]
- I arrived three days ago je suis arrivé il y a trois jours [zhuh sweez aree-vay eel ya trwah zhoor]
- I'd like to do a round trip in a day je voudrais faire l'aller-retour dans la journée [zhuh voodreh fehr lalay-ruhtoor dON la zhoornay]
- how much is it a day? c'est combien par jour ? [seh kONbyAN par zhoor]
- I prefer traveling by day je préfère voyager de jour [zhuh prayfehr vwaya-zhay duh zhoor]

dead mort(e) [mor(mort)]
- he was pronounced dead at the scene il a été déclaré mort sur les lieux [eel a aytay dayklka-ray mor sUr lay lyuh]
- the battery's dead la batterie est morte [la batree eh mort]

dead end l'impasse *f* [ANpas], la voie sans issue [vwa sONz eesU]
- it's a dead end c'est une impasse [seht Un ANpas]

deal *(business agreement)* l'affaire *f* [afehr], le marché [marshay]
- I got a good deal on the room j'ai fait une affaire sur le prix de la chambre [zhay feht Un afehr sUr luh pree duh la shONbr]

death la mort [mor]
- there were two deaths il y a eu deux morts [eel ya U duh mor]

decaf, decaffeinated coffee
- a decaf/decaffeinated coffee, please un déca/un décaféiné, s'il vous plaît [AN dayka/AN dayka-fay-eenay seel voo play]

December décembre [daysONbr]
- December 10th le dix décembre [luh dee daysONbr]

decide choisir [shwazeer]
- we haven't decided yet nous n'avons pas encore choisi [noo navON paz ONkor shwazee]

deck *(of ship)* le pont [pON]; *(of cards)* le jeu [zhuh]
- how do I get to the upper deck? comment fait-on pour aller sur le pont supérieur ? [komON feht-ON poor alay sUr luh pON sUpayr-yuhr]

deckchair la chaise longue [shez IONg]
- I'd like to rent a deckchair je voudrais louer une chaise longue [zhuh voodreh lway Un shez IONg]

declare déclarer [daykla-ray]
- I have nothing to declare je n'ai rien à déclarer [zhuh nay ryAN a daykla-ray]
- I have a bottle of spirits to declare j'ai une bouteille d'alcool à déclarer [zhay Un bootey dalkol a daykla-ray]

definitely certainement [serten-mON]
> we'll definitely find them on va certainement les retrouver [ON va serten-mON lay ruhtroo-vay]

degree le degré [duhgray]
> it's 5 degrees below freezing il fait moins cinq (degrés) [eel feh mwAN sANk (duhgray)]

delay le retard [ruhtar]
> there's going to be a short delay to your flight votre vol aura un léger retard [votr vol ohra AN layzhay ruhtar]

delayed retardé(e) [ruhtar-day]
> how long will the flight be delayed? le vol sera retardé de combien de temps ? [luh vol suhra ruhtar-day duh kONbyAN duh tON]

delighted enchanté(e) [OnshON-tay], ravi(e) [ravee]
> we're delighted you could make it nous sommes ravis que vous ayiez pu venir [noo som ravee kuh vooz a-yay pU vuhneer]

dentist le dentiste [dONteest]
> I need to see a dentist urgently je dois voir un dentiste de toute urgence [zhuh dwah vwar AN dONteest duh toot UrzhOns]

department *(in store)* le service [servees], le rayon [reyON]
> I'm looking for the menswear department je cherche le rayon hommes [zhuh shersh luh reyON om]

department store le grand magasin [grON maga-zAN]
> where are the department stores? où sont les grands magasins ? [oo sON lay grON maga-zAN]

departure le départ [daypar]
> all departures are subject to delays tous les départs sont susceptibles d'être retardés [toolay daypar sON sUsep-teebl detr ruhtar-day]

departure lounge la salle d'embarquement [sal dONbark-mON]
> where's the departure lounge? où se trouve la salle d'embarquement ? [oo suh troov la sal dONbark-mON]

deposit *(against loss or damage)* la caution [kohsyON]; *(down payment)* l'acompte *m* [akONt], les arrhes *f* [ar]
> is there a deposit to pay on the equipment? faut-il payer une caution pour le matériel ? [foht-eel peyay Un kohsyON poor luh matay-ryel]
> how much is the deposit? quel est le montant de la caution ? [kel eh luh mONtON duh la kohsyON]

desk *(in office, home)* le bureau [bUroh]; *(at reception)* la réception [raysep-syON]; *(for cashier)* la caisse [kehs]; *(at airport)* le comptoir [kONtwar]
> ask at the desk demandez à la réception [duhmON-day a la raysep-syON]
> where can I find the Air France desk ? où est le comptoir d'Air France ? [oo eh luh kONtwar dehr frONs]

dessert le dessert [dayser]
▸ what desserts do you have? qu'est-ce que vous avez comme desserts ? [keskuh vooz avay kom dayser]

dessert wine le vin doux [vAN doo]
▸ can you recommend a good dessert wine? que pouvez-vous nous recommander comme vin doux ? [kuh poovay-voo noo ruhko-mONday kom vAN doo]

develop développer [dayvlo-pay]
▸ how much does it cost to develop a 36-exposure film? combien ça coûte pour développer une pellicule de trente-six poses ? [kONbyAN sa koot poor dayvlo-pay Un pelee-kUl duh trONt-sees poz]

diabetic diabétique [dyabay-teek]
▸ I'm diabetic and I need a prescription for insulin je suis diabétique et il me faudrait une ordonnance d'insuline [zhuh swee dyabay-teek ay eel muh fohdreht Un ordo-nONs dANsU-leen]

diarrhea la diarrhée [dyaray]
▸ I'd like something for diarrhea je voudrais un médicament contre la diarrhée [zhuh voodreh AN maydee-kamON kONtr la dyaray]

difference *(in price, cost)* la différence [deefay-rONs]
▸ will you pay the difference? tu veux bien payer la différence ? [tU vuh byAN peyay la deefay-rONs]

difficult difficile [deefee-seel]
▸ there are some sounds which are difficult to pronounce il y a des sons difficiles à prononcer [eel ya day sON deefee-seel a pronON-say]

difficulty *(trouble)* la difficulté [deefee-kUltay]; *(problem)* le problème [problem]
▸ the main difficulty is the pronunciation la principale difficulté, c'est la prononciation [la prANsee-pal deefee-kUltay seh la pronON-syasyON]
▸ did you have any difficulty finding the place? vous avez eu du mal à trouver ? [vooz avay U dU mal a troovay]

digital camera l'appareil *m* photo numérique [apa-rey fotoh nUmay-reek]
▸ my digital camera's been stolen on m'a volé mon appareil photo numérique [ON ma volay mON apa-rey fotoh nUmay-reek]

dining room la salle à manger [sal a mONzhay]
▸ do you have to have breakfast in the dining room? est-ce qu'on est obligé de prendre le petit déjeuner dans la salle à manger ? [eskON eht oblee-zhay duh prONdr luh puhtee dayzhuh-nay dON la sal a mONzhay]

dinner le dîner [deenay]
▸ up to what time do they serve dinner? jusqu'à quelle heure servent-ils le dîner ? [zhUska kel uhr serv-teel luh deenay] ▸ see box on p. 40

direct direct(e) [deerekt]
▸ is that train direct? s'agit-il d'un train direct ? [sazheet-eel dAN trAN deerekt]

dinner

The French tend to eat dinner relatively late, at about 8 o'clock at the earliest. *Le dîner* is more often than not a three-course meal consisting of an *entrée* (starter), a *plat principal* (main course) and a *dessert*, but sometimes you will also be offered extra courses such as *la salade* and *le fromage* before dessert. Obviously, all of this takes time, so it's quite common to spend several hours at the dinner table.

direction *(heading)* la direction [deerek-syON]
 ▶ am I heading in the right direction for the Louvre? suis-je bien dans la direction du Louvre ? [sweezh byAN dON la deerek-syON dU loovr]

directory assistance les renseignements *m* [rONsen-yuhmON]
 ▶ what's the number for directory assistance? quel est le numéro des renseignements ? [kel eh luh nUmay-roh day rONsen-yuhmON]

dirty *(room, tablecloth)* sale [sal]
 ▶ the sheets are dirty les draps sont sales [lay drah sON sal]

disability le handicap [ONdee-kap]
 ▶ do you have facilities for people with disabilities? êtes-vous équipés pour les handicapés ? [et-vooz aykee-pay poor lay ONdeeka-pay]

disabled handicapé(e) [ONdee-kapay]
 ▶ you can't park in a disabled parking space vous ne pouvez pas vous garer à une place pour handicapés [voo nuh poovay pah voo garay a Un plas poor ONdee-kapay]

disco *(club)* la discothèque [deesko-tek]
 ▶ are there any discos around here? est-ce qu'il y a des discothèques ici ? [eskeel ya day deesko-tek eesee]

discount le rabais [rabeh]
 ▶ is there any chance of a discount? ce n'est pas possible d'avoir un petit rabais ? [suh neh pah poseebl davwar AN puhtee rabeh]

dish le plat [plah] ◆ **dishes** la vaisselle [vehsel]
 ▶ what's the dish of the day? quel est le plat du jour ? [kel eh luh plah dU zhoor]
 ▶ can I help you with the dishes? je peux vous aider à faire la vaisselle ? [zhuh puh vooz ayday a fehr la vehsel]

disposable jetable [zhuhtabl]
 ▶ I need some disposable razors j'ai besoin de rasoirs jetables [zhay buhzwAN duh razwar zhuhtabl]
 ▶ do you sell disposable cameras? est-ce que vous vendez des appareils photo jetables ? [eskuh voo vONday dayz apa-rey fotoh zhuhtabl]

distance la distance [deestONs]
 ▶ the hotel is only a short distance from here l'hôtel n'est pas très loin d'ici [lotel neh pas treh lwAN deesee]

district (*of town*) le quartier [kartyay], l'arrondissement *m* [arON-deesmON]
  ▸ which district of Paris do you live in? vous habitez dans quel quartier de Paris ? [vooz abee-tay dON kel kartyay duh paree]

dive plonger [plONzhay] ◆ le plongeon [plONzhON]
  ▸ can we do a night dive? peut-on plonger de nuit ? [puht-ON plONzhay duh nwee]

diversion la déviation [dayvya-syON]
  ▸ is there a diversion? y a-t-il une déviation ? [ee ateel Un dayvya-syON]

diving la plongée [plONzhay]
  ▸ what's the diving like around here? la plongée est bonne par ici ? [la plONzhay eh bon par eesee]
  ▸ I'd like to take diving lessons j'aimerais prendre des cours de plongée [zhemuh-reh prONdr day koor duh plONzhay]
  ▸ do you rent out diving equipment? louez-vous du matériel de plongée ? [lway-voo dU matay-ryel duh plONzhay]

diving board le plongeoir [plONzhwar]
  ▸ is there a diving board? y a-t-il un plongeoir ? [ee ateel AN plONzhwar]

dizzy spell le vertige [vehrteezh]
  ▸ I've been having dizzy spells j'ai des vertiges [zhay day vehrteezh]

do faire [fehr]
  ▸ what do you do for a living? que faites-vous comme métier ? [kuh fet-voo kom maytyay]
  ▸ is there anything I can do (to help)? puis-je faire quelque chose (pour vous aider) ? [pweezh fehr kelkuh shohz (poor vooz ayday)]
  ▸ what are you doing tonight? qu'est-ce que tu fais ce soir ? [keskuh tU feh suh swar]
  ▸ what is there to do here on Sundays? que peut-on faire ici le dimanche ? [kuh puht-ON fehr eesee luh deeMONsh]
  ▸ we did 150 kilometers in two hours nous avons fait cent cinquante kilomètres en deux heures [nooz avON feh sON sANkONt keelo-metr ON duhz uhr]

doctor le médecin [maydsAN]
  ▸ I have to see a doctor je dois voir un médecin [zhuh dwah vwar AN maydsAN]

dollar le dollar [dolar]
  ▸ I'd like to change some dollars into euros je voudrais changer des dollars en euros [zhuh voodreh shONzhay day dolar ON uhroh]

door la porte [port]
  ▸ do you want me to answer the door? tu veux que j'aille ouvrir ? [tU vuh kuh zha-yuh oovreer]

dormitory (*in youth hostel*) le dortoir [dortwar]; (*for students*) la cité universitaire [seetay Unee-versee-tehr]
  ▸ are you staying in the dormitory? tu loges en cité universitaire ? [tU lozh ON seetay Unee-versee-tehr]

double double [doobl] ◆ le double de [luh doobl duh] ◆ doubler [dooblay]
  ▸ it's spelled with a double l ça s'écrit avec deux l [sa saykree avek duhz el]
  ▸ prices have doubled since last year les prix ont doublé depuis l'an dernier [lay pree ON dooblay duhpwee lON dernyay]

double bed le grand lit [grON lee]
  ▸ does the room have a double bed? la chambre a-t-elle un grand lit ? [la shONbr a-tel AN grON lee]

double room la chambre double [shONbr doobl]
  ▸ I'd like to book a double room for 5 nights, please je voudrais réserver une chambre pour deux personnes pour cinq nuits, s'il vous plaît [zhuh voodreh rayzer-vay Un shONbr poor duh person poor sANk nwee seel voo play]

downtown central(e) [sONtral] ◆ au centre-ville [ohN sONtr-veel] ◆ le centre-ville [luh sONtr-veel]
  ▸ we're looking for a good downtown hotel on cherche un bon hôtel central [ON shersh AN bon otel sONtral]
  ▸ does this bus go downtown? est-ce que ce bus va au centre-ville ? [eskuh suh bUs va oh sONtr-veel]
  ▸ is it easy to park in the downtown? c'est facile de se garer dans le centre-ville ? [seh faseel duh suh garay dON luh sONtr-veel]

draft beer la (bière) pression [(byehr) presyON]
  ▸ a draft beer, please une bière pression, s'il vous plaît [Un byehr presyON seel voo play]

dream le rêve [rev] ◆ rêver [revay]
  ▸ to have a dream faire un rêve [fehr AN rev]
  ▸ I dreamt (that)... j'ai rêvé que... [zhay revay kuh]

drink la boisson [bwasON], la consommation [kONso-masyON] ◆ boire [bwar]
  ▸ I'll have a cold drink je vais prendre une boisson fraîche [zhuh veh prONdr Un bwasON fresh]
  ▸ I could do with a drink je boirais bien un coup [zhuh bwareh byAN AN koo]
  ▸ what kind of hot drinks do you have? qu'est-ce que vous avez comme boissons chaudes ? [keskuh vooz avay kom bwasON shohd]
  ▸ shall we go for a drink? on va boire un verre ? [ON va bwar AN vehr]
  ▸ can I buy you a drink? je peux vous offrir un verre ? [zhuh puh vooz ofreer AN vehr]

drive *(in vehicle)* la promenade [promnad], le tour [toor] ◆ conduire [kONdweer]
  ▸ is it a long drive? est-ce que c'est loin en voiture ? [eskuh seh lwAN ON vwatUr]
  ▸ I'm not used to driving a manual je n'ai pas l'habitude de conduire une voiture à boîte manuelle [zhuh nay pah labee-tUd duh kONdweer Un vwatUr a bwat manUel]
  ▸ could you drive me home? pourriez-vous me raccompagner ? [pooryay-voo muh rakON-panyay]
  ▸ she was driving too close elle roulait trop près [el rooleh troh preh]

driver conducteur [kONdUk-tuhr], conductrice [kONdUk-trees]; *(of taxi)* le chauffeur [shohfuhr]

▸ the other driver wasn't looking where he was going l'autre conducteur ne regardait pas où il allait [lohtr kONdUk-tuhr nuh ruhgar-deh paz oo eel aleh]

driver's license le permis de conduire [permee duh kONdweer]

▸ here's my driver's license voici mon permis de conduire [vwasee mON permee duh kONdweer]

drop *(of liquid)* la goutte [goot]; *(small amount)* le doigt [dwah] ◆ *(let fall)* laisser tomber [laysay tONbay]; *(let out of vehicle)* déposer [daypo-zay]

▸ could I just have a drop of milk? je peux avoir juste une goutte de lait ? [zhuh puhz avwar zhUst Un goot duh leh]

▸ I dropped my scarf j'ai laissé tomber mon foulard [zhay laysay tONbay mON foolar]

▸ could you drop me at the corner? est-ce que vous pourriez me déposer au coin ? [eskuh voo pooryay muh daypo-zay oh kwAN]

drop off *(let out of vehicle)* déposer [daypo-zay]

▸ could you drop me off here? est-ce que vous pourriez me déposer ici ? [eskuh voo pooryay muh daypo-zay eesee]

drown se noyer [suh nwa-yay]

▸ he's drowning: somebody call for help il est en train de se noyer, il faut appeler de l'aide [eel eht ON trAN duh suh nwa-yay eel foht aplay duh lehd]

drugstore la pharmacie [farma-see]

▸ where is the nearest drugstore? où se trouve la pharmacie la plus proche ? [oo suh troov la farma-see la plU prosh]

drunk ivre [eevr]

▸ he's drunk il est ivre [eel eht eevr]

dry sec [sek], sèche [sesh] ◆ *(gen)* sécher [sayshay]; *(with a cloth, a towel)* essuyer [eswee-yay]

▸ a small glass of dry white wine un petit verre de vin blanc sec [AN puhtee vehr duh vAN blON sek]

at a drugstore

▸ I'd like something for a headache/a sore throat/diarrhea je voudrais un médicament contre les maux de tête/le mal de gorge/la diarrhée [zhuh voodreh AN maydee-kamON kONtr lay moh duh tet/luh mal duh gorzh/la dyaray]

▸ I'd like some aspirin/some Band-Aids® je voudrais de l'aspirine/des sparadraps [zhuh voodreh duh laspee-reen/day spara-drah]

▸ could you recommend a doctor? pourriez-vous me recommander un médecin ? [pooryay-voo muh ruhko-mONday AN maydsAN]

▸ where can I put my towel to dry? où est-ce que je peux mettre ma serviette à sécher ? [oo eskuh zhuh puh metr ma servyet a saychay]

dry cleaner's le pressing [preseeng]
  ▸ is there a dry cleaner's nearby? y a-t-il un pressing dans les environs ? [ee ateel AN preseeng dON layz ONvee-rON]

dryer *(for laundry)* le séchoir (à linge) [sayshwar (a lANzh)]
  ▸ is there a dryer? est-ce qu'il y a un séchoir ? [eskeel ya AN sayshwar]

dub *(movie)* doubler [dooblay]
  ▸ do they always dub English-language movies? est-ce que tous les films en anglais sont doublés ? [eskuh too lay feelm ON ONglay sON dooblay]

during pendant [pONdON]
  ▸ I heard a noise during the night j'ai entendu un bruit pendant la nuit [zhay ONtON-dU AN brwee pONdON la nwee]

duty la taxe [taks], le droit [drwah]
  ▸ do I have to pay duty on this? je dois payer une taxe là-dessus ? [zhuh dwah payay Un taks la-duhsU]
  ▸ I want to see the doctor on duty je veux voir le médecin de garde [zhuh vuh vwar luh maydsAN duh gard]

duty-free shop la boutique hors taxes [booteek or taks], le duty-free [dUtee-free]
  ▸ where are the duty-free shops? où sont les boutiques hors taxes ? [oo sON lay booteek or taks]

DVD le DVD [dayvay-day]
  ▸ which region is this DVD? ce DVD est de quelle zone ? [suh dayvay-day eh duh kel zon]

ear l'oreille *f* [orey]
  ▸ I have a ringing in my ears j'ai un bourdonnement dans l'oreille [zhay AN boordon-mON dON lorey]

earache le mal aux oreilles [mal ohz orey]
  ▸ he has an earache il a mal aux oreilles [eel a mal ohz orey]

ear infection l'otite *f* [oteet]
  ▸ I have an ear infection j'ai une otite [zhay Un oteet]

early *(in the day)* tôt [toh]; *(before the expected time)* en avance [ON avONs]
  ◆ *(at the beginning)* au début [oh daybU]
  ▸ is there an earlier one? il n'y en a pas plus tôt ? [eel nyON a pa plU toh]
  ▸ we arrived early nous sommes arrivés en avance [noo somz aree-vay ON avONs]

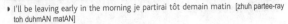

▸ I'll be leaving early in the morning je partirai tôt demain matin [zhuh partee-ray toh duhmAN matAN]

Easter Pâques [pahk]

▸ Happy Easter! joyeuses Pâques ! [zhwayuhz pahk]

easy facile [faseel]

▸ is it easy to use? est-ce que le maniement est simple ? [eskuh luh manee-mON eh sANpl]

▸ I'd like something easy to carry je voudrais quelque chose de facile à transporter [zhuh voodreh kelkuh shohz duh faseel a trONspor-tay]

eat manger [mONzhay]

▸ I'm afraid I don't eat meat désolé, je ne mange pas de viande [dayzo-lay zhuh nuh mONzh pa duh vyONd]

▸ where can we get something to eat? où pouvons-nous manger un morceau ? [oo poovON-noo mONzhay AN morsoh]

economy class la classe économique [klas ayko-nomeek]

▸ are there any seats in economy class? il y a des places en classe économique ? [eel ya day plas ON klas ayko-nomeek]

▸ I'd prefer to go economy class je préfèrerais voyager en classe économique [zhuh prayfay-ruhreh vwa-yazhay ON klas ayko-nomeek]

egg l'œuf m [uhf]

▸ how would you like your eggs? comment voulez-vous vos œufs? [komON voolay-voo vohz uhf]

eight huit [weet]

▸ there are eight of us nous sommes huit [noo som weet]

electric heater le radiateur électrique [radya-tuhr aylek-treek]

▸ do you have an electric heater? auriez-vous un radiateur électrique ? [ohryay-vooz AN radya-tuhr aylek-treek]

electricity l'électricité f [aylek-treesee-tay]

▸ there's no electricity in the room il n'y a pas d'électricité dans la chambre [eel nya pa daylek-treesee-tay dON la shONbr]

electric razor, electric shaver le rasoir électrique [razwar aylek-treek]

▸ where can I plug in my electric razor? où y a-t-il une prise pour mon rasoir électrique ? [oo ee ateel Un preez poor mON razwar aylek-treek]

elevator l'ascenseur m [asON-suhr]

▸ is there an elevator? est-ce qu'il y a un ascenseur ? [eskeel ya AN asON-suhr]

▸ the elevator is out of order l'ascenseur est en panne [lasON-suhr eht ON pan]

eleven onze [ONz]

▸ there are eleven of us nous sommes onze [noo som ONz]

emergencies

In a medical emergency, you can reach *SAMU* (*Service d'Assistance Médicale d'Urgence*) by dialing *15*, or the *Pompiers* (fire department), whose ambulances are often the fastest to arrive, by dialing *18*. Fire stations also often provide first aid and emergency treatment. The emergency number for the police is *17*.

e-mail l'e-mail *m* [eemel]
- I'd like to send an e-mail je voudrais envoyer un e-mail [zhuh voodreh ONvwa-yay AN eemel]
- where can I check my e-mail? où puis-je consulter mes e-mails ? [oo pweezh kONsUl-tay mayz eemel]

e-mail address l'adresse *f* électronique [adres aylek-troneek]
- do you have an e-mail address? tu as une adresse électronique ? [tU a Un adres aylek-troneek]

emergency l'urgence *f* [UrzhONs]
- it's an emergency! c'est urgent ! [seht UrzhON]
- what number do you call in an emergency? quel numéro faut-il appeler en cas d'urgence ? [kel nUmay-roh foht-eel aplay ON kas dUrzhONs]

emergency brake le frein à main [frAN a mAN]
- I'm sure I put the emergency brake on je suis sûr d'avoir serré le frein à main [zhuh swee sUr avvwar seray luh frAN a mAN]

emergency cord la sonnette d'alarme [sonet dalarm]
- someone's pulled the emergency cord quelqu'un a tiré la sonnette d'alarme [kelkAN a teeray la sonet dalarm]

emergency exit la sortie de secours [sortee duh suhkoor]
- where is the emergency exit? où se trouve la sortie de secours ? [oo suh troov la sortee duh suhkoor]

emergency room (le service des) urgences [(servees dayz) UrzhONs]
- can you tell me where the nearest emergency room is? pouvez-vous me dire où se trouve les urgences les plus proches ? [poovay-voo muh deer oo suh troov layz UrzhONs lay plU prosh]

emergency services les secours *m* [suhkoor]
- we have to call the emergency services il faut appeler les secours [eel foht aplay lay suhkoor]

end (*conclusion, finish*) la fin [fAN]
- at the end of July fin juillet [fAN zhweeyeh]

engine le moteur [motuhr]
- the engine is making a funny noise le moteur fait un drôle de bruit [luh motuhr feht AN drol duh brwee]

English anglais(e) [ONglay(ONglez)] ◆ *(language)* l'anglais *m* [ONglay]

‣ that's not how you say it in English ce n'est pas comme ça que vous dites en anglais [suh neh pa kom sa kuh voo deet ON ONglay]

‣ do you understand English? est-ce que vous comprenez l'anglais ? [eskuh voo kONpruh-nay lONglay]

enjoy apprécier [apray-syay]

‣ to enjoy oneself s'amuser [samU-zay]

‣ enjoy your meal! bon appétit ! [bon apay-tee]

‣ did you enjoy your meal? êtes-vous content de votre repas ? [et-voo kONtON duh votr ruhpah]

enough assez (de) [asay(duh)]

‣ I don't have enough money je n'ai pas assez d'argent [zhuh nay pasz asay darzhON]

‣ that's enough! ça suffit ! [sa sUfee]

‣ no thanks, I've had quite enough non, merci, j'ai bien mangé [nON mersee zhay byAN mONzhay]

en-suite bathroom salle *f* de bains comprise [sal duh bAN kONpreez]

‣ how much is a room with en-suite bathroom? combien coûte une chambre avec salle de bains ? [kONbyAN koot Un shONbr avek sal duh bAN]

enter *(type in)* taper [tapay]

‣ do I enter my PIN number now? je dois taper mon code maintenant ? [zhuh dwah tapay mON kod mANtuh-nON]

entrance l'entrée *f* [ONtray]

‣ where's the entrance to the subway? où est l'entrée du métro ? [oo eh lONtray dU maytroh]

entry *(to place)* l'entrée *f* [ONtray]

‣ entry to the exhibit is free l'exposition est gratuite [lekspo-zeesyON eh gratweet], entrée libre à l'exposition [ONtray leebr a lekspo-zeesyON]

envelope l'enveloppe *f* [ONvlop]

‣ I'd like a pack of envelopes je voudrais un paquet d'enveloppes [zhuh voodreh AN pakeh dONvlop]

equipment le matériel [matay-ryel]

‣ do you provide the equipment? est-ce que vous fournissez le matériel ? [eskuh voo foornee-say luh matay-ryel]

escalator l'escalier *m* roulant [eskal-yay roolON]

‣ is there an escalator? est-ce qu'il y a un escalier roulant ? [eskeel ya AN eskal-yay roolON]

euro l'euro *m* [uhroh]

‣ I'd like to change some dollars into euros je voudrais changer des dollars en euros [zhuh voodreh shONzhay day dolar ON uhroh]

evening *(gen)* le soir [swar]; *(expressing duration)* la soirée [swaray]
- why don't we meet up this evening? on n'a qu'à se retrouver dans la soirée [ON na ka suh ruhtroo-vay dON la swaray]
- in the evening *(of every day)* le soir [luh swar]

event *(cultural)* la manifestation [manee-festa-syON]
- what's the program of events? quel est le programme des manifestations ? [kel eh luh program day manee-festa-syON]

ever *(at any time)* jamais [zhameh]; *(before now)* déjà [dayzha]
- have you ever been to Bordeaux? es-tu déjà allé à Bordeaux ? [eh-tU dayzha alay a bordoh]

everything tout [too]
- that's everything, thanks ça sera tout, merci [sa sura too mersee]
- we didn't have time to see everything on n'a pas eu le temps de tout voir [ON na pas U luh tON duh too vwar]

excess baggage l'excédent *m* de bagages [eksay-dON duh bagazh]
- do I have excess baggage? est-ce que j'ai un excédent de bagages ? [eskuh zhay AN eksay-dON duh bagazh]

exchange échanger [ayshON-zhay]
- I'd like to exchange this T-shirt j'aimerais échanger ce T-shirt [zhehmuh-reh ayshON-zhay suh teeshuhrt]

exchange rate change [shONzh]
- what is your exchange rate? vous appliquez quel taux de change ? [vooz aplee-kay kel toh duh shONzh]

excursion l'excursion *f* [ekskUr-syON]
- I'd like to sign up for the excursion on Saturday j'aimerais m'inscrire pour l'excursion de samedi [zhehmuh-reh mANskreer poor lekskUr-syON duh samdee]

excuse *(behavior, person)* excuser [ekskU-zay]
- excuse me? *(asking for repetition)* pardon ? [pardON]
- excuse me! *(to get attention)* s'il vous plaît ! [seel voo play]; *(when interrupting, to apologize)* excusez-moi [ekskU-zay-mwa]; *(to get by)* pardon ! [pardON]; *(when leaving)* désolé [dayzo-lay]; *(expressing disagreement)* excusez-moi ? [ekskU-zay-mwa]
- you'll have to excuse my (poor) French pardonnez mon (mauvais) français [pardo-nay mON (mohveh) frONsay]

exhaust le pot d'échappement [poh dayshap-mON]
- the exhaust is making a strange noise le pot d'échappement fait un drôle de bruit [luh poh dayshap-mON feht AN drol duh brwee]

exhausted *(tired)* épuisé(e) [aypwee-zay]
- I'm exhausted je n'en peux plus [zhuh nON puh plus]

exhibit l'exposition *f* [ekspo-zeesyON]
- I'd like a ticket for the temporary exhibit je voudrais une entrée pour

l'exposition temporaire [zhuh voodreh Un ONtray poor lekspo-zeesyON tONpo-rehr]

> is this ticket valid for the exhibit too? le ticket est valable aussi pour l'exposition ? [luh teekeh eh valabl ohsee poor lekspo-zeesyON]

exit la sortie [sortee]

> where's the exit? où est la sortie ? [oo eh la sortee]
> it's the next exit c'est la prochaine sortie [seh la proshen sortee]

expect *(event, letter)* attendre [atONdr]

> I'll be expecting you at eight o'clock at... je vous attends à huit heures à... [zhuh vooz atON a weet uhr a]
> when do you expect it to be ready? quand pensez-vous que ce sera prêt ? [kON pONsay-voo kuh suh suhra preh]

expensive cher [shehr], chère [shehr]

> do you have anything less expensive? n'avez-vous pas quelque chose de moins cher ? [navay-voo pa kelkuh shohz duh mwAN shehr]

expire *(visa)* expirer [ekspee-ray]

> my passport has expired mon passeport n'est plus valable [mON paspor neh plU valabl]

explain expliquer [eksplee-kay]

> can you explain to me how to get to the airport? pouvez-vous m'expliquer comment aller à l'aéroport ? [poovay-voo meksplee-kay komONt alay a la-ayro-por]
> can you explain what this means? peux-tu m'expliquer ce que cela veut dire ? [puh-tU meksplee-kay suh kuh suhla vuh deer]

express (train) le TGV [tayzhay-vay], le train rapide [trAN rapeed]

> how long does it take by express? combien de temps ça met en TGV ? [kONbyAN duh tON sa met ON tayzhay-vay]

extension le poste [post]; *(cord)* la rallonge [ralONzh]

> could I have extension 358, please? pourrais-je avoir le poste trois cent cinquante-huit, s'il vous plaît ? [poorehzh avwar luh post trwah sON sANkONt-weet seel voo play]

extra supplémentaire [sUplay-mONtehr]

> is it possible to add an extra bed? est-ce qu'il est possible d'ajouter un lit supplémentaire ? [eskeel eh poseebl dazhoo-tay AN lee sUplay-mONtehr]
> is it possible to stay an extra night? est-il possible de rester une nuit de plus ? [ehteel poseebl duh restay Un nwee duh plUs]

extra charge le supplément [sUplay-mON]

> is there an extra charge for this service? il faut payer un supplément pour ce service ? [eel foh peyay AN sUplay-mON poor suh servees]
> at no extra charge sans supplément de prix [sON sUplay-mON duh pree]

eye l'œil *m* [oy]

> she has blue eyes elle a les yeux bleus [ell a layz yuh bluh]

▸ can you keep an eye on my bag for a few minutes? pouvez-vous garder mon sac quelques instants ? [poovay-voo garday mON sak kelkuhz ANstON]

eye drops les gouttes *f* pour les yeux [goot poor layz yuh]
 ▸ do you have any eye drops? avez-vous des gouttes pour les yeux ? [avay-voo day goot poor layz yuh]

eye shadow l'ombre *f* à paupières [ONbr a pohpyehr]
 ▸ is this the only eye shadow you've got? c'est tout ce que vous avez comme ombres à paupières ? [seh toos kuh vooz avay kom ONbr a pohpyehr]

eyesight la vue [vU]
 ▸ I don't have very good eyesight je n'ai pas une très bonne vue [zhuh nay paz Un treh bon vU]

face *(of person)* le visage [veezazh]
 ▸ did you see the man's face? avez-vous vu le visage de l'homme ? [avay-voo vU luh veezazh duh lom]

facilities les équipements *m* [aykeep-mON], les installations *f* [ANsta-lasyON]
 ▸ what kind of facilities do you have here? quelles installations avez-vous ici ? [kel ANsta-lasyON avay-voo eesee]
 ▸ do you have facilities for people with disabilities? êtes-vous équipés pour les handicapés ? [et-vooz aykee-pay poor lay ONdee-kapay]
 ▸ are there facilities for children? y a-t-il des installations pour les enfants ? [ee ateel dayz ANsta-lasyON poor layz ONfON]

faint s'évanouir [sayvan-weer]
 ▸ I fainted je me suis évanoui [zhuh muh sweez ayvan-wee]

fair *(gen)* juste [zhUst]; *(hair)* blond(e) [blON(blONd)]; *(skin, complexion)* clair(e) [klehr]
 ▸ it's not fair! ce n'est pas juste ! [suh neh pa zhUst]

fall tomber [tONbay]
 ▸ I fell on my back je suis tombé sur le dos [zhuh swee tONbay sUr luh doh]

family la famille [fameey]
 ▸ have you any family? tu as de la famille ? [tU a duh la fameey]

fan le ventilateur [vONtee-latuhr]
 ▸ how does the fan work? comment marche le ventilateur ? [komON marsh luh vONtee-latuhr]

far loin [lwAN]
 ▸ am I far from the village? suis-je loin du village ? [sweezh lwAN dU veelazh]

- is it far to walk? est-ce que c'est loin à pied ? [eskuh seh lwAN a pyay]
- is it far by car? est-ce que c'est loin en voiture ? [eskuh seh lwAN ON vwatUr]
- how far is the market from here? à quelle distance se trouve le marché ? [a kel deestONs suh troov luh marshay]
- far away/off *(in distance, time)* loin [lwAN]
- so far jusqu'ici [zhUsk-eesee]
- I haven't drunk a single local beer so far jusqu'ici je n'ai pas bu une seule bière locale [zhUsk-eesee zhuh nay pa bU Un suhl byehr lokal]

fast rapide [rapeed] ◆ vite [veet]
- please don't drive so fast s'il vous plaît, ne conduisez pas si vite [seel voo play nuh kONdwee-zay pa see veet]
- to be fast *(watch, clock)* avancer [avON-say]
- my watch is five minutes fast ma montre avance de 5 minutes [ma mONtr avONs duh sANk meenUt]

fat *(in diet)* les matières *f* grasses [matyehr gras]
- it's low in fat c'est pauvre en matières grasses [seh pohvr ON matyehr gras]

father le père [pehr]
- this is my father voici mon père [vwasee mON pehr]

fault *(responsibility)* la faute [foht]
- it was my fault c'est moi qui suis en tort [seh mwa kee sweez ON tor]

favor *(kind act)* le service [servees], la faveur [favuhr]
- can I ask you a favor? je peux vous demander un service ? [zhuh puh voo duhmON-day AN servees]

favorite préféré(e) [prayfay-ray]
- it's my favorite book c'est mon livre préféré [seh mONleevr prayfay-ray]

February février [fayvree-yay]
- February 8th le huit février [luh weet fayvree-yay]

feed donner à manger à [donay a mONzhay a]
- where can I feed the baby? où puis-je donner à manger au bébé ? [oo pweezh donay a mONzhay oh baybay]

feel sentir [sONteer] ◆ *(physically)* se sentir [suh sONteer]
- I can't feel my feet je ne sens plus mes pieds [zhuh nuh sON plU may pyay]
- I don't feel well je ne me sens pas bien [zhuh nuh muh sON pa byAN]

ferry le ferry [feree]
- when does the next ferry leave? à quelle heure part le prochain ferry ? [a kel uhr par luh proshAN feree]

ferry terminal le terminal ferry [termee-nal feree]
- is the ferry terminal that way? c'est bien par là, le terminal ferry ? [seh byAN par la luh termee-nal feree]

fever la fièvre [fyehvr]
> the baby's got a fever le bébé a de la fièvre [luh baybay a duh la fyehvr]

few peu de [puh duh] • **a few** quelques [kelkuh]
> there are few sights worth seeing around here il y a peu de choses à voir dans le coin [eel ya puh duh shohz a vwar dON luh kwAN]
> we're thinking of staying a few more days nous pensons rester quelques jours de plus [noo pONsON restay kelkuh zhoor duh plUs]
> I spent a month in France a few years ago j'ai passé un mois en France il y a quelques années [zhay pasay AN mwah ON frONs eel ya kelkuhz anay]

fifth cinquième [sANkyem] • *(gear)* la cinquième [sANkyam]
> I can't get it into fifth je n'arrive pas à passer la cinquième [zhuh nareev paz a pasay la sANkyem]

filling *(in a tooth)* le plombage [plONbazh]
> a filling has come out j'ai un plombage qui est parti [zhahy AN plONbazh kee eh partee]

fill up *(with gas)* faire le plein [fehr luh plAN]
> fill it up, please le plein, s'il vous plaît [luh plAN seel voo play]
> we need to fill up with gas il faut faire le plein d'essence [eel foh fehr luh plAN desONs]

film *(for camera)* la pellicule [pelee-kUl] • filmer [feelmay]
> I'd like to have this film developed je voudrais faire développer cette pellicule [zhuh voodreh fehr dayvlo-pay set pelee-kUl]
> do you have black-and-white films? est-ce que vous avez des pellicules noir et blanc ? [eskuh vooz avay day pelee-kUl nwar ay blON]
> is it allowed to film in the museum? on a le droit de filmer dans ce musée ? [ON a luh drwah duh feelmay dON suh mUzay]

find trouver [troovay]; *(lost object)* retrouver [ruh-troovay]
> has anyone found a watch? quelqu'un aurait-il trouvé une montre ? [kelkAN ohreht-eel troovay Un mONtr]
> where can I find a doctor on a Sunday? où est-ce que je peux trouver un médecin un dimanche ? [oo eskuh zhuh puh troovay AN maydsAN AN deemONsh]
> to find oneself se retrouver [suh ruh-troovay]

find out se renseigner [suh rONsen-yay]
> I need to find out the times of trains to Berlin j'ai besoin de renseignements sur les horaires de trains pour Berlin [zhay buhzwAN duh rONsen-yuhmON sUr layz orehr duh trAN poor berlAN]

fine *(in health etc.)* bien [byAN] • l'amende *f* [amONd]
> fine thanks, and you? bien, merci, et vous ? [byAN mersee ay voo]
> how much is the fine? l'amende est de combien ? [lamONd eh duh kONbyAN]

finger le doigt [dwah]
> I've twisted my finger je me suis tordu le doigt [zhuh muh swee tordU luh dwah]

finish terminer [termee-nay]
> we'll leave as soon as we've finished our meal nous partirons dès que nous aurons terminé le repas [noo partee-rON deh kuh noo zohrON termee-nay luh ruhpah]

fire le feu [fuh]; *(out of control)* l'incendie *m* [ANsON-dee]
> to make a fire faire du feu [fehr dU fuh]
> on fire *(forest, house)* en feu [ON fuh]

fire department les pompiers *m* [pONpyay]
> call the fire department, please! appelez les pompiers, s'il vous plaît ! [aplay lay pONpyay seel voo play]

fireworks le feu d'artifice [fuh dartee-fees]
> what time do the fireworks start? à quelle heure démarre le feu d'artifice ? [a kel uhr daymar luh fuh dartee-fees]

first premier [pruhmyay], première [pruhmyehr]
> it's the first time I've been here c'est la première fois que je viens ici [seh la pruhmyehr fwah kuh zhuh vyANz eesee]
> you have to take the first left after the lights il faut prendre la première rue à gauche après le feu [eel foh prONdr la pruhmyehr rU a gohsh apreh luh fuh]
> our seats are in first nous avons des places en première [nooz avON day plas ON pruhmyehr]
> put it into first passe la première [pas la pruhmyehr]

first-aid kit la trousse de secours [troos duh suhkoor]
> do you have a first-aid kit? avez-vous une trousse de secours ? [avay-vooz Un troos duh suhkoor]

first class *(on train)* la première classe [prumyehr klas] ♦ *(mail)* en tarif normal [ON tareef normal]
> are there any seats in first class? est-ce qu'il y a des places en première classe ? [eskeel ya day plas ON pruhmyehr klas]
> I'd like to send this first class je voudrais envoyer ça en tarif normal [zhuh voodreh ONvwa-yay sa ON tareef normal]
> I prefer to travel first class je préfère voyager en première (classe) [zhuh prayfehr vwa-yazhay ON pruhmyehr (klas)]

fish le poisson [pwasON]
> I don't eat fish je ne mange pas de poisson [zhuh nuh mONzh pa duh pwasON]

fishing permit le permis de pêche [permee duh pesh]
> do you need a fishing permit to fish here? est-ce qu'il faut un permis de pêche pour pêcher ici ? [eskeel foht AN permee duh pesh poor payshay eesee]

fit *(of laughter, tears)* la crise [kreez] ♦ *(be correct size for)* convenir [kONvneer], aller [alay] ♦ *(be correct size)* rentrer [rONtray]

- ▶ I think she's having some kind of fit je crois qu'elle fait une crise [zhuh krwah kel feht Un kreez]
- ▶ those pants fit you better ce pantalon te va mieux [suh pONta-lON tuh va myuh]
- ▶ the key doesn't fit in the lock la clé ne rentre pas dans la serrure [la klay nuh rONtr pa dON la serUr]
- ▶ we won't all fit around one table nous ne tiendrons pas tous autour de la table [noo nuh tyANdrON pa toos ohtoor duh la tabl]

fit in rentrer [rONtray]

- ▶ I can't get everything to fit in my suitcase je n'arrive pas à tout rentrer dans ma valise [zhuh nareev paz a too rONtray dON ma valeez]
- ▶ you can fit six people in this car on tient à six dans cette voiture [ON tyAN a sees dON cet vwatUR]

fitting room la cabine d'essayage [kabeen de-seyazh]

- ▶ where are the fitting rooms? où sont les cabines d'essayage ? [oo sON lay kabeen de-seyazh]

five cinq [sANk]

- ▶ there are five of us nous sommes cinq [noo som sANk]

fix réparer [raypa-ray]

- ▶ where can I find someone to fix my bike? où puis-je trouver quelqu'un pour réparer mon vélo ? [oo pweezh troovay kelkAN poor raypa-ray mON vayloh]

fixed price le forfait [forfeh]

- ▶ do taxis to the airport charge a fixed price? est-ce que les taxis prennent un forfait pour l'aéroport ? [eskuh lay taksee pren AN forfeh poor la-ayro-por]

flash le flash [flash]

- ▶ I'd like some batteries for my flash je voudrais des piles pour mon flash [zhuh voodreh day peel poor mON flash]

flash photography la photo avec flash [fotoh avek flash]

- ▶ is flash photography allowed here? on peut faire des photos avec flash ici ? [ON puh fehr day fotoh avek flash eesee]

flat *(tire)* à plat [a plah]

- ▶ the tire's flat le pneu est à plat [luh pnuh eht a plah]

flavor *(of food)* le goût [goo]; *(of ice cream, yogurt)* le parfum [parfAN]

- ▶ I'd like an ice-cream with three different flavors j'aimerais une glace avec trois parfums [zhemuh-reh AN glas avek trwa parfAN]

flea market le marché aux puces [marshay oh pUs]

- ▶ where's the flea market? où est le marché aux puces ? [oo eh luh marshay oh pUs]

flight le vol [vol]

- ▶ how many flights a day are there? combien y a-t-il de vols par jour ? [kONbyAN ee ateel duh vol par zhoor]

‣ your flight's been canceled votre vol est annulé [votr vol eht anU-lay]
‣ what time is the flight at? l'avion est à quelle heure ? [lavyON eht a kel uhr]

flight of stairs l'escalier *m* [eskal-yay]

‣ your rooms are up that flight of stairs vos chambres sont en haut de cet escalier [voh shONbr sON ON oht duh set eskal-yay]

floor *(story)* l'étage *m* [aytazh]

‣ which floor is it on? c'est à quel étage ? [seht a kel aytazh]
‣ it's on the top floor c'est au dernier étage [seht oh dernyehr aytazh]

flower la fleur [fluhr]

‣ do you sell flowers? est-ce que vous vendez des fleurs ? [eskuh voo vONday day fluhr]

flu la grippe [greep]

‣ I'd like something for the flu je voudrais quelque chose contre la grippe [zhuh voodreh kelkuh shohz kONtr la greep]

flush la chasse d'eau [shas doh] ✦ *(toilet)* tirer la chasse [teeray la shas]

‣ the toilet won't flush la chasse d'eau ne marche pas [la shas doh nuh marsh pa]

fog le brouillard [broo-yar]

‣ is there fog on the roads? est-ce qu'il y a du brouillard sur les routes ? [eskeel ya dU brwee-yar sUr lay root]

food l'alimentation *f* [alee-mONta-syON]

‣ we need to buy some food il faut faire les courses [eel foh fehr lay koors]
‣ the food here is excellent la nourriture est excellente, ici [la nooree-tUr eht ekse-lONt eesee]

food cart *(on train, plane)* le chariot de boissons [sharyoh duh bwasON]

‣ is there a food cart service on this train? est-ce qu'il y a un service de vente ambulante dans ce train ? [eskeel ya AN servees duh vONt ONbU-lONt dON suh trAN]

food section *(in store)* le rayon alimentation [reyON alee-mONta-syON]

‣ where's the food section? où se trouve le rayon alimentation ? [oo suh troov luh reyON alee-mONta-syON]

foot le pied [pyay]

‣ on foot à pied [a pyay]

for pour [poor]; *(indicating duration)* pendant [pONdON]; *(since)* depuis [duhpwee]

‣ what's that for? ça sert à quoi, ça ? [sa sehr a kwa sa]
‣ the flight for London le vol pour Londres [luh vol poor lONdr]
‣ is this the right train for Bordeaux? ce train va bien à Bordeaux ? [suh trAN va byAN a bordoh]
‣ I'm staying for two months je suis là pour deux mois [zhuh swee la poor duh mwah]

- I've been here for a week je suis là depuis une semaine [zhuh swee la duhpweez Un suhmen]
- I need something for a cough j'aurais besoin de quelque chose contre la toux [zhohreh buhzwAN duh kelkuh shohz kONtr la too]
- I'm for leaving earlier je suis d'accord pour partir plus tôt [zhuh swee dakor poor parteer plU toh]

foreign *(country, language)* étranger [aytrON-zhay], étrangère [aytrON-zhehr]

- I don't speak any foreign languages je ne parle aucune langue étrangère [zhuh nuh parl ohkUn lONg aytrON-zhehr]

foreign currency les monnaies *f* étrangères [monehz aytrON-zhehr]

- do you change foreign currency? est-ce que vous échangez les monnaies étrangères ? [eskuh vooz ayshON-zhay lay monehz aytrON-zhehr]

foreigner étranger [aytrON-zhay], étrangère [aytrON-zhehr]

- I'm a foreigner je suis étranger [zhuh sweez aytrON-zhay]

fork la fourchette [foorshet]

- could I have a fork? pourriez-vous m'apporter une fourchette ? [pooryay-voo mapor-tay Un foorshet]

forward faire suivre [fehr sweevr]

- can you forward my mail? est-ce que vous pouvez faire suivre mon courrier ? [eskuh voo povay fehr sweevr mON kooryay]

four quatre [katr]

- there are four of us nous sommes quatre [noo som katr]

fourth quatrième [katree-yem] ♦ *(gear)* la quatrième [katree-yem]

- it's hard to get it into fourth la quatrième ne passe pas bien [la katree-yem nuh pas pa byAN]

four-wheel drive le 4X4 [katr-katr]

- I'd like a four-wheel drive je voudrais un 4X4 [zhuh voodreh AN katr-katr]

fracture la fracture [fraktUr]

- I think I have a fracture je pense que j'ai une fracture [zhuh pONs kuh zhay Un fraktUr]

France la France [frONs]

- are you from France? vous venez de France ? [voo vuhnay duh frONs]
- do you live in France? vous habitez en France ? [vooz abee-tay ON frONs]
- I've never been to France before je ne suis jamais venu en France avant [zhuh nuh swee zhameh vuhnU ON frONs avON]

free *(not paid for)* gratuit(e) [gratwee(gratweet)]; *(not occupied)* libre [leebr]; *(available)* disponible [deespo-neebl]

- is it free? c'est gratuit ? [seh gratwee]
- is this seat free? est-ce que cette place est libre ? [eskuh set plas eh leebr]

▸ are you free on Thursday evening? êtes-vous disponible jeudi soir ? [et-voo deespo-neebl zhuhdee swar]

freeway l'autoroute *f* [otoroot]
▸ what is the speed limit on freeways? quelle est la vitesse limite sur les autoroutes ? [kel eh la veetess leemeet sUr layz otoh-root]
▸ how do I get onto the freeway? comment est-ce que je peux rejoindre l'autoroute ? [komONt eskuh zhuh puh ruhzhwANdr lotoh-root]

freezing (cold) *(room, day)* glacé(e) [glasay]
▸ I'm freezing (cold) je suis glacé [zhuh swee glasay]

French français [frONsay], française [frONsehz]
▸ are you French? vous êtes français ? [vooz et frONsay]
▸ I'm sorry, I don't speak French je m'excuse, je ne parle pas français [zhuh meksUz zhuh nuh parl pa frONsay]
▸ are all the tours in French? toutes les visites sont en français ? [toot lay veezeet sONt ON frONsay]
▸ the French les Français [lay frONsay]

Frenchman le Français [frONsay]
▸ I'm dating a Frenchman je sors avec un Français [zhuh sor avek AN frONsay]

Frenchwoman la Française [frONsehz]
▸ I'm married to a Frenchwoman je suis marié à une Française [zhuh swee maryay a Un frONsehz]

frequent fréquent(e) [fraykON(fraykONt)]
▸ how frequent are the trains to the city? quelle est la fréquence des trains vers la ville ? [kel eh la fraykONs day trAN vehr la veel]

fresh *(food)* frais [freh], fraîche [fresh]
▸ I'd like some fresh orange juice je voudrais un jus d'oranges frais [zhuh voodreh AN zhU dorONzh freh]

Friday vendredi *m* [vONdruh-dee]
▸ we're arriving/leaving on Friday nous arrivons/partons vendredi [noo zaree-vON/partON vONdruh-dee]

fried egg l'œuf *m* sur le plat [uhf sUr luh plah]
▸ I'd prefer a fried egg je préférerais un œuf sur le plat [zhuh prayfay-ruhrehz AN uhf sUr luh plah]

friend l'ami *m* [amee], l'amie *f* [amee]
▸ are you with friends? êtes-vous avec des amis ? [et-vooz avek dayz amee]
▸ I've come with a friend je suis venu avec un ami [zhuh swee vuhnU avek AN amee]
▸ I'm meeting some friends je suis venu rejoindre des amis [zhuh swee vuhnU ruhzhwANdr dayz amee]

from *(expressing origin)* de [duh]; *(leaving from)* au départ de [oh daypar duh]

- I'm from the United States je viens des États-Unis [zhuh vyAN dayz aytaz-Unee]
- how many flights a day are there from Paris to JFK? combien y a-t-il de vols par jour pour JFK au départ de Paris ? [kONbyAN ee ateel duh vol par zhoor poor zhee-ef-ka oh daypar duh paree]

front *(of train)* la tête [tet] ◆ **in front (of)** devant [duhvON]

- the car in front braked suddenly la voiture de devant a brusquement freiné [la vwatUr duh duhvON a brUskmON frehnay]
- I'll meet you in front of the museum on se retrouve devant le musée [ON suh ruhtroov duhvON luh mUzay]

front door la porte d'entrée [port dONtray]

- which is the key to the front door? quelle est la clé pour la porte d'entrée ? [kel eh la klay poor la port dONtray]
- the front door is closed la porte de devant est fermée [la port duh duhvON eh fermay]

frozen *(person)* glacé(e) [glasay], gelé(e) [zhuhlay]; *(pipes)* bloqué(e) [blokay]

- I'm absolutely frozen je suis complètement gelé [zhuh swee kONplet-mON zhuhlay]
- the lock is frozen la serrure est bloquée [la serUr eh blokay]

frozen food les surgelés *m* [sUrzhuh-lay]

- is that all the frozen food you have? c'est tout ce que vous avez comme surgelés ? [seh toos kuh vooz avay kom sUrzhuh-lay]

fruit juice le jus de fruit [zhU duh frwee]

- what types of fruit juice do you have? qu'est-ce que vous avez comme jus de fruit ? [keskuh vooz avay kom zhU duh frwee]

full *(completely filled)* plein(e) [plAN(plen)]; *(hotel, restaurant, train)* complet [kONpleh], complète [kONplet]; *(with food)* rassasié(e) [rasaz-yay]

- is it full? c'est complet ? [seh kONpleh]
- I'm quite full, thank you je n'ai plus faim, merci [zhuh nay plU fAN mersee]

full up *(with food)* repu(e) [ruhpU]

- I'm full up je n'en peux plus [zhuh nON peuh plU]

fun *(pleasure, amusement)* le plaisir [playzeer], l'amusement *m* [amUz-mON]

- to have fun s'amuser [samU-zay]

g

gallery *(for art)* le musée [mUzay]
- what time does the gallery open? à quelle heure ouvre le musée ? [a kel uhr oovr luh mUsay]

game *(fun activity)* le jeu [zhuh]; *(of sport)* la partie [partee]
- do you want to have a game of tennis tomorrow? veux-tu faire une partie de tennis demain matin ? [vuh-tU fehr Un partee duh tenees duhmAN matAN]

garage le garage [garazh]
- is there a garage near here? est-ce qu'il y a un garage par ici ? [eskeel ya AN garazh par eesee]
- could you tow me to a garage? pourriez-vous me remorquer jusqu'à un garage ? [pooryay-voo muh ruhmor-kay zhUska AN garazh]

garbage can la poubelle [poobel]
- put it in the garbage can mets-le à la poubelle [meh-luh a la poobel]

gas *(for vehicle)* l'essence *f* [esONs]; *(for domestic use)* le gaz [gaz]; *(at dentist)* le gaz anesthésiant [gaz anes-tayzyON]
- where can I get gas? où puis-je trouver de l'essence ? [oo pweezh troovay duh lesONs]
- I've run out of gas je suis en panne d'essence [zhuh sweez ON pan desONs]
- can you smell gas? vous sentez l'odeur de gaz ? [voo sONtay loduhr duh gaz]

gas station la station-service [stasyON-servees]
- where can I find a gas station? où est-ce que je peux trouver une station-service ? [oo eskuh zhuh puh troovay Un stasyON-servees]

gas tank le réservoir d'essence [rayzer-vwar desONs]
- the gas tank is leaking il y a une fuite dans le réservoir d'essence [eel ya Un fweet dON la rayzer-vwar desONs]

gate *(of a garden, a town)* la porte [port]; *(at an airport)* la porte (d'embarquement) [port (dONbark-mON)]
- where is gate number 2? où se trouve la porte (d'embarquement) deux ? [oo suh troov la port (dONbark-mON) duh]

gear *(of a car, a bike)* la vitesse [veetes]
- how many gears does the bike have? il y a combien de vitesses sur ce vélo ? [eel ya kONbyAN duh veetes sUr suh vayloh]

get *(obtain)* avoir [avwar], obtenir [obtuh-neer]; *(understand)* comprendre [kONprONdr] ◆ *(make one's way)* arriver [aree-vay], aller [alay]
- where can we get something to eat at this time of night? où peut-on acheter à manger à cette heure-ci ? [oo puht-ON ashtay a mONzhay a set uhr-see]

- now I get it ça y est, j'ai compris maintenant [sa yeh zhay kONpree mANt-nON]
- I got here a month ago je suis arrivé il y a un mois [zhuh sweez aree-vay eel ya AN mwah]
- can you get there by car? est-ce que c'est accessible en voiture ? [eskuh seht akseh-seebl ON vwatUr]
- how can I get to... comment puis-je aller à... [komON pweezh alay a]
- could you tell me the best way to get to Cannes? pourriez-vous m'indiquer la meilleure façon de me rendre à Cannes ? [pooray-voo mANdee-kay la meyuhr fasON duh muh rONdr a kan]
- how do we get to Terminal 2? comment se rend-on au terminal deux ? [komON suh rONd-ON oh termee-nal duh]

get back *(money)* récupérer [raykU-payray]

- I just want to get my money back je veux juste récupérer mon argent [zhuh vuh zhUst raykU-payray mON arzhON]

get back onto *(road)* rejoindre [ruhzhwANdr]

- how can I get back onto the freeway? comment est-ce que je peux rejoindre l'autoroute ? [komON eskuh zhuh puh ruhzhwANdr lotoh-root]

get in *(arrive)* arriver [aree-vay]; *(gain entry)* entrer [ONtray] ◆ *(car)* monter dans [mONtay dON]

- what time does the train get in to Paris? à quelle heure le train arrive-t-il à Paris ? [a kel uhr luh trAN areev-teel a paree]
- what time does the flight get in? quelle est l'heure d'atterrissage ? [kel eh luhr dateh-reesazh]
- do you have to pay to get in? l'entrée est payante ? [lONtray eh peyONt]
- hurry up and get in the car dépêche-toi et monte dans la voiture [daypesh-twa ay mONt dON la vwatUr]

get off descendre (de) [desONdr (duh)]; *(road)* sortir de [sorteer duh]

- where do I get off the freeway? je dois sortir de l'autoroute à quel endroit ? [zhuh dwah sorteer duh lotoh-root a kel ONdrwah]
- where do I get off? où dois-je descendre ? [oo dwazh desONdr]

get on *(train, bus)* monter dans [mONtay dON]; *(plane)* monter à bord de [mONtay a bor dON] ◆ *(have good relationship)* bien s'entendre avec [byAN sONtONdr avek]

- get on quickly if you want a seat dépêche-toi de monter si tu veux une place [daypesh-twa duh mONtay see tU vuh Un plas]
- as a rule, I get on well with everyone en principe, je m'entends bien avec tout le monde [ON prANseep zhuh mONtON byAN avek too luh mONd]

get past passer [pasay]

- can I get past, please? je voudrais passer, s'il vous plaît [pardON zhuh voodreh pasay seel voo play]

get up *(in morning)* se lever [suh luhvay]
- I got up very early je me suis levé très tôt [zhuh muh swee luhvay treh toh]

gift-wrap emballer [ONba-lay], faire un paquet-cadeau [fehr AN pakeh-kadoh]
- could you gift-wrap it for me? pourriez-vous me faire un paquet-cadeau ? [pooryay-voo muh fehr AN pakeh-kadoh]

girl la fille [feey]
- who is that girl? qui est cette fille ? [kee eh set feey]
- I've got two girls j'ai deux filles [zhay duh feey]

girlfriend la copine [kopeen], la (petite) amie [(puhteet) amee]
- is she your girlfriend? est-ce que c'est ta copine ? [eskuh seh ta kopeen]

gîte le gîte rural [zheet rUral]
- are there any gîtes around here? est-ce qu'il y a des gîtes ruraux dans le coin ? [eskeel ya day zheet rUroh dON luh kwAN]

give donner [donay]
- I can give you my e-mail address je peux te donner mon adresse e-mail [zhuh puh tuh donay mON adress eemel]
- can you give me a hand? tu peux me donner un coup de main ? [tU puh muh donay AN koo duh mAN]

glass le verre [vehr] ◆ **glasses** les lunettes *f* [lUnet]
- can I have a clean glass? pourrais-je avoir un verre propre ? [poorehzh avwar AN vehr propr]
- would you like a glass of champagne? voulez-vous une coupe de champagne ? [voolay-vooz Un koop duh shONpan-yuh]
- I've lost my glasses j'ai perdu mes lunettes [zhay perdU may lUnet]

glove le gant [gON]
- I've lost a glove j'ai perdu un gant [zhay perdU AN gON]

go *(move, travel)* aller [alay]; *(depart)* partir [parteer]; *(lead)* mener [muhnay]; *(vehicle)* rouler [roolay]
- let's go to the beach allons à la plage [alONz a la plazh]
- where can we go for breakfast? où pouvons-nous prendre le petit-déjeuner ? [oo poovON-noo prONdr luh puhtee-dayzhuh-nay]
- where does this path go to? où mène ce chemin ? [oo men suh shuhmAN]
- I must be going je dois y aller [zhuh dwaz ee alay]
- we're going home tomorrow on rentre chez nous demain [ON rONtr shay noo duhmAN]

go away *(person)* s'en aller [sON alay]; *(pain)* passer [pasay]
- go away and leave me alone! allez-vous-en et laissez-moi tranquille ! [alay-vooz-ON ay laysay-mwa trONkeel]

go back *(return)* retourner [ruhtoor-nay]
- we're going back home tomorrow on retourne chez nous demain [ON rutoorn shay noo duhmAN]

▸ you have to go back up the street il faut remonter la rue [eel foh ruhmON-tay la rU]

gold *(metal)* l'or *m* [or]

▸ is it made of gold? est-ce que c'est en or ? [eskuh seht ON or]

golf le golf [golf]

▸ I play golf je fais du golf [zhuh feh dU golf]

golf club le club de golf [kluhb duh golf]

▸ where can I rent golf clubs? où peut-on louer des clubs de golf ? [oo puht-ON lway day kluhb duh golf]

golf course le (terrain de) golf [(terAN duh) golf]

▸ is there a golf course nearby? est-ce qu'il y a un golf par ici ? [eskeel ya AN golf par eesee]

good bon(ne) [bON(bon)]; *(high-quality)* bien [byAN]

▸ this isn't a very good restaurant ce restaurant n'est pas terrible [suh resto-rON neh pa tereebl]

▸ you're really good at surfing! vous êtes très doué en planche ! [vooz et treh dway ON plONsh]

▸ we had a good time on s'est bien amusés [ON seh byAN amU-zay]

▸ when's a good time for you? quand est-ce que ça t'arrange ? [kONt eskuh sa tarONzh]

good afternoon bonjour ! [bONzhoor]

▸ good afternoon! isn't it a beautiful day? bonjour ! quelle belle journée ! [bONzhoor kel bel zhoornay]

goodbye au revoir [oh ruhvwar]

▸ I'd better say goodbye now je vous dis au revoir [zhuh voo dee oh ruhvwar]

good evening bonsoir ! [bONswar]

▸ good evening! how are you tonight? bonsoir ! comment allez-vous ? [bONswar komONt alay-voo]

good morning bonjour ! [bONzhoor]

▸ good morning! how are you today? bonjour ! comment allez-vous ? [bONzhoor komONt alay-voo]

good night *(when leaving)* bonsoir ! [bONswar]; *(when going to bed)* bonne nuit ! [bon nwee]

▸ I'll say good night, then je vous dis bonne nuit, alors [zhuh voo dee bon nwee alor]

go out sortir [sorteer]; *(tide)* descendre [desONdr]

▸ the tide's going out la mer descend [la mehr desON]

grapefruit le pamplemousse [pONpl-moos]

▸ I'll just have the grapefruit je vais juste prendre le pamplemousse [zhuh veh zhUst prONdr luh pONpl-moos]

great *(very good)* super [sUpehr], formidable [formee-dabl], génial [zhaynyal]
▶ that's great! c'est formidable ! [seh formee-dabl]
▶ it was really great c'était vraiment super [sayteh vrehmON supehr]

green vert(e) [vehr(vehrt)]
▶ the green one le vert [luh vehr], la verte [la vehrt]

grocery store l'épicerie *f* [aypee-sree]
▶ is there a grocery store around here? il y a une épicerie dans le coin ? [eel ya Un aypee-sree dON luh kwAN]

ground cloth le tapis de sol [tapee duh sol]
▶ I brought a ground cloth j'ai emporté un tapis de sol [zhay ONpor-tay AN tapee duh sol]

group le groupe [groop]
▶ there's a group of 12 of us nous sommes un groupe de douze personnes [noo somz AN groop duh dooz person]
▶ are there reductions for groups? y a-t-il des réductions pour les groupes ? [ee ateel day raydUk-syON poor lay groop]

group rate la réduction pour les groupes [raydUk-syON poor lay groop]
▶ are there special group rates? y a-t-il des réductions pour les groupes ? [ee ateel day raydUk-syON poor lay groop]

guarantee la garantie [garON-tee]
▶ it's still under guarantee c'est encore sous garantie [seht ONkor soo garON-tee]

guesthouse la pension (de famille) [pONsyON (duh fameey)]
▶ can you tell me where I can find a guesthouse? pouvez-vous m'indiquer une pension de famille ? [poovay-voo mANdee-kay Un pONsyON duh fameey]
▶ we're looking for a guesthouse for the night on cherche un gîte pour la nuit [ON shersh AN zheet poor la nwee]

guide le guide [geed]
▶ does the guide speak English? est-ce que le guide parle anglais ? [eskuh luh geed parl ONglay]

guidebook le guide [geed]
▶ do you have a guidebook in English? avez-vous un guide en anglais ? [avay-vooz AN geed ON ONglay]

guided tour la visite guidée [veezeet geeday]
▶ what time does the guided tour begin? à quelle heure commence la visite guidée ? [a kel uhr komONs la veezeet geeday]
▶ is there a guided tour in English? y a-t-il une visite en anglais ? [ee ateel Un veezeet ON ONglay]
▶ are there guided tours of the museum? y a-t-il des visites guidées pour le musée ? [ee ateel day veezeet geeday poor luh mUzay]

h

hair les cheveux *m* [shuhvuh]
- she has short hair elle a les cheveux courts [el a lay shuhvuh koor]
- he has red hair il a les cheveux roux [eel a lay shuhvuh roo]

hairbrush la brosse à cheveux [bros a shuhvuh]
- do you sell hairbrushes? vous vendez des brosses à cheveux ? [voo vONday day bros a shuhvuh]

hairdryer le sèche-cheveux [sesh-shuhvuh]
- do you have a hairdryer? auriez-vous un sèche-cheveux ? [ohryay-voo AN sesh-shuhvuh]

hair salon le salon de coiffure [salON duh kwafUr]
- does the hotel have a hair salon? est-ce qu'il y a un salon de coiffure dans l'hôtel ? [eskeel ya AN salON duh kwafUr dON lotel]

half demi(e) [duhmee] ◆ la moitié [mwatyay]
- shall we meet in half an hour? on se retrouve dans une demi-heure ? [ON suh ruhtroov dONz Un duhmee-uhr]
- it's half past eight il est huit heures et demie [eel eh weet uhr ay duhmee]

half-bottle la demi-bouteille [duhmee-bootey]
- a half-bottle of red wine, please servez-nous une demi-bouteille de vin rouge [servay-nooz Un duhmee-bootey duh vAN roozh]

ham le jambon [zhONbON]
- I'd like five slices of ham je voudrais cinq tranches de jambon [zhuh voodreh sANk trONsh duh zhONbON]

hand la main [mAN]
- where can I wash my hands? où puis-je me laver les mains ? [oo pweezh muh lavay lay mAN]

handbag le sac à main [sak a mAN]
- someone's stolen my handbag on m'a volé mon sac à main [ON a volay mON sak a mAN]

hand baggage les bagages *m* à main [bagazh a mAN]
- one suitcase and one piece of hand baggage une valise et un bagage à main [Un valeez ay UN bagazh a mAN]

handkerchief le mouchoir [mooshwar]
- do you have a spare handkerchief? auriez-vous un mouchoir à me donner ? [ohryay-vooz AN mooshwar a muh donay]

handle la poignée [pwanyay]

▸ the handle's broken la poignée est cassée [la pwanyay eh kasay]

handmade fait(e) à la main [feh(feht) a la mAN]

▸ is this handmade? est-ce que c'est fait à la main ? [eskuh seh feh a la mAN]

happen *(occur)* arriver [aree-vay], se passer [suh pasay]

▸ what happened? que s'est-il passé ? [kuh seht-eel pasay]

▸ these things happen ce sont des choses qui arrivent [suh sON day shohz kee areev]

happy *(not sad)* heureux [uhruh], heureuse [uhruhz]; *(satisfied)* content(e) [kONtON(kONtONt)]

▸ I'd be happy to help ça me ferait plaisir de vous aider [sa muh fuhreh playzeer duh vooz ayday]

▸ Happy Birthday! joyeux anniversaire ! [zhwa-yuhz anee-versehr]

▸ Happy New Year! bonne année ! [bon anay]

hard-boiled egg l'œuf *m* dur [uhf dUr]

▸ I'll just have a hard-boiled egg je prendrai juste un œuf dur [zhuh prONdray zhUst AN uhf dUr]

hat le chapeau [shapoh]

▸ I think I left my hat here j'ai dû laisser mon chapeau ici [zhay dU laysay mON shapoh eesee]

hate détester [daytes-tay]

▸ I hate golf je déteste le golf [zhuh daytest luh golf]

have avoir [avwar]; *(meal, drink)* prendre [prONdr] ◆ *(be obliged)* devoir [duhvwar]

▸ do you have any bread? avez-vous du pain ? [avay-voo dU pAN]

▸ do you have them in red? est-ce que vous les avez en rouge ? [eskuh voo layz avay ON roozh]

▸ he has brown hair il a les cheveux bruns [eel a ley shuhvuh brAN]

▸ where should we go to have a drink? où peut-on aller pour prendre un verre [oo puht-ON alay poor prONdr AN vehr]

▸ I have to be at the airport by six (o'clock) je dois être à l'aéroport à six heures [zhuh dwahz etr a la-ayro-por a seez uhr]

▸ we have to go il faut y aller [eel foht ee alay]

head *(of a person)* la tête [tet]; *(of a shower)* la pomme [pom]

▸ I hit my head when I fell je me suis cogné la tête en tombant [zhuh muh swee konyay la tet ON tONbON]

headache le mal de tête [mal duh tet]

▸ I've got a headache j'ai mal à la tête [zhay mal a la tet]

▸ do you have anything for a headache? auriez-vous quelque chose pour les maux de têtes ? [ohryay-voo kelkuh shohz poor lay moh duh tet]

headlight le phare [far]

▸ one of my headlights got smashed l'un de mes phares est brisé [lAN duh may far eh breezay]

headphones le casque (à écouteurs) [kask (a aykoo-tuhr)]
▸ did you find my headphones? tu as trouvé mon casque ? [tU a troovay mON kask]

health la santé [sONtay]
▸ in good/poor health en bonne/mauvaise santé [ON bon/mohvez sONtay]

hear entendre (dire) [ONtONdr (deer)]
▸ I've heard a lot about you j'ai beaucoup entendu parler de vous [zhay bohkoo ONtON-dU parlay duh voo]
▸ I've heard there's an old abbey that you can visit on m'a dit qu'il y a une ancienne abbaye à visiter [ON ma dee keel ya Un ONsyen aba-yee a veezee-tay]

heart le cœur [kuhr]
▸ I think there's something wrong with my heart je crois que j'ai un problème au cœur [zhuh krwah kuh zhay AN problem oh kuhr]

heart attack l'infarctus *m* [ANfark-tUs], la crise cardiaque [kreez kardyak]
▸ he had a heart attack il a fait un infarctus [eel a feht AN ANfark-tUs]
▸ I nearly had a heart attack! j'ai frisé la crise cardiaque ! [zhay freezay la kreez kardyak]

heart condition
▸ to have a heart condition être cardiaque [etr kardyak]

heat la chaleur [shaluhr]; *(for cooking)* le feu [fuh]
▸ there's no heat from the radiator in my room le radiateur de ma chambre ne chauffe pas [luh radya-tuhr duh ma shONbr nuh shohf pa]

heating le chauffage [shohfazh]
▸ how does the heating work? comment marche le chauffage ? [komON marsh luh shohfazh]

heavy lourd(e) [loor(loord)]

heel le talon [talON]
▸ can you put new heels on these shoes? pouvez-vous remettre un talon à ces chaussures ? [poovay-voo ruhmetr AN talON a say shohsUr]

hello *(as a greeting)* bonjour ! [bONzhoor]; *(on the phone)* allô [aloh]
▸ hello, is this...? allô, est-ce que je suis bien chez... ? [aloh eskuh zhuh swee byAN shay]

helmet le casque [kask]
▸ do you have a helmet you could lend me? auriez-vous un casque à me prêter ? [ohryay-vooz AN kask a muh prehtay]

help *(assistance)* l'aide *f* [ehd]; *(emergency aid)* le secours [suhkoor] ◆ aider [ayday]
▸ help! au secours ! [oh suhkoor], à l'aide ! [a lehd]
▸ go and get help quickly! allez vite chercher de l'aide ! [alay veet shershay duh lehd]

‣ thank you for your help je vous remercie de votre aide [zhuh voo ruhmer-see duh votr ehd]

‣ could you help me? pourriez-vous m'aider ? [pooryay-voo mayday]

‣ could you help us to push the car? pouvez-vous nous aider à pousser la voiture ? [poovay-voo nooz ayday a poosay la vwatUr]

‣ let me help you with that je vais vous aider [zhuh veh vooz ayday]

‣ could you help me to find a hotel? pouvez-vous m'aider à trouver un hôtel ? [poovay-voo mayday a troovay AN otel]

‣ could you help me with my bags? pourriez-vous m'aider à porter mes bagages ? [pooryay-voo mayday a portay may bagazh]

herbal tea la tisane [teezan], l'infusion *f* [ANfU-zyON]

‣ I'd like a herbal tea j'aimerais une tisane [zhehmuh-rehz Un teezan]

here ici [eesee] ◆ *(giving)* tiens/tenez [tyAN/tuhnay]

‣ I've been here two days je suis là depuis deux jours [zhuh swee la duhpwee duh zhoor]

‣ I came here three years ago je suis venu ici il y a trois ans [zhuh swee vuhnU eesee eel ya trwaz ON]

‣ are you from around here? tu es d'ici ? [tU eh deesee]

‣ I'm a stranger here myself excusez-moi, je ne suis pas d'ici non plus [ekskU-zay-mwa zhuh nuh swee pa deesee nON plu]

‣ it's five minutes from here c'est à cinq minutes d'ici [seht a sANk meenUt deesee]

‣ here is/are... voici... [vwasee]

‣ here are my passport and ticket voici mon passeport et mon billet [vwasee mON paspor ay mON beeyeh]

‣ here: take that tenez, prenez ça [tuhnay pruhnay sa]

hi salut ! [salU]

‣ hi, I'm Julia bonjour, moi c'est Julia [bONzhoor mwa seh Julia]

‣ say hi to the others! donne mon bonjour aux autres ! [don mON bONzhoor ohz ohtr]

high beam le (plein) phare [(plAN) far], le feu de route [fuh duh root]

‣ put your lights on high beam mets tes feux de route [meh tay fuh duh root]

high chair la chaise haute [shehz oht]

‣ could we have a high chair for the baby? pourrions-nous avoir une chaise haute pour le bébé ? [pooryON-noo avwar Un shehz oht poor luh baybay]

high season la haute saison [oht sehzON]

‣ is it very expensive in the high season? les prix augmentent-ils beaucoup en haute saison ? [lay pree ohgmONt-teel bohkoo ON oht sehzON]

high tide la marée haute [maray oht]

‣ what time is high tide? à quelle heure est la marée haute ? [a kel uhr eh la maray oht]

highways

If you drive on those parts of the French road network that are privately run, which correspond, for the most part, to the major highways linking the big cities, you will have to pay a toll at a *péage*. Tolls must also be paid to go over major bridges and through tunnels. Road signs warn you that a *péage* is coming up, and machines accept coins or credit cards.

highway l'autoroute *f* [otoroot]
- what is the speed limit on highways? quelle est la vitesse limite sur les autoroutes ? [kel eh la veetes leemeet sUr layz otoh-root]
- how do I get onto the highway? comment est-ce que je peux rejoindre l'autoroute ? [komONt eskuh zhuh puh ruhzhwANdr lotoh-root]

hike la randonnée [rONdo-nay]
- are there any good hikes around here? y a-t-il des randonnées sympas à faire dans le coin ? [ee ateel day rONdo-nay sANpah a fehr dON luh kwAN]

hiking la marche [marsh], la randonnée [rONdo-nay]
- to go hiking faire de la randonnée (pédestre) [fehr duh la rANdo-nay paydestr]
- are there any hiking trails? est-ce qu'il y a des sentiers de randonnée ? [eskeel ya day sONtyay duh rONdo-nay]

hiking boots les chaussures *f* de randonnée [shohsUr duh rONdo-nay]
- do you need to wear hiking boots? est-ce qu'il faut avoir des chaussures de randonnée ? [eskeel foht avwar day shohsUr duh rONdo-nay]

hitchhike faire du stop [fehr dU stop], faire de l'auto-stop [fehr duh lotoh-stop]
- we hitchhiked here on est venu en stop [ON eh vuhnU ON stop]

hitchhiking l'auto-stop *m* [otoh-stop]
- to go hitchhiking faire de l'auto-stop [fehr duh lotoh-stop]

holiday la fête [fet], le jour férié [zhoor fayryay]
- is tomorrow a holiday? c'est férié, demain ? [seh fayryay duhmAN]

home *(house)* la maison [mehzON]
- to stay at home rester à la maison [restay a la mehzON]
- we're going home tomorrow on rentre chez nous demain [ON rONtr shay noo duhmAN]

homemade fait(e) maison [feh(feht) mehzON]
- is it homemade? c'est fait maison ? [seh feh mehzON]

hood *(of car)* le capot [kapoh]
- I've dented the hood j'ai fait une bosse sur le capot [zhay feht Un bos sUr luh kapoh]

horrible *(weather, day)* sale [sal]; *(person)* horrible [oreebl]
- what horrible weather! quel sale temps ! [kel sal tON]

horseback riding l'équitation *f* [aykee-tasyON]
- can we go horseback riding? peut-on faire de l'équitation ? [puht-ON fehr duh laykee-tasyON]

hospital l'hôpital *m* [opee-tal]
- where is the nearest hospital? où est l'hôpital le plus proche ? [oo eh lopee-tal luh plU prosh]

hot *(in temperature)* chaud(e) [shoh(shohd)]; *(spicy)* épicé(e) [aypee-say]
- I'm too hot j'ai trop chaud [zhay troh shoh]
- it's really hot il fait vraiment chaud [eel feh vrehmON shoh]
- there's no hot water il n'y a pas d'eau chaude [eel nya pa doh shohd]

hotel l'hôtel *m* [otel]
- do you have a list of hotels in this area? avez-vous une liste des hôtels de la région ? [avay-vooz Un leest dayz otel duh la rayzhyON]
- are there any reasonably priced hotels near here? y a-t-il des hôtels pas trop chers par ici ? [ee ateel dayz otels pa troh shehr par eesee]
- is the hotel downtown? est-ce que l'hôtel est près du centre ? [eskuh lotel eh preh dU sONtr]
- could you recommend another hotel? pourriez-vous me recommander un autre hôtel ? [pooryay-voo muh ruhko-mONday AN ohtr otel]

hour l'heure *f* [uhr]
- I'll be back in an hour je reviens dans une heure [zhuh ruhvyAN dONz Un uhr]
- the flight takes three hours le vol dure trois heures [luh vol dUr trwaz uhr]

house la maison [mehzON]
- is this your house? c'est chez vous ? [seh shay voo]

house wine le vin de la maison [vAN duh la mehzON], la cuvée du patron [kUvay dU patrON]
- a bottle of house wine une bouteille de la cuvée du patron [Un bootey duh la kUvay dU patrON]

---

at the hotel

- we'd like a double room/two single rooms nous voudrions une chambre double/deux chambres simples [noo voodree-yONz Un shONbr doobl/duh shONbr sANpl]
- I have a reservation in the name of Jones j'ai réservé une chambre au nom de Jones [zhahy rayzer-vay Un shONbr oh nON duh Jones]
- what time is breakfast/dinner served? à quelle heure est le petit déjeuner/dîner ? [a kel uhr eh luh puhtee dayzhuh-nay/deenay]
- could I have a wake-up call at 7 a.m.? pourriez-vous me réveiller à sept heures ? [pooryay-voo muh ray-veyay a set uhr]

how comment [komON]
- how are you? comment vas-tu/allez-vous ? [komON va tU/alay-voo]
- how do you spell it? comment ça s'écrit ? [komON sa saykree]
- how about a drink? on va boire un verre ? [ON va bwar AN vehr]

humid humide [Umeed]
- it's very humid today il fait humide aujourd'hui [eel feht Umeed ohzhoor-dwee]

hungry
- to be hungry avoir faim [avwar fAN]
- I'm starting to get hungry je commence à avoir faim [zhuh komONs a avwar fAN]

hurry
- to be in a hurry être pressé [etr presay]

hurry up se dépêcher [suh daypay-shay]
- hurry up! dépêchez-vous ! [daypay-shay-voo]

hurt blesser [blesay] ♦ faire mal [fehr mal]
- you're hurting me! vous me faites mal ! [voo muh fet mal]
- to hurt oneself se blesser [suh blesay]
- I hurt myself je me suis fait mal [zhuh muh swee feh mal]
- I hurt my hand je me suis blessé à la main [zhuh muh swee blesay a la mAN]
- it hurts ça fait mal [sa feh mal]

ice la glace [glas]; *(cubes)* les glaçons *m* [glasON]
- the car skidded on the ice la voiture a dérapé sur le verglas [la vwatUr a dayra-pay sUr luh verglah]
- a Diet Coke® without ice, please un Coca Light® sans glaçons, s'il vous plaît [AN coca light sON glasON seel voo play]

ice cream la glace [glas]
- I'd like an ice cream j'aimerais une glace [zhehmuh-rehz Un glas]

ice cube le glaçon [glasON]
- could I have a carafe of water with no ice cubes in it? pourrais-je avoir une carafe d'eau sans glaçons ? [poorehzh avwar Un karaf doh sON glasON]

iced coffee le café glacé [kafay glasay]
- I'd like an iced coffee je voudrais un café glacé [zhuh voodreh AN kafay glasay]

ice rink la patinoire [pateen-war]
- is there an ice rink? est-ce qu'il y a une patinoire ? [eskeel ya Un pateen-war]

ID cards

All French citizens carry an ID card which they must show to a police officer or public transport official upon request. It's also used when paying by check, taking exams, opening a bank account, etc. and can be used like a passport for travel within the EU.

ice skate le patin à glace [patAN a glas]
- I'd like to rent some ice skates j'aimerais louer des patins à glace [zhehmuh-reh lway day patAN a glas]

ID card la carte d'identité [kart deedON-teetay]
- I don't have an ID card: will a passport do instead? je n'ai pas de carte d'identité, est-ce qu'un passeport fait l'affaire ? [zhuh nay pa duh kart deedON-teetay eskAN paspor feh lafehr]

if si [see]
- we'll go if you want si tu veux, on y va [see tU vuh ON ee va]

ill malade [malad]
- my son is ill mon fils est malade [mON fees eh malad]

immediately tout de suite [toot sweet]
- can you do it immediately? pouvez-vous le faire tout de suite ? [poovay-voo luh fehr toot sweet]

improve améliorer [amay-lyoray]
- I'm hoping to improve my French while I'm here j'espère améliorer mon français pendant mon séjour [zhespehr amay-lyoray mON frONsay pONdON mON sayzhoor]

in dans [dON]; *(with towns, countries)* à [a]
- our bags are still in the room nos bagages sont encore dans la chambre [noh bagazh sONt ONkor dON la shONbr]
- do you live in Paris? tu vis à Paris ? [tU vee a paree]

included inclus(e) [ANklU(ANklUz)], compris(e) [kONpree(kONpreez)]
- is breakfast included? est-ce que le petit déjeuner est inclus ? [eskuh luh puhtee dayzhuh-nay eht ANklU]
- is sales tax included? est-ce que la TVA est comprise ? [eskuh la tayvay-ah eh kONpreez]
- is service charge included? est-ce que le service est compris ? [eskuh luh servees eh kONpree]

indoor intérieur(e) [ANtay-ryuhr], couvert(e) [koovehr(koovehrt)]
- is there an indoor pool? est-ce qu'il y a une piscine couverte ? [eskeel ya Un peeseen koovehrt]

infection l'infection *f* [ANfek-syON]

▸ I have an eye infection j'ai une infection à l'œil [zhay Un ANfek-syON a loy]

information *(facts)* l'information *f* [ANfor-masyON]; *(services)* les renseignements *m* [rONsen-yuhmON]

▸ a piece of information un renseignement [AN rONsen-yuhmON]

▸ may I ask you for some information? je peux vous demander un renseignement ? [zhuh puh voo duhmON-day AN rONsen-yuhmON]

▸ where can I find information on...? où est-ce que je peux trouver des informations sur... ? [oo eskuh zhuh puh troovay dayz ANfor-masyON sUr]

▸ I'm looking for information on the region je cherche de la documentation sur la région [zhuh shersh duh la dokU-mONta-syON sUr la rayzhyON]

▸ could you give me some information about crossings between Calais and Dover? pourriez-vous me renseigner sur les traversées Calais-Douvres ? [pooryay-voo muh rONsen-yay sUr lay traver-say kaleh-doovr]

injection *(medicine)* la piqûre [peekUr]

▸ am I going to need an injection? est-ce qu'une piqûre est nécessaire ? [eskUn peekUr eh nayseh-sehr]

injure blesser [blesay]

▸ to injure oneself se blesser [suh blesay]

▸ I injured myself je me suis blessé [zhu muh swee blesay]

inside à l'intérieur (de) [a lANtayr-yuhr (duh)]

▸ are you allowed inside the castle? on peut entrer dans le château ? [ON puht ONtray dON luh shatoh]

▸ we'd prefer a table inside nous aimerions mieux une table à l'intérieur [nooz ehmuh-ryONz Un tabl a lANtayr-yuhr]

insurance l'assurance *f* [asU-rONs]

▸ what does the insurance cover? quelles garanties l'assurance couvre-t-elle ? [kel garON-tee lasU-rONs koovruh-tel]

insure *(house, car)* assurer [asU-ray]

▸ are you insured? êtes-vous assuré ? [et-vooz asU-ray]

interesting intéressant(e) [ANtay-resON(-resONt)]

▸ it's not a very interesting place cet endroit n'est pas très intéressant [set ON drwah neh pa trez ANtay-resON]

international call la communication internationale [komU-neeka-syON ANter-nasyo-nal]

▸ I'd like to make an international call je voudrais faire une communication internationale [zhuh voodreh fehr Un komU-neeka-syON ANter-nasyo-nal]

Internet l'Internet *m* [ANter-net]

▸ do you have Internet? vous avez Internet ? [vooz avay ANter-net]

introduce *(present)* présenter [prayzON-tay]

▸ to introduce oneself se présenter [suh prayzON-tay]

▸ allow me to introduce myself: I'm Michael je me présente, je m'appelle Michael [zhuh muh prayzONt zhuh mapel Michael]

invite inviter [ANvee-tay]
▸ I'd really like to invite you to dinner next weekend j'aimerais beaucoup vous inviter à dîner le week-end prochain [zhehmuh-reh bohkoo vooz ANvee-tay a deenay luh weekend proshAN]

iron *(for ironing)* le fer à repasser [fehr a ruhpa-say] ✦ repasser [ruhpa-say]
▸ I need an iron j'ai besoin d'un fer à repasser [zhay buhzwAN dAN fehr a ruhpa-say]

itch la démangeaison [daymON-zhehzON]
▸ I've got an itch j'ai une démangeaison [zhay Un daymON-zhehzON]

itinerary l'itinéraire *m* [eetee-nayrehr]
▸ is it possible to modify the itinerary planned for this tour? est-il possible de modifier l'itinéraire prévu dans ce circuit ? [eht-eel poseebl duh modee-fyay leetee-nayrehr prayvU dON suh seerkwee]

January janvier [zhONvyay]
▸ January 4th le quatre janvier [luh katr zhONvyay]

Jet Ski® le scooter des mers [skootuhr day mehr]
▸ I'd like to rent a Jet Ski® j'aimerais louer un scooter des mers [zhehmuh-reh lway AN skootuhr day mehr]

job *(employment)* l'emploi *m* [ONplwa], le job [dzhob]
▸ I'm looking for a summer job in the area je cherche un job d'été dans la région [zhuh shersh AN dzhob daytay dON la rayzhyON]

joke la plaisanterie [plehzON-tree] ✦ plaisanter [plehzON-tay]
▸ it's beyond a joke! la plaisanterie a assez duré ! [la plehzON-tree a asay dUray]
▸ I was just joking j'ai dit ça pour rire [zhay dee sa poor reer]

journey le voyage [vwa-yazh]
▸ how long does the journey take? combien de temps dure le voyage ? [kONbyAN duh tON dUr luh vwa-yazh]

juice *(from fruit)* le jus [zhU]
▸ what types of juice do you have? qu'est-ce que vous avez comme jus de fruit ? [keskuh vooz avay kom zhU duh frwee]

July juillet [zhweeyeh]
▸ July 4th le quatre juillet [luh katr zhweeyeh]

June juin [zhwAN]
▸ June 2nd le deux juin [luh duh zhwAN]

just juste [zhUst]; *(at that moment)* tout de suite [toot sweet]
> he just left il vient juste de partir [eel vyAN zhUst duh parteer]
> (I'm) just coming j'arrive tout de suite [zhareev toot sweet]
> I'll just have one j'en prendrai un seul [zhON prONdray AN suhl]

k

kayak le kayak [ka-yak]
> can we rent kayaks? peut-on louer des kayaks ? [puht-ON lway day ka-yak]

keep garder [garday]; *(promise, appointment)* tenir [tuhneer]
> can you keep an eye on my bag for a few minutes? pouvez-vous garder mon sac quelques instants ? [poovay-voo garday mON sak kelkuz ANstON]
> keep the change gardez la monnaie [garday la moneh]

key *(for a door, a container)* la clé [klay]; *(on a keyboard)* la touche [toosh]; *(of a phone)* la touche [toosh]
> which is the key to the front door? quelle est la clé pour la porte d'entrée ? [kel eh la klay poor la port dONtray]

kilometer le kilomètre [keelo-metr]
> how much is it per kilometer? y a-t-il un tarif au kilomètre ? [ee ateel AN tareef oh keelo-metr]

kind *(nice)* gentil(le) [zhONtee(zhONteey)] ♦ *(sort, type)* la sorte [sort], le style [steel]
> that's very kind of you c'est très gentil [seh treh zhONtee]
> what's your favorite kind of music? quel style de musique préfères-tu ? [kel steel duh mUzeek prayfehr-tU]

kitchen la cuisine [kweezeen]
> is the kitchen shared? c'est une cuisine commune ? [seht Un kweezeen komUn]

Kleenex® le mouchoir en papier [mooshwar ON papyay]
> do you have a Kleenex®, please? vous auriez un mouchoir en papier, s'il vous plaît ? [vooz ohryay AN mooshwar ON papyay, seel voo play]

knife le couteau [kootoh]
> could I have a knife? pourrais-je avoir un couteau ? [poorehzh avwar AN kootoh]

know *(fact)* savoir [savwar]; *(person, place)* connaître [konehtr]
> I don't know what it is je ne sais pas ce que c'est [zhuh nuh seh pa suh kuh seh]
> I know the basics but no more than that je connais les bases mais pas plus [zhuh koneh lay baz meh pa plUs]
> I don't know a lot of people here, do you? je ne connais pas grand-monde ici, et vous ? [zhuh nuh koneh pa grON-mONd eesee ay voo]

▸ do you know each other? est-ce que vous vous connaissez ? [eskuh voo voo koneh-say]

knowledge la connaissance [koneh-sONs]
▸ she has a good knowledge of French elle a un bon niveau de français [el a AN bON neevoh duh frONsay]
▸ not to my knowedge pas à ma connaissance [paz a ma koneh-sONs]
▸ without my knowledge à mon insu [a mON ANsU]

l

ladies' room les toilettes *f* pour dames [twalet poor dam]
▸ where's the ladies' room? où sont les toilettes pour dames ? [oo sON lay twalet poor dam]

lake le lac [lak]
▸ can you go swimming in the lake? peut-on se baigner dans le lac ? [puht-ON suh baynyay dON luh lak]

lamp la lampe [lONp]
▸ the lamp doesn't work la lampe ne fonctionne pas [la lONp nuh fONksyon pa]

land *(plane)* se poser [suh pohzay]
▸ the plane has just landed l'avion vient seulement de se poser [lavyON vyAN suhlmON duh suh pohzay]

landmark le point de repère [pwAN duh raypehr]
▸ do you recognize any landmarks? est-ce que vous retrouvez des points de repère ? [eskuh voo ruhtroo-vay day pwAN duh raypehr]

lane *(on a highway)* la voie [vwah]; *(for a bus)* le couloir [koolwar]
▸ a four-lane highway un autoroute à quatre voies [AN otoh-root a katr vwah]

laptop l'ordinateur *m* portable [ordee-natuhr portabl]
▸ my laptop's been stolen on m'a volé mon ordinateur portable [ON ma volay mON ordee-natuhr portabl]

last dernier [dernyay], dernière [dernyehr] ♦ *(go on)* durer [dUray]; *(weather)* tenir [tuhneer]
▸ when does the last bus go? à quelle heure part le dernier bus ? [a kel uhr pahr luh dernyay bUs]
▸ when is the last subway train? à quelle heure est le dernier métro ? [a kel uhr eh luh dernyay maytroh]
▸ how long do the batteries last for? combien de temps durent les piles ? [kONbyAN duh tON dUr lay peel]

last name le nom de famille [nON duh famey]
▸ could I have your last name? puis-je avoir votre nom de famille ? [pweezh avwar votr nON duh famey]

late en retard [ON ruhtar], de retard [duh ruhtar]
▸ the plane was two hours late l'avion a eu deux heures de retard [lavyON a U duhz uhr duh ruhtar]
▸ could you tell me if the 13:17 to Paris is running late? pourriez-vous me dire si le train de treize heures dix-sept pour Paris a du retard ? [pooryay-voo muh deer see luh trAN duh trehz uhr dees-set poor pa-ree a dU ruhtar]

later plus tard [plU tar]
▸ is there a later train? il n'y a pas de train plus tard ? [eel nya pa duh trAN plU tar]
▸ see you later! à plus tard ! [a plU tar], à tout à l'heure ! [a toot a luhr]

latest (most recent) dernier [dernyay], dernière [dernyehr]
▸ what's the latest time we can check out? jusqu'à quelle heure peut-on rester dans la chambre ? [zhuska kel uhr puht-ON restay dON la shONbr]

laugh le rire [reer] ♦ rire [reer]
▸ I just did it for a laugh j'ai fait ça pour rire [zhay feh sa poor reer]

Laundromat® la laverie [lavree]
▸ is there a Laundromat® nearby? y a-t-il une laverie près d'ici ? [ee ateel Un lavree preh deesee]

laundry (clothes) la lessive [leseev]; (business) la blanchisserie [blONshees-ree]; (room) la buanderie [bU-ONdree]
▸ where can we do our laundry? où peut-on faire une lessive ? [oo puht-ON fehr Un leseev]
▸ is there a laundry nearby? est-ce qu'il y a une blanchisserie près d'ici ? [eskeel ya Un blONshees-ree preh deesee]

lawyer avocat [avo-kah], avocate [avo-kat]
▸ I'm a lawyer je suis avocat [zhuh sweez avo-kah]
▸ I need a lawyer j'ai besoin d'un avocat [zhay buhzwAN dAN avo-kah]

leaflet le prospectus [prospek-tUs], le dépliant [dayplee-yON]
▸ do you have any leaflets in English? vous avez des prospectus en anglais ? [vooz avay day prospek-tUs ON ONglay]

learn apprendre [aprONdr]
▸ I've just learned a few words from a book j'ai appris quelques mots avec un bouquin [zhay apree kelkuh moh avek AN bookAN]

least le moins [luh mwAN], la moins [la mwAN] ♦ **at least** au moins [oh mwAN]
▸ it's the least I can do c'est la moindre des choses [seh la mwANdr day shohz]
▸ not in the least pas le moins du monde [pa luh mwAN dU mOnd]
▸ to say the least le moins qu'on puisse dire [luh mwAN kON pwees deer]
▸ it's at least a three-hour drive il y a au moins trois heures de route [eel ya oh mwAN trwaz uhr duh root]

leave *(go away from)* quitter [keetay]; *(let stay)* laisser [laysay]; *(forget to take)* oublier [ooblee-yay] ◆ *(go away)* partir [parteer]

- can I leave my backpack at reception? est-ce que je peux laisser mon sac à dos à la réception ? [eskuh zhuh puh laysay mON sak a doh a la raysep-syON]
- can I leave the car at the airport? pourrais-je rendre la voiture à l'aéroport ? [poorehzh rONdr la vwatUr a la-ayro-por]
- leave us alone! laissez-nous tranquilles ! [laysay-noo trONkeel]
- I've left something on the plane j'ai oublié quelque chose dans l'avion [zhay ooblee-yay kelhuh shohz dON lavyON]
- I will be leaving at nine o'clock tomorrow morning je partirai demain matin à neuf heures [zhu partee-ray duhmAN matAN a nuhv uhr]
- what platform does the train for Paris leave from? de quel quai part le train pour Paris ? [duh kel keh par luh trAN poor paree]

left *(not right)* gauche [gohsh]

- on the left (of) à gauche (de) [a gohsh (duh)]
- to be left rester [restay]
- are there any tickets left for...? est-ce qu'il vous reste des places pour... ? [eskeel voo rest day plas poor]

left-hand (de) gauche [(duh) gohsh]

- on your left-hand side à votre gauche [a votr gohsh]

leg la jambe [zhONb]

- I have a pain in my leg j'ai mal à la jambe [zhay mal a la zhONb]
- I can't move my leg je ne peux pas bouger ma jambe [zhuh nuh puh pa boozhay ma zhONb]

lemon le citron [seetrON]

- can I have half a kilo of lemons? puis-je avoir une livre de citrons ? [pweezh avwar Un leevr duh seetrON]

lend prêter [prehtay]

- could you lend us your car? est-ce que vous pourriez nous prêter votre voiture ? [eskuh voo pooryay noo prehtay votr vwatUr]

lens *(of camera)* l'objectif *m* [obzhek-teef]; *(contact lens)* la lentille [lONteey]

- there's something on the lens il y a quelque chose sur l'objectif [eel ya kelkuh shohz sUr lobzhek-teef]
- I have hard/soft lenses j'ai des lentilles dures/souples [zhay lay lONteey dUr/soopl]

less moins [mwAN]

- less and less de moins en moins [duh mwANz ON mwAN]
- a little less un peu moins [AN puh mwAN]

lesson la leçon [luhsON], le cours [koor]

- how much do lessons cost? combien coûtent les cours ? [kONbyAN koot lay koor]
- can we take lessons? pouvons-nous prendre des leçons ? [poovON-noo prONdr day luhsON]

license plates

The last two digits of a French license plate refer to the *département* where the vehicle was registered. So, for example, 75 denotes Paris and 94 Val-de-Marne.

let off *(allow to disembark)* laisser descendre [laysay desOndr]
▸ could you let me off here, please? pourriez-vous me laisser descendre ici, s'il vous plaît ? [pooryay-voo muh laysay desONdr eesee seel voo play]

letter la lettre [letr]
▸ I would like to send this letter to the States je voudrais envoyer cette lettre aux États-Unis [zhuh voodreh ONvwa-yay set letr ohz aytaz-Unee]
▸ I confirmed my booking by letter j'ai confirmé ma réservation par lettre [zhay kONfeer-may ma rayzer-vasyON par letr]

level le niveau [neevoh]
▸ do you know if cabin 27 is on this level? savez-vous si la cabine vingt-sept se trouve à ce niveau ? [savay-voo see la kabeen vANt-set suh troov a suh neevoh]

license la licence [leesONs], l'autorisation f [otoh-reeza-syON]; *(for driving)* le permis (de conduire) [permee (duh kONdweer)]
▸ does the restaurant not have a license? le restaurant n'a pas de licence ? [luh resto-rON na pa duh leesONs]

license number le numéro d'immatriculation [nUmay-roh deema-treekU-lasyON]
▸ I got the license number j'ai relevé le numéro d'immatriculation [zhay ruhluh-vay luh nUmay-roh deema-treekU-lasyON]

license plate la plaque d'immatriculation [plak deema-treekU-lasyON]
▸ the car had false license plates la voiture avait de fausses plaques (d'immatriculation) [la vwatUr aveh duh fohs plak (deema-treekU-lasyON)]

lifebelt la bouée de sauvetage [bway duh sohvtazh]
▸ throw me a lifebelt! lancez-moi une bouée de sauvetage ! [lONsay-mwa Un bway duh sohvtazh]

lifeboat le canot de sauvetage [kanoh duh sohvtazh]
▸ how many lifeboats are there? il y a combien de canots de sauvetage ? [eel ya kONbyAN duh kanoh duh sohvtazh]

lifejacket le gilet de sauvetage [zheeleh duh sohvtazh]
▸ are there any lifejackets? est-ce qu'il y a des gilets de sauvetage ? [eskeel ya day zheeleh duh sohvtazh]

light *(brightness)* la lumière [lUmyehr]; *(on a car)* le phare [far], le feu [fuh]; *(regulating traffic)* le feu tricolore [fuh treeko-lor]; *(for a cigarette)* le feu [fuh]
▸ there's no light il n'y a pas de lumière [eel nya pa duh lUmyehr]

likes

- I really love that painting j'aime beaucoup ce tableau [zhem bohkoo suh tabloh]
- I like your brother j'aime bien ton frère [zhem byAN tON frehr]
- I've a soft spot for her j'ai un faible pour elle [zhay AN fehbl poor el]
- I think she's very nice je la trouve très sympathique [zhuh la troov treh sANpa-teek]

- the light doesn't work la lumière ne fonctionne pas [la lUmyehr nuh fONksyon pa]
- you've left your lights on vous avez laissé vos phares allumés [vooz avay laysay voh far alU-may]
- could you check the lights? pourriez-vous vérifier les phares ? [pooryay-voo vayree-fyay lay far]
- stop at the lights arrêtez-vous au feu [areh-tay-voo oh fuh]
- do you have a light? avez-vous du feu ? [avay-voo dU fuh]

lighter le briquet [breekeh]
- can I borrow your lighter? je peux vous emprunter votre briquet ? [zhuh puh vooz ONprAN-tay votr breekeh]

lighthouse le phare [far]
- are there boat trips to the lighthouse? y a-t-il des balades en bateau jusqu'au phare ? [ee ateel day balad ON batoh zhUskoh far]

like comme [kom] ◆ aimer [aymay]
- it's like last year c'est comme l'an dernier [seh kom lON dernyay]
- it's quite like English ça ressemble pas mal à l'anglais [sa ruhsONbl pa mal a lONglay]
- I like it ça me plaît [sa muh pleh]
- I don't like it ça ne me plaît pas [sa nuh muh pleh pa]
- do you like it here? tu te plais ici ? [tU tuh pleh eesee]
- I like French food very much j'aime beaucoup la cuisine française [zhem bohkoo la kweezeen frONsehz]

dislikes

- I hate football je déteste le foot [zhuh daytest luh foot]
- I can't stand him je ne peux pas le supporter [zhuh nuh puh pa luh sUpor-tay]
- I don't really like him/her je ne l'aime pas trop [zhuh nuh lem pa troh]
- I'm not really into walking je ne suis pas très branché rando [zhuh nuh swee pa treh brONshay rONdoh]

▸ do you like the movies? aimes-tu le cinéma ? [em-tU luh seenay-ma]

▸ would you like a drink? - yes, I'd love one tu prends un verre ? - oui, avec plaisir [tU prON AN vehr – wee avek playzeer]

▸ I'd like to speak to the manager je voudrais parler au responsable [zhuh voodreh parlay oh respON-sabl]

lime le citron vert [seetrON vehr]

▸ can I have half a kilo of limes? puis-je avoir une livre de citrons verts ? [pweezh avwar Un leevr duh seetrON vehr]

limit la limite [leemeet] ◆ limiter [leemee-tay]

▸ that area is off limits cette zone est interdite d'accès [set zon eht ANter-deet dakseh]

▸ do they limit the number of visitors at any one time? est-ce que le nombre de personnes par visite est limité ? [eskuh luh nONbr duh person par veezeet eh leemee-tay]

line la ligne [leenyuh]; *(of people waiting)* la queue [kuh]

▸ it's a bad line la ligne est mauvaise [la leenyuh eh mohvez]

▸ we had to stand in line for quarter of an hour on a dû faire la queue un quart d'heure [ON a dU fehr la kuh AN kar duhr]

▸ which line do I take to get to...? quelle ligne dois-je prendre pour... ? [kel leenyuh dwazh prONdr poor]

▸ where's the stop for line 63 to...? où faut-il prendre la ligne soixante-trois vers... ? [oo foht-eel prONdr la leenyuh swasONt-trwah vehr]

lipstick le rouge à lèvres [roozh a levr]

▸ I need to buy some lipstick il faut que j'achète du rouge à lèvres [eel foh kuh zhashet dU roozh a levr]

listen écouter [aykoo-tay]

▸ listen, I really need to see a doctor écoutez, il faut absolument que je voie un médecin [aykoo-tay eel foht abso-lUmON kuh zhuh vwah AN maydsAN]

▸ listen to me carefully écoute-moi bien [aykoot-mwa byAN]

liter le litre [leetr]

▸ a liter of milk un litre de lait [AN leetr duh leh]

little petit(e) [puhtee(puhteet)] ◆ peu [puh] ◆ **a little** un peu (de) [AN puh (duh)]

▸ it's for a little girl of four c'est pour une petite fille de quatre ans [seh poor Un puhteet feey duh katr ON]

▸ as little as possible le moins possible [luh mwAN poseebl]

▸ a little bit un petit peu [AN puhtee puh]

▸ a little less un peu moins [AN puh mwAN]

▸ a little more un peu plus [AN puh plUs]

▸ I speak a little French je parle un peu français [zhuh parl AN puh frONsay]

▸ we've only got a little money left il ne nous reste qu'un peu d'argent [eel nuh noo rest kAN puh darzhON]

live habiter [abee-tay]
- do you live around here? tu habites le quartier ? [tU abeet luh kartyay]
- I live in Lille j'habite à Lille [zhabeet a leel]

live music le concert [kONsehr]
- I'd like to go to a bar with live music j'aimerais bien aller à un concert dans un café [zhehmuh-reh byAN alay a AN kONsehr dONz AN kafay]

living room le salon [salON]
- I can sleep in the living room je peux dormir dans le salon [zhuh puh dormeer dON luh salON]

loaf le pain [pAN]
- I'd like one of those large loaves je voudrais un de ces gros pains [zhuh voodreh AN duh say groh pAN]

local local(e) [lokal]
- what's the local specialty? quelle est la spécialité locale ? [kel eh la spaysya-leetay lokal]

lock la serrure [serUr] ◆ fermer [fermay]
- the lock's broken la serrure est cassée [la serUr eh kasay]
- I locked the door j'ai fermé la porte à clé [zhay fermay la port a klay]

lock out
- to lock oneself out s'enfermer dehors [sONfer-may duhor]
- I've locked myself out je me suis enfermé à l'extérieur [zhuh muh sweez ONfer-may a lekstayr-yuhr]

long long(ue) [lON(lONg)] ◆ de long [duh lON]
- it's 10 meters long ça fait dix mètres de long [sa feh dee metr duh lON]
- I waited for a long time j'ai attendu longtemps [zhay atON-dU lONtON]
- how long? combien de temps ? [kONbyAN duh tON]
- how long will it take? ça va prendre combien de temps ? [sa va prONdr kONbyAN duh tON]
- we're not sure how long we're going to stay on ne sait pas combien de temps on va rester [On nuh seh pa kONbyAN duh tON ON va restay]

look (with eyes) le regard [ruhgar]; (appearance) l'air m [ehr] ◆ (with eyes) regarder [ruhgar-day]; (seem) avoir l'air [avwar lehr]
- could you have a look at my car? pourriez-vous jeter un coup d'œil à ma voiture ? [pooray-voo zhuhtay AN koo doy a ma vwatUr]
- no, thanks, I'm just looking non, merci, je regarde seulement [nON mersee zhuh ruhgard suhlmON]
- you're looking better today tu as l'air d'aller mieux aujourd'hui [tU a lehr dalay myuh ohzhoor-dwee]
- what does she look like? à quoi elle ressemble ? [a kwa el ruhsONbl]
- you look like your brother tu ressembles à ton frère [tU ruhsONbl a tON frehr]

▸ it looks like it's going to rain on dirait qu'il va pleuvoir [ON deereh keel va pluhvwar]

look after *(child, invalid)* garder [garday]; *(customer)* s'occuper de [sokU-pay duh]; *(luggage)* surveiller [sUr-veyay]

▸ can someone look after the children for us? est-ce que quelqu'un peut garder les enfants (pour nous) ? [eskuh kelkAN puh garday layz ONfON (poor noo)]

▸ someone's looking after me, thank you on s'occupe de moi, merci [ON sokUp duh mwa mersee]

▸ can you look after my things for a minute? pouvez-vous surveiller mes affaires un instant ? [poovay-voo sUr-veyay mayz afehr AN ANstON]

look for chercher [shershay]

▸ I'm looking for a good traditional restaurant je cherche un bon restaurant traditionnel [zhuh shersh AN bON resto-rON tradee-syonel]

lose perdre [perdr]

▸ I've lost the key to my room j'ai perdu la clé de ma chambre [zhay perdU la klay duh ma shONbr]

▸ I've lost my way je me suis perdu [zhuh muh swee perdU]

lost perdu(e) [perdU]

▸ who do you have to see about lost luggage? à qui doit-on s'adresser quand on a perdu ses bagages ? [a kee dwat-ON sadreh-say kONt ON a perdU say bagazh]

▸ could you help me? I seem to be lost pourriez-vous m'aider ? je crois que je suis perdu [pooryay-voo mayday zhuh krwah kuh zhuh swee perdU]

▸ to get lost se perdre [suh perdr]

▸ get lost! va te faire voir ! [va tuh fehr vwar]

lost-and-found le bureau des objets trouvés [bUroh dayz obzheh troovay]

▸ where's the lost-and-found? où est le bureau des objets trouvés ? [oo eh luh bUroh dayz obzheh troovay]

lot

▸ a lot of... beaucoup de... [bohkoo duh]

▸ are there a lot of things to see around here? est-ce qu'il y a beaucoup de choses à voir ici ? [eskeel ya bohkoo duh shohz a vwar eesee]

▸ will there be a lot of other people there? est-ce qu'il y aura beaucoup de monde ? [eskeel yohra bohkoo duh mONd]

▸ I don't have a lot of money je n'ai pas beaucoup d'argent [zhuh nay pa bohkoo darzhON]

▸ that's a lot better c'est beaucoup mieux [seh bohkoo myuh]

▸ thanks a lot merci beaucoup [mersee bohkoo]

loud *(noise)* puissant(e) [pweesOn(pweesONt)]; *(voice, music)* fort(e) [for(fort)]

▸ the television is too loud la télévision est trop forte [la taylay-veezyON eh troh fort]

▸ they've been playing loud music all evening ils ont mis la musique très forte toute la soirée [eelz ON mee la mUzeek treh fort toot la swaray]

loudly *(speak)* fort [for]
> can you speak a little more loudly? est-ce que vous pouvez parler un peu plus fort ? [eskuh voo poovay parlay AN puh plU for]

love aimer [aymay]
> I love you je t'aime [zhuh tem]
> I love the movies j'adore le cinéma [zhador luh seenay-ma]
> I love cooking j'adore cuisiner [zhador kweezee-nay]
> I'd love some more! j'en reprendrais volontiers ! [zhON ruhprON-dreh volON-tyay]

lovely beau [boh], belle [bel]
> what a lovely room! quelle jolie chambre ! [kel jolee shONbr]
> it's lovely today il fait bon aujourd'hui [eel feh bON ohzhoor-dwee]
> it's really lovely here, isn't it? c'est vraiment un endroit très agréable, non ? [seh vrehmON AN ON drwah trez agray-abl nON]

low *(temperature)* bas(se) [bah(bas)]; *(speed)* réduit(e) [raydwee(raydweet)]
> temperatures are in the low twenties il fait un peu plus de vingt degrés [eel feht AN puh plUs duh vAN duhgray]
> cook over a low heat faites cuire à feu doux [fet kweer a fuh doo]

low beam les feux *m* de croisement [fuh duh krwazmON]
> keep your lights on low beam gardez vos feux de croisement [garday voh fuh duh krwazmON]

lower baisser [baysay]
> is it OK if I lower the blind a little? ça ne vous dérange pas si je baisse un peu le store ? [sa nuh voo dayrONzh pa see zhuh bes AN puh luh stor]

low-fat *(yogurt)* maigre [mehgr]
> do you have any low-fat yogurt? auriez-vous des yaourts maigres ? [ohryay-voo day ya-oort mehgr]

low season la basse saison [bas sehzON]
> what are prices like in the low season? quels sont les prix en basse saison ? [kel sON lay pree ON bas sehzON]

low tide la marée basse [maray bas]
> what time is low tide today? à quelle heure la marée est-elle au plus bas aujourd'hui ? [a kel uhr la maray eht-el oh plU bas ohzhoor-dwee]

luck la chance [shONs]
> good luck! bonne chance ! [bon shONs]

luggage les bagages *m* [bagazh]
> my luggage hasn't arrived mes bagages ne sont pas arrivés [may bagazh nuh sON paz aree-vay]
> I'd like to report the loss of my luggage je voudrais faire une déclaration de perte pour mes bagages [zhu voodreh fehr Un daykla-rasyON duh pert poor may bagazh]

lunch

Nowadays, *le déjeuner* in France is often little more than a sandwich eaten on the go, although the French do enjoy long leisurely lunches in summer when they are on vacation. Some stores do still close at lunchtime, however.

luggage cart le chariot [sharyoh]
 ▶ I'm looking for a luggage cart je cherche un chariot pour mes bagages [zhuh shersh AN sharyoh poor may bagazh]

lunch le déjeuner [dayzhuh-nay]
 ▶ to have lunch déjeuner [dayzhuh-nay]
 ▶ what time is lunch served? le déjeuner est servi à quelle heure ? [luh dayzhuh-nay eh servee a kel uhr]

m

machine-washable lavable en machine [lavabl ON masheen]
 ▶ is it machine-washable? est-ce lavable en machine ? [es lavabl ON masheen]

maid la femme de chambre [fam duh shONbr]
 ▶ what time does the maid come? à quelle heure passe la femme de chambre ? [a kel uhr pas la fam duh shONbr]

maid service le service de ménage [servees duh maynazh]
 ▶ is there a maid service? est-ce qu'il y a un service de ménage ? [eskeel ya AN servees duh maynazh]

mailbox la boîte aux lettres [bwat oh letr]
 ▶ where's the nearest mailbox? où se trouve la boîte aux lettres la plus proche ? [oo suh troov la bwat oh letr la plU prosh]

main course le plat principal [plah prANsee-pal]
 ▶ what are you having for your main course? que prenez-vous comme plat principal ? [kuh pruhnay-voo kom plah prANsee-pal]

mainline de grande ligne [duh grOnd leenyuh]
 ▶ where are the mainline trains? où sont les grandes lignes ? [oo sON lay grOnd leenyuh]

make *(create, produce)* faire [fehr]; *(cause to become)* rendre [rOndr]
 ▶ the neighbor makes a lot of noise le voisin fait beaucoup de bruit [luh vwazAN feh bohkoo duh brwee]
 ▶ how is this dish made? comment ce plat est-il préparé ? [komON suh plah eht-eel praypa-ray]

> I hope to make new friends here j'espère me faire de nouveaux amis ici [zhespehr muh fehr duh noovohz amee eesee]

make up *(compensate for)* récupérer [raykU-payray]; *(prepare)* préparer [praypa-ray]
> will we be able to make up the time we've lost? est-ce qu'on pourra récupérer le temps qu'on a perdu ? [eskON poora raykU-payray luh tON kON a perdU]
> can the pharmacist make up the prescription for me now? est-ce que le pharmacien peut préparer mon ordonnance maintenant ? [eskuh luh farma-syAN puh praypa-ray mon ordo-nONs mANt-nON]
> can you make up my bill, please? vous pouvez préparer ma note, s'il vous plaît ? [voo poovay praypa-ray ma not seel voo play]

man l'homme *m* [om]
> is that man bothering you? est-ce que cet homme vous importune ? [eskuh set om vooz ANpor-tUn]

man-made synthétique [sANtay-teek]
> it's man-made c'est du synthétique [seh dU sANtay-teek]

many beaucoup de [bohkoo duh]
> there are many good restaurants here il y a beaucoup de bons restaurants ici [eel ya bohkoo duh bON resto-rON eesee]
> how many? combien ? [kONbyAN]
> how many days will you be staying? combien de jours restez-vous ? [kONbyAN duh zhoor restay-voo]

map *(of a country)* la carte [kart]; *(of a town, a network)* le plan [plON]
> where can I buy a map of the area? où puis-je acheter une carte de la région ? [oo pweezh ashtay Un kart duh la rayzhyON]
> can you show me where we are on the map? pouvez-vous me montrer sur le plan où nous sommes ? [poovay-voo muh mONtray sUr luh plON oo noo som]
> I'd like a map of the city je voudrais un plan de la ville [zhuh voodreh AN plON duh la veel]
> can I have a map of the subway? est-ce que je peux avoir un plan du métro ? [eskuh zhuh puh avwar AN plON dU maytroh]

March mars [mars]
> March 1st le 1er mars [luh pruhmyay mars]

market le marché [marshay]
> is there a market in the square every day? il y a un marché sur la place tous les jours ? [eel ya UN marshay sUr la plas too lay zhoor]

married marié(e) [maryay]
> are you married? es-tu marié ? [eh-tU maryay]

mass *(religious)* la messe [mes]
> what time is mass at? à quelle heure est la messe ? [a kel uhr eh la mes]

match *(for lighting)* l'allumette *f* [alU-met]
> do you have any matches? avez-vous des allumettes ? [avay-voo dayz alU-met]

meat

France is famous for its food and one of the highlights is its *charcuterie*. This term covers cooked meats, hams, *saucissons* (salami), *pâtés*, *rillettes* (a kind of *pâté* made from shredded pork or duck) and *foie gras*. In every town you'll find *charcuteries* (delicatessens) bursting with tempting delicacies for you to try.

matter importer [ANpor-tay]
▸ it doesn't matter ça ne fait rien [sa nuh feh ryAN]

mattress le matelas [matlah]
▸ the mattresses are saggy les matelas sont défoncés [lay matlah sON dayfON-say]

May mai [meh]
▸ May 9th le neuf mai [luh nuhf meh]

maybe peut-être [puht-etr]
▸ maybe the weather will be better tomorrow peut-être que le temps va s'améliorer demain [puht-etr kuh luh tON va samay-lyoray duhmAN]

meal le repas [ruhpah]
▸ are meals included? les repas sont-ils compris ? [lay ruhpah sONt-eel kONpree]
▸ what times are meals served at? les repas sont servis à quelle heure ? [lay ruhpah sON servee a kel uhr]

meat la viande [vyONd]
▸ I don't eat meat je ne mange pas de viande [zhuh nuh mONzh pa duh vyONd]

mechanic le garagiste [gara-zheest]
▸ what did the mechanic say was wrong with the car? qu'est-ce qui ne va pas avec la voiture, selon le garagiste ? [kes kee nuh va paz avek la vwatUr suhlON luh gara-zheest]

medication le médicament [maydee-kamON]
▸ I'm not taking any other medication at the moment je ne prends pas d'autres médicaments en ce moment [zhuh nuh prON pa dohtruh maydee-kamON ON suh momON]

medicine le médicament [maydee-kamON]
▸ don't forget to take your medicine n'oublie pas de prendre ton médicament [nooblee pa duh prONdr tON maydee-kamON]

medium *(size)* moyen(ne) [mwa-yAN(-yen)] ♦ *(in size)* la taille moyenne [ta-yuh mwa-yen]
▸ do you have this in a medium? vous l'avez en taille moyenne ? [voo lavay ON ta-yuh mwa-yen]

to kiss or to shake hands?

French people usually shake hands when they meet, or, with closer friends or family, they kiss each other on both cheeks (*faire la bise*). This can be tricky, as sometimes they kiss each other twice, once on each cheek, sometimes three times, and sometimes even four times, depending on the region of France and the people concerned. Young people tend to go for three or four kisses, and dispense kisses more liberally, while older people often prefer a handshake.

▸ I'd like my steak medium, please je voudrais mon steak à point, s'il vous plaît [zhuh voodreh mON stek a pwAN seel voo play]

meet (se) rencontrer [(suh) rONkON-tray]; (*by arrangement*) rejoindre [ruhzh-wANdr]; (*wait for, collect*) attendre [atONdr], venir chercher [vuhneer shershay]
◆ (*by arrangement*) se retrouver [suh ruhtroo-vAY]; (*become acquainted*) faire connaissance [fehr koneh-sONs]

▸ meet you at 9 o'clock in front of the town hall rendez-vous à neuf heures devant l'hôtel de ville [rONday-vooz a nuhv uhr duhvON lotel duh veel]
▸ I have to meet my friend at 9 o'clock je dois rejoindre mon ami à neuf heures [zhuh dwah ruhzhwANdr mON amee a nuhv uhr]
▸ I'm supposed to meet someone inside je dois retrouver quelqu'un à l'intérieur [zhuh dwah ruhtroo-vay kelkAN a lANtayr-yuhr]
▸ pleased to meet you enchanté [ONshON-tay]
▸ it was a pleasure meeting you j'ai été très heureux de faire ta connaissance [zhay aytay trez uhruh duh fehr ta koneh-sONs]
▸ goodbye! it was nice meeting you au revoir! enchanté d'avoir fait votre connaissance [oh ruhvwar ONshON-tay davwar feh votr koneh-sONs]
▸ Claude, I'd like you to meet Jane Claude, je te présente Jane [Claude zhuh tuh prayzONt Jane]
▸ where shall we meet? on se retrouve où? [ON suh ruhtroov oo]
▸ what time are we meeting tomorrow? on se voit vers quelle heure demain? [ON suh vwah vehr kel uhr duhmAN]
▸ I don't think we've met je ne crois pas que nous nous connaissions [zhuh nuh krwah pa kuh noo noo koneh-syON]

member (*of a club*) le membre [mONbr]

▸ do you have to be a member? doit-on être membre? [dwaht-ON ehtr mONbr]

men's room les toilettes *f* pour hommes [twalet poor om]

▸ where's the men's room? où sont les toilettes pour hommes? [oo sON lay twalet poor om]

menu la carte [kart]

▸ can we see the menu? pouvons-nous voir la carte, s'il vous plaît? [poovON-noo vwar la kart seel voo play]

▶ do you have a menu in English? avez-vous une carte en anglais ? [avay-vooz Un kart ON ONglay]

▶ do you have a children's menu? avez-vous un menu enfant ? [avay-vooz AN muhnU ONfON]

message le message [mesazh]

▶ can you take a message? pouvez-vous prendre un message ? [poovay-voo prONdr AN mesazh]

▶ can I leave a message? puis-je laisser un message ? [pweezh laysay AN mesazh]

▶ did you get my message? tu as eu mon message ? [tU a U mON mesazh]

▶ don't forget to give him the message n'oublie pas de lui transmettre mon message [nooblee pa duh lwee trONSmetr mON mesazh]

meter *(measurement)* le mètre [mehtr]; *(device)* le compteur [kONtuhr]

▶ I'm 1.75 meters tall je fais un mètre soixante-quinze [zhuh feh AN mehtr swasONt-kANz]

▶ what does the meter say? qu'indique le compteur ? [kANdeek luh kONtuhr]

midday midi *m* [meedee]

▶ we have to be there for midday il faut qu'on y soit à midi [eel foh kON ee swah a meedee]

midnight minuit *m* [meenwee]

▶ it's midnight il est minuit [eel eh meenwee]

mileage *(distance)* le kilométrage [keelo-maytrazh]

▶ is there unlimited mileage? y a-t-il un kilométrage illimité ? [ee ateel AN keelo-maytrazh elee-meetay]

milestone *(on the road)* la borne [born]

▶ what did it say on the last milestone? qu'est-ce qui était marqué sur la dernière borne ? [kes kee ayteh markay sUr la dernyehr born]

milk le lait [leh]

▶ a liter of milk un litre de lait [AN leetr duh leh]

▶ a tea with milk un thé au lait [AN tay oh leh]

milk chocolate le chocolat au lait [shoko-lah oh leh]

▶ I prefer milk chocolate je préfère le chocolat au lait [zhuh prayfehr luh shoko-lah oh leh]

mind *(object)* être dérangé (par) [ehtr dayrONzhay par]

▶ I don't mind ça m'est égal [sa meht aygal]

▶ do you mind if I smoke? ça te dérange si je fume ? [sa tuh dayrONzh see zhuh fUm]

▶ do you mind if I open the window? ça vous dérange si j'ouvre la fenêtre ? [sa voo dayrONzh see zhoovr la fuhnetr]

▶ never mind ça ne fait rien [sa nuh feh ryAN]

mineral water l'eau *f* minérale [oh meenay-ral]

▶ could I have a bottle of mineral water, please? pourriez-vous m'apporter une bouteille d'eau minérale, s'il vous plaît ? [pooryay-voo mapor-tay Un bootey doh meenay-ral seel voo play]

minus moins [mwAN]
- it's minus two il fait moins deux [eel feh mwAN duh]

minute la minute [meenUt]
- we'll go in a minute on ira dans une minute [ON eera dONz Un meenUt]

mirror la glace [glas], le miroir [meerwar]
- the mirror's cracked la glace est fendue [la glas eh fONdu]

miss *(be too late for)* manquer [mONkay], rater [ratay]; *(regret the absence of)* regretter [ruhgreh-tay], manquer [mONkay]
- I've missed my connection j'ai raté ma correspondance [zhay ratay ma kores-pONdONs]
- we're going to miss the train on va rater le train [ON va ratay luh trAN]
- I missed the train by five minutes j'ai manqué le train de cinq minutes [zhay mONkay luh trAN duh sANk meenUt]
- I missed you tu m'as manqué [tU ma mONkay]

missing manquant(e) [mONkON(mONkONt)]
- one of my bags is missing il me manque une valise [eel muh mONk Un valeez]

mistake l'erreur *f* [eruhr]
- I think there's a mistake with the bill je crois qu'il y a une erreur dans l'addition [zhuh krwah keel ya Un eruhr dON ladee-syON]
- to make a mistake se tromper [suh trONpay]
- you've made a mistake with my change vous avez fait une erreur en me rendant la monnaie [vooz avay feht Un eruhr ON muh rONdON la moneh]

money l'argent *m* [arzhON]
- I don't have much money je n'ai pas beaucoup d'argent [zhuh nay pa bohkoo darzhON]
- I have run out of money je n'ai plus d'argent [zhuh nay plU darzhON]
- where can I change money? où puis-je changer de l'argent ? [oo pweezh shONzhay duh larzhON]
- I want my money back je veux être remboursé [zhuh vuh ehtr rONboor-say]

Monday lundi *m* [lANdee]
- we're arriving/leaving on Monday nous arrivons/partons lundi [noo zaree-vON/partON lANdee]

month le mois [mwah]
- I'm leaving in a month je repars dans un mois [zhuh ruhpar dONz AN mwah]

monument le monument [monU-mON]
- what does this monument commemorate? qu'est-ce que ce monument commémore ? [keskuh suh monU-mON komay-mor]

more plus [plU]

- can we have some more bread? est-ce qu'on peut avoir encore du pain ? [eskON puht avwar ONkor dU pAN]
- a little more un peu plus [AN puh plUs]
- could I have a little more wine? pourrais-je reprendre un peu de vin ? [poorehzh ruhprONdr AN puh duh vAN]
- I don't want any more, thank you je n'en veux plus, merci [zhuh nON vuh plU mersee]
- I don't want to spend any more je ne veux pas dépenser plus [zhuh nuh vuh pa daypON-say plUs]

morning le matin [matAN]; *(expressing duration)* la matinée [matee-nay]

- the museum is open in the morning le musée est ouvert le matin [luh mUzay eht oovehr luh matAN]

morning-after pill la pilule du lendemain [peelUl dU lOnduh-mAN]

- I need the morning-after pill j'ai besoin de la pilule du lendemain [zhay buhzwAN duh la peelUl dU lONduh-mAN]

mosque la mosquée [moskay]

- where's the nearest mosque? où est la mosquée la plus proche ? [oo eh la moskay la plU prosh]

most *(the majority of)* la plupart (de) [la plUpar (duh)]; *(the largest amount of)* le plus (de) [luh plU duh] ◆ *(the largest amount)* la majeure partie [la mazhuhr partee] ◆ *(very)* très [treh]

- are you here most days? vous êtes ici la plupart du temps ? [vooz et eesee la plUpar dU tON]
- that's the most I can offer c'est le mieux que je puisse faire [seh luh myuh kuh zhuh pwees fehr]

mother la mère [mehr]

- this is my mother voici ma mère [vwasee ma mehr]

motorboat le bateau à moteur [batoh a motuhr]

- can we rent a motorboat? pouvons-nous louer un bateau à moteur ? [poovON-noo lway AN batoh a motuhr]

motorcycle la moto [motoh]

- I'd like to rent a motorcycle j'aimerais louer une moto [zhemuh-reh lway Un motoh]

mountain la montagne [mONtan-yuh]

- in the mountains à la montagne [a la mONtan-yuh]

mountain hut le refuge (de montagne) [ruhfUzh (duh mONtan-yuh)]

- we slept in a mountain hut nous avons dormi dans un refuge [nooz avON dormee dONz AN ruhfUzh]

mouth la bouche [boosh]

- I've got a strange taste in my mouth j'ai un drôle de goût dans la bouche [zhay AN drol duh goo dON la boosh]

museums

Most national museums are closed on Tuesdays, while municipal museums usually close on Mondays. An admission fee is usually charged, or you will be expected to make a donation. Some museums offer reduced rates on Sundays. In Paris, the *Carte Musées et Monuments* is a good investment as it offers free admission to many tourist attractions and also means that you don't have to stand in line.

move *(movement)* le mouvement [moovmON]; *(step)* le pas [pah], la démarche [daymarsh] ♦ bouger [boozhay]
> I can't move my leg je ne peux pas bouger la jambe [zhuh nuh puh pa boozhay la zhONb]
> don't move him ne le bougez pas [nuh luh boozhay pa]

movie le film [feelm]
> have you seen...'s latest movie? as-tu vu le dernier film de... ? [a-tU vU luh dernyay feelm duh]
> it's a subtitled movie c'est un film sous-titré [seht AN feelm soo-teetray]
> where is the movie... showing? où passe le film... ? [oo pas luh feelm]

movie theater le cinéma [seenay-ma]
> where is there a movie theater? où y a-t-il un cinéma ? [oo ee ateel AN seenay-ma]
> what's on at the movie theater? qu'est-ce qui passe au cinéma ? [keskee suh pas oh seenay-ma]

much beaucoup (de) [bohkoo (duh)]
> I don't have much money je n'ai pas beaucoup d'argent [zhuh nay pa bohkoo darzhON]
> how much is it for one night? c'est combien pour une nuit ? [seh kONbyAN poor Un nwee]
> how much is it per day and per person? combien ça coûte par jour et par personne ? [kONbyAN sa koot par zhoor ay par person]
> how much does it cost per hour? c'est combien de l'heure ? [seh kONbyAN duh luhr]
> how much is a ticket to Paris? combien coûte un billet pour Paris ? [kONbyAN koot AN beeyeh poor paree]

museum le musée [mUzay]
> what time does the museum open? à quelle heure ouvre le musée ? [a kel uhr oovr luh mUzay]

music la musique [mUzeek]
> what kind of music do they play in that club? c'est quel genre de musique dans cette boîte ? [seh kel zhONr duh mUzeek dON set bwat]

must devoir [duhvwar]
▸ that must cost a lot ça doit coûter cher [sa dwah kootay shehr]

mustard la moutarde [mootard]
▸ is it strong mustard? c'est de la moutarde forte ? [seh duh la mootard fort]

n

nail *(on a finger, a toe)* l'ongle *m* [ONgl]
▸ I need to cut my nails il faut que je me coupe les ongles [eel foh kuh zhuh muh koop layz ONgl]

nail polish le vernis à ongles [vernee a ONgl]
▸ I'd like to find nail polish in this shade j'aimerais trouver du vernis à ongles de cette teinte [zhemuh-reh troovay dU vernee a ONgl duh set tANt]

name le nom [nON]
▸ what is your name? comment vous appelez-vous ? [komON vooz aplay-voo]
▸ my name is Patrick je m'appelle Patrick [zhuh mapel Patrick]
▸ hello, my name's John bonjour, moi c'est John [bONzhoor mwa seh John]
▸ I have a reservation in the name of Jackson j'ai une réservation au nom de Jackson [zhay Un rayzer-vasyON oh nON duh Jackson]

napkin la serviette (de table) [servyet (duh tabl)]
▸ could I have a clean napkin, please? pourrais-je avoir une serviette propre ? [poorehzh avwar Un servyet propr]

national holiday la fête nationale [fet nasyo-nal]
▸ tomorrow is a national holiday demain, c'est une fête nationale [duhmAN seht Un fet nasyo-nal]

nationality la nationalité [nasyo-nalee-tay]
▸ what nationality are you? de quelle nationalité êtes-vous ? [duh kel nasyo-nalee-tay et-voo]

nature la nature [natUr]
▸ I like to take long walks outdoors and enjoy nature j'aime faire de longues promenades dans la nature [zhem fehr duh lONg promnad dON la natUr]

nausea la nausée [nohzay]
▸ are you suffering from nausea? êtes-vous sujet aux nausées ? [et-voo sUzheh oh nohzay]

near près (de) [preh (duh)], proche (de) [prosh (duh)]
▸ where's the nearest subway station? où se trouve la station de métro la plus proche ? [oo suh troov la stasyON duh maytroh la plU prosh]
▸ it's near the station c'est près de la gare [seh preh duh la gar]
▸ very near (to)... à deux pas de... [a duh pah duh]

nearby près d'ici [preh deesee]
- is there a supermarket nearby? est-ce qu'il y a un supermarché près d'ici ? [eskeel ya AN sUper-marshay preh deesee]

neck le cou [koo]
- I have a stiff neck j'ai un torticolis [zhay AN tortee-kolee]

need le besoin [buhzwAN] ♦ avoir besoin de [avwar buhzwAN duh] ♦ devoir [duhvwar]
- I need something for a cough j'aurais besoin de quelque chose contre la toux [zhohreh buhzwAN duh kelkuh shohz kONtr la too]
- I need to be at the airport by six (o'clock) je dois être à l'aéroport à six heures [zhu dwaz etr a la-ayro-por a seez uhr]
- we need to go il faut y aller [eel foht ee alay]

neither aucun(e) [ohkAN(ohkUn)] ♦ ni… ni [nee… nee] ♦ non plus [nON plU]
- neither of us aucun de nous [ohkAN duh noo]
- me neither moi non plus [mwa nON plU]

neutral le point mort [pwAN mor]
- make sure the car's in neutral vérifie que la voiture est au point mort [vayree-fyay kuh la vwatUr eht oh pwAN mor]

never jamais [zhameh]
- I've never done it before je n'en ai jamais fait [zhuh nON ay zhameh feh]

new nouveau [noovoh], nouvelle [noovel]
- could we have a new tablecloth, please? pourrions-nous avoir une nouvelle nappe, s'il vous plaît ? [pooryON-nooz avwar Un noovel nap seel voo play]

news *(information)* la nouvelle [noovel]; *(on TV, radio)* les informations *f* [ANformasyON]
- a piece of news une nouvelle [Un noovel]
- that's great news! ça, c'est une bonne nouvelle ! [sa seht Un bon noovel]
- I've listened to the news j'ai écouté les informations [zhay aykoo-tay layz ANformasyON]

newspaper le journal [zhoornal]
- do you have any English newspapers? est-ce que vous avez des journaux en anglais ? [eskuh vooz avay day zhoornoh ON ONglay]

New Year le nouvel an [noovel ON]
- Happy New Year! bonne année ! [bon anay]

New Year's Day le jour de l'An [zhoor duh lON]
- are stores open on New Year's Day? est-ce que les boutiques sont ouvertes le jour de l'An ? [eskuh lay booteek sONt oovehrt luh zhoor duh lON]

next prochain(e) [proshAN(proshen)] ♦ next to à côté de [a kotay duh]
- when is the next guided tour? à quelle heure est la prochaine visite guidée ? [a kel uhr eh la proshen veezeet geeday]
- when is the next train to Paris? à quelle heure est le prochain train pour Paris ? [a kel uhr eh luh proshAN trAN poor paree]

> what time is the next flight to London? quand partira le prochain vol pour Londres ? [kON partee-ra luh proshAN vol poor lONdr]
> can we park next to the tent? peut-on se garer à côté de la tente ? [puht-ON suh garay a kotay duh la tONt]

nice *(vacation, food)* bon(ne) [bON(bon)]; *(kind)* gentil(le) [zhONtee(zhONteey)]; *(likable)* sympa [sANpa]

> have a nice vacation! bonnes vacances ! [bon vakONs]
> we found a really nice little hotel on a trouvé un petit hôtel très sympa [ON a troovay AN puhteet otel treh sANpa]
> goodbye! it was nice meeting you au revoir ! enchanté d'avoir fait votre connaissance [oh ruhvwar ONshON-tay davvar feh votr koneh-sONs]

night la nuit [nwee]

> how much is it per night? c'est combien pour une nuit ? [seh kONbyAN poor Un nwee]
> I'd like to stay an extra night je voudrais rester une nuit supplémentaire [zhuh voodreh restay Un nwee sUplay-mONtehr]

nightclub la boîte (de nuit) [bwat (duh nwee)]

> are there any good nightclubs in this town? est-ce qu'il y a de bonnes boîtes de nuit dans cette ville ? [eskeel ya duh bon bwat duh nwee dON set veel]

nine neuf [nuhf]

> there are nine of us nous sommes neuf [noo som nuhf]
> we have a reservation for nine (o'clock) nous avons une réservation pour neuf heures [nooz avON Un rayzer-vasyON poor nuhv uhr]

no non [nON] ◆ pas de [pa duh]

> no thanks! non, merci ! [nON mersee]
> one tea, no milk or sugar, please un thé nature, s'il vous plaît [AN tay natUr seel voo play]

nobody personne [person]

> there's nobody at reception il n'y a personne à la réception [eel nya person a la raysep-syON]

noise le bruit [brwee]

> to make a noise faire du bruit [fehr dU brwee]
> I heard a funny noise j'ai entendu un drôle de bruit [zhay ONtON-dU AN drol duh brwee]

noisy bruyant(e) [brwee-yON(brwee-yONt)]

> I'd like another room: mine is too noisy j'aimerais changer de chambre, la mienne est trop bruyante [zhemuh-reh shONzhay duh shONbr la myen eh troh brwee-yONt]

nonsmoker non-fumeur [nON-fUmuhr], non-fumeuse [nON-fUmuhz]

> we're nonsmokers nous sommes non-fumeurs [noo som nON-fUmuhr]

nonsmoking non-fumeur [nON-fUmuhr]

> is this restaurant nonsmoking? est-ce que c'est un restaurant non-fumeur ? [eskuh seht AN resto-rON nON-fUmuhr]

nonsmoking compartment le compartiment non-fumeur [kONpar-teemON nON-fUmuhr]

▸ I'd like a seat in a nonsmoking compartment je voudrais une place dans un compartiment non-fumeur [zhuh voodreh Un plas dONz AN kONpar-teemON nON-fUmuhr]

nonsmoking section la zone non-fumeur [zon nON-fUmuhr]

▸ do you have a nonsmoking section? vous avez une zone non-fumeur ? [vooz avay Un zon nON-fUmuhr]

nonstop sans arrêt [sONz areh], sans escale [sONz eskal]

▸ I'd like a nonstop flight from Lyons to London je voudrais un vol Lyon-Londres sans escale [zhuh voodreh AN vol lyON-lONdr sONz eskal]

noon midi *m* [meedee]

▸ we leave at noon nous partons à midi [noo partON a meedee]

no one personne [person]

▸ no one wants any trouble personne ne veut de problème [person nuh vuh duh problem]

normal normal(e) [normal] ✦ la normale [normal]

▸ is it normal for it to rain as much as this? c'est normal qu'il pleuve autant ? [seh normal keel pluhv ohtON]

not pas [pa]

▸ I don't like spinach je n'aime pas les épinards [zhuh nem pa layz aypee-nar]

▸ I don't think so je crois que non [zhuh krwah kuh nON]

▸ not at all pas du tout [pa dU too]

note la note [not], le message [mesazh]

▸ someone left this note for you quelqu'un a laissé ce message pour vous [kelkAN a laysay suh mesazh poor voo]

nothing rien [ryAN]

▸ there's nothing to do here in the evening il n'y a rien à faire ici le soir [eel nya ryAN a fehr eesee luh swar]

▸ there's nothing I can do about it je n'y peux rien [zhuh nee puh ryAN]

November novembre [novONbr]

▸ November 7th le sept novembre [luh set novONbr]

now maintenant [mANt-nON]

▸ are you doing anything now? vous faites quelque chose maintenant ? [voo fet kelkuh shohz mANt-nON]

number le numéro [nUmay-roh]; (*numeral, quantity*) le nombre [nONbr]

▸ my name is... and my number is... mon nom est... et mon numéro est le... [mON nON eh... ay mON nUmay-roh eh luh]

occupied occupé(e) [okU-pay]

> the restroom's occupied les toilettes sont occupées [lat twalet sONt okU-pay]

o'clock

> it's eight o'clock il est huit heures [eel eh weet uhr]

October octobre [oktobr]

> October 12th le douze octobre [luh dooz oktobr]

of de [duh]

> one of us l'un d'entre nous [lAN dONtr noo]

off *(at a distance from)* loin [lwAN]; *(deducted from)* en moins [ON mwAN]

> right, I'm off bon, j'y vais [bON zhee veh]
> an island off the coast of France une île au large de la France [Un eel oh larzh duh la frONs]
> can you give me something off it? vous ne pouvez pas me faire un petit rabais ? [voo nuh poovay pa muh fehr AN puhtee rabeh]

offer offrir [ofreer]

> can I offer you a cigarette? puis-je vous offrir une cigarette ? [pweezh vooz ofreer Un seega-ret]

office le bureau [bUroh], le guichet [geesheh]

> ask at the office demandez au guichet [duhmON-day oh geesheh]

often souvent [soovON]

> how often does the ferry sail? quelle est la fréquence des traversées ? [kel eh la fraykONs day traver-say]

oil l'huile *f* [weel]

> could you check the oil, please? pouvez-vous vérifier le niveau d'huile ? [poovay-voo vayree-fyay luh neevoh dweel]

OK bon [bON], bonne [bon] ◆ *(expressing agreement)* d'accord ! [dakor]

> that's OK ce n'est pas grave [suh neh pa grav]

old vieux [vyuh], vieille [vyey]

> how old are you? quel âge as-tu ? [kel azh a-tU]
> I'm 18 years old j'ai dix-huit ans [zhay deez-weet ON]
> have you visited the old town? vous avez visité la vieille ville ? [vooz avay veezee-tay la vyey veel]

on *(position)* sur [sUr]; *(working)* allumé(e) [alU-may]; *(happening)* qui se joue [keek suh zhoo]

▸ I'm on the 6 o'clock Air France flight je suis sur le vol Air France de dix-huit heures [zhuh swee sUr luh vol ehr frONs duh deez-weet uhr]

▸ how long is it on for? ça se joue jusqu'à quand ? [sa suh zhoo zhUska kON]

once *(on one occasion)* une fois [Un fwah]; *(previously)* avant [avON] ◆ **at once** *(immediately)* tout de suite [toot sweet]; *(at the same time)* en même temps [ON mem tON]

▸ I've been here once before je suis déjà venu une fois ici [zhuh swee dayzha vuhnU Un fwah eesee]

one un(e) [AN(Un)]

▸ a table for one, please une table pour une personne, s'il vous plaît [Un tabl poor Un person seel voo play]

one-way (ticket) l'aller *m* (simple) [alay (sANpl)]

▸ how much is a one-way ticket downtown? combien coûte un aller pour le centre-ville ? [kONbyAN koot AN alay poor luh sONtr-veel]

▸ a one-way ticket to Cannes un aller simple pour Cannes [AN alay sANpl poor kan]

only seulement [suhlmON]

▸ that's the only one left c'est le seul qui reste [seh luh suhl kee rest]

open ouvert(e) [oovehr(oovehrt)] ◆ **ouvrir** [oovreer]

▸ is the bank open at lunchtime? la banque est-elle ouverte à l'heure du déjeuner ? [la bONk eht-el oovehrt a luhr dU dayzhuh-nay]

▸ is the museum open all day? le musée est-il ouvert toute la journée ? [luh mUzay eht-eel oovehr toot la zhoornay]

▸ at what time is... open? à quelle heure... est-il ouvert ? [a kel uhr... eht-eel oovehr]

▸ can I open the window? puis-je ouvrir la fenêtre ? [pweezh oovreer la fuhnetr]

▸ what time do you open at? à quelle heure ouvrez-vous ? [a kel uhr oovray-voo]

open-air en plein air [ON plAN ehr]

▸ is there an open-air swimming pool? y a-t-il une piscine en plein air ? [ee ateel Un peeseen ON plAN ehr]

operating room la salle d'opération [sal dopay-rasyON]

▸ is she still in the operating room? elle est toujours en salle d'opération ? [el eh toozhoor ON sal dopay-rasyON]

opinion l'opinion *f* [opee-nyON]

▸ in my opinion,... selon moi,... [suhlON mwa] ▸ see box on p. 98

orange *(fruit)* l'orange *f* [orONzh]; *(color)* l'orange *m* [orONzh]

▸ I'd like a kilo of oranges je voudrais un kilo d'oranges [zhuh voodreh AN keeloh dorONzh]

orange juice le jus d'orange [zhU dorONzh]

▸ I'll have a glass of orange juice je vais prendre un verre de jus d'orange [zhuh veh prONdr AN vehr duh zhU dorONzh]

opinions

- personally, I don't think it's fair d'après moi, ce n'est pas juste [dapreh mwa suh neh pa zhUst]
- I think he's right je pense qu'il a raison [zhuh pONs keel a rehzON]
- I wouldn't like to say c'est difficile à dire [seh deefee-seel a deer]
- I'm not sure je ne sais pas trop [zhuh nuh seh pa troh]
- no idea! aucune idée ! [ohkUn eeday]
- it depends ça dépend [sa daypON]

order la commande [komONd] ◆ commander [komONday]
- this isn't what I ordered: I asked for... ce n'est pas ce que j'ai commandé, j'avais demandé... [suh neh pa suh kuh zhay komON-day zhaveh duhmON-day]
- I ordered a coffee j'ai commandé un café [zhay komON-day AN kafay]

organize organiser [orga-neezay]
- can you organize the whole trip for us? pouvez-vous vous occuper d'organiser notre séjour ? [poovay-voo vooz okU-pay dorga-neezay notr sayzhoor]

other autre [ohtr]
- I'll have the other one je vais prendre l'autre [zhuh veh prONdr lohtr]
- on the other side of the street de l'autre côté de la rue [duh lohtr kotay duh la rU]

out-of-date périmé(e) [payree-may]
- my passport is out-of-date mon passeport est périmé [mON paspor eh payree-may]

outside call l'appel *m* à l'extérieur [apel ekstayr-yuhr]
- I'd like to make an outside call je voudrais téléphoner à l'extérieur [zhuh voodreh taylay-fonay a lekstayr-yuhr]

outside line la ligne extérieure [leenyuh ekstayr-yuhr]
- how do you get an outside line? comment on accède à la ligne extérieure ? [komONt ON aksehd a la leenyuh ekstayr-yuhr]

overheat chauffer [shohfay]
- the engine is overheating le moteur chauffe [luh motuhr shohf]

owner propriétaire [propree-aytehr]
- do you know who the owner is? vous savez qui est le propriétaire ? [voo savay kee eh luh propree-aytehr]

p

pack *(of cigarettes, chewing-gum)* le paquet [pakeh] • *(for a trip)* faire sa valise [fehr sa valeez]

▸ how much is a pack of cigarettes? combien coûte un paquet de cigarettes ? [kONbyAN koot AN pakeh duh seega-ret]
▸ I need to pack il faut que je fasse ma valise [eel foh kuh zhuh fas ma valeez]

package *(wrapped object)* le colis (postal) [kolee (postal)], le paquet [pakeh]; *(of butter)* la plaque [plak]; *(vacation deal)* le forfait vacances [forfeh vakONs]

▸ I'd like to send this package to New York by airmail je voudrais envoyer ce colis à New York par avion [zhuh voodreh ONvwa-yay suh kolee a New York par avyON]
▸ do you have weekend packages? avez-vous des forfaits week-end ? [avay-voo day forfeh weekend]

package tour le voyage organisé [vwa-yazh orga-neezay]

▸ it's my first time on a package tour c'est la première fois que je pars en voyage organisé [seh la pruhm-yehr fwah kuh zhuh par ON vwa-yazh orga-neezay]

padlock le cadenas [kadnah]

▸ is there a padlock for the bike? est-ce qu'il y a un cadenas pour le vélo ? [eskeel ya AN kadnah poor luh vayloh]

pain *(physical)* la douleur [dooluhr]

▸ I'd like something for the pain j'aimerais quelque chose contre la douleur [zhemuh-reh kelkuh shohz kONtr la dooluhr]
▸ I have a pain here j'ai mal là [zhay mal la]

painkiller le calmant [kalmON]

▸ can you give me a painkiller, please? je voudrais un calmant [zhuh voodreh AN kalmON]

pair *(of gloves, socks)* la paire [pehr]

▸ a pair of shoes une paire de chaussures [Un pehr duh shohsUr]
▸ a pair of pants un pantalon [AN pONta-lON]
▸ a pair of scissors une paire de ciseaux [Un pehr duh seezoh]

pants le pantalon [pONta-lON]

▸ a pair of pants un pantalon [AN pONta-lON]
▸ there is a hole in these pants il y a un trou à ce pantalon [eel ya AN troo a suh pONta-lON]

pantyhose le collant [kolON]

▸ I got a run in my pantyhose j'ai filé mes collants [zhay feelay may kolON]

paper *(for writing on)* le papier [papyay]; *(newspaper)* le journal [zhoornal]
- **papers** *(official documents)* papiers (d'identité) [papyay (deedON-teetay)]
  - here are my papers voici mes papiers [vwasee may papyay]

parasol le parasol [para-sol]
- can you rent parasols? est-ce que l'on peut louer des parasols? [eskuh lON puh lway day para-sol]

pardon *(forgiveness)* le pardon [pardON] • *(forgive)* pardonner [pardo-nay]
- I beg your pardon! *(asking for repetition)* pardon? [pardON]; *(to apologize)* je m'excuse [zhuh mekskUz]; *(showing disagreement)* je vous demande pardon! [zhuh voo duhmONd pardON]
- pardon me! *(asking for repetition)* comment? [komON]; *(to get past)* excusez-moi [ekskU-zay-mwa]; *(to apologize)* je m'excuse [zhuh mekskUz]; *(showing disagreement)* je vous demande pardon! [zhuh voo duhmONd pardON]

park (se) garer [(suh) garay]
- can we park our trailer here? pouvons-nous installer notre caravane ici? [poovON-nooz ANsta-lay notr kara-van eesee]
- am I allowed to park here? est-ce que j'ai le droit de me garer ici? [eskuh zhay luh drwah duh muh garay eesee]

parking le parking [parkeeng]
- is there any parking near the hostel? y a-t-il des endroits où se garer près de l'auberge? [ee ateel dayz ONdrwah oo suh garay preh duh loberzh]

parking lot le parking [parkeeng]
- is there a parking lot nearby? y a-t-il un parking dans les environs? [ee ateel UN parkeeng dON layz ONvee-rON]

parking space l'emplacement *m* [ONplas-mON]
- is it easy to find a parking space in town? c'est facile de trouver à se garer en ville? [seh faseel duh troovay a suh garay ON veel]

part *(piece)* la partie [partee]; *(area)* la région [rayzhyON]
- what part of France are you from? de quelle région de France êtes-vous? [duh kel rayzhyON duh frONs et-voo]
- I've never been to this part of France before c'est la première fois que je viens dans cette région de France [seh la pruhmyehr fwah kuh zhuh vyAN dON set rayzhyON duh frONs]

party la fête [fet], la soirée [swaray] • faire la fête [fehr la fet]
- I'm planning a little party tomorrow j'organise une petite soirée demain [zhorga-neez Un puhteet swaray duhmAN]

pass *(hand)* passer [pasay]; *(in a car)* doubler [dooblay]
- can you pass me the salt? tu peux me passer le sel? [tU puh muh pasay luh sel]
- can you pass on this road? est-ce qu'on peut doubler sur cette route? [eskON puh dooblay sUr set root]

passenger le passager [pasa-zhay], la passagère [pasa-zhehr]
 ▸ is this where the passengers from the Toulouse flight arrive? c'est bien ici qu'arrivent les passagers du vol de Toulouse ? [seh byAN eesee kareev lay pasa-zhay dU vol duh toolooz]

passport le passeport [paspor]
 ▸ I've lost/forgotten my passport j'ai perdu/oublié mon passeport [zhay perdU/ ooblee-yay mON paspor]
 ▸ my passport has been stolen on m'a volé mon passeport [ON ma volay mON paspor]

path *(track)* chemin [shuhmAN], sentier [sONtyay]
 ▸ is the path waymarked? est-ce que le sentier est balisé ? [eskuh luh sONtyay eh balee-zay]

pay payer [peyay]
 ▸ do I have to pay a deposit? est-ce qu'il y a des arrhes à verser ? [eskeel ya dayz ar a versay]
 ▸ can you pay by credit card? peut-on régler par carte ? [puht-ON rayglay par kart]
 ▸ we're going to pay separately on va payer séparément [ON va peyay sayparaymON]

pay-per-view TV la télévision à péage [taylay-veezyON a peyazh]
 ▸ is there pay-per-view TV in the room? il y a la télévision à péage dans la chambre ? [eel ya la taylay-veezyON a peyazh dON la shONbr]

pay-per-view channel la chaîne à péage [shen a peyazh]
 ▸ are there any pay-per-view channels? est-ce qu'il y a des chaînes à péage ? [eskeel ya day shen a peyazh]

pedestrian mall la zone piétonne [zon pyayton]
 ▸ can you direct me to the pedestrian mall? pouvez-vous m'indiquer la zone piétonne ? [poovay-voo mANdee-kay la zon pyayton]

pen le stylo [steeloh]
 ▸ can you lend me a pen? pouvez-vous me prêter un stylo ? [poovay-voo muh prehtay AN steeloh]

pencil le crayon [kreyOn]
 ▸ can you lend me a pencil? pouvez-vous me prêter un crayon (de papier) ? [poovay-voo muh prehtay AN kreyON (duh papyay)]

penicillin la pénicilline [paynee-seeleen]
 ▸ I'm allergic to penicillin je suis allergique à la pénicilline [zhuh sweez aler-zheek a la paynee-seeleen]

pepper le poivre [pwavr]
 ▸ pass the pepper, please passe-moi le poivre, s'il te plaît [pas-mwa luh pwavr see tuh play]

per cent pour cent [poor sON]

> could you knock 10 per cent off the price? pourriez-vous me faire un rabais de dix pour cent ? [pooray-voo muh fehr AN rabeh duh dee poor sON]

performance *(show)* la représentation [raypray-zONta-syON]; *(in a movie theater)* la séance [sayONs]

> what time does the performance begin? à quelle heure commence la représentation ? [a kel uhr komONs la ruhpray-zONta-syON]

perfume le parfum [parfAN]

> how much is this perfume? combien coûte ce parfum ? [kONbyAn koot suh parfAN]

perhaps peut-être [puht-etr]

> perhaps you can help me? peut-être pouvez-vous m'aider ? [puht-etr poovay-voo mayday]

person la personne [person]

> how much is it per hour and per person? combien ça coûte par heure et par personne ? [kONbyAN so koot par uhr ay par person]

pet l'animal *m* domestique [anee-mal domes-teek]

> are pets allowed? les animaux domestiques sont-ils admis ? [layz anee-moh domes-teek sONt-eel admee]

phone le téléphone [taylay-fon] ◆ téléphoner [taylay-fonay]

> can I use the phone? puis-je appeler quelqu'un ? [pweezh aplay kelkAN]
> we haven't used the phone nous n'avons pas utilisé le téléphone [noo navON paz Utee-leezay luh taylay-fon]

phone booth la cabine (téléphonique) [kabeen (taylay-foneek)]

> is there a phone booth near here? y a-t-il une cabine téléphonique près d'ici ? [ee ateel Un kabeen taylay-foneek preh deesee]

on the phone

> hello? allô ? [aloh]
> John Bing speaking John Bing à l'appareil [John Bing a lapa-rey]
> I'd like to speak to Jack Adams je voudrais parler à Jack Adams [zhuh voodreh parlay a Jack Adams]
> hold the line ne quittez pas [nuh keetay pa]
> can you call back in ten minutes? rappelez dans dix minutes, s'il vous plaît [raplay dON dee meenUt seel voo play]
> would you like to leave a message? voulez-vous lui laisser un message ? [voolay-voo lwee laysay AN mesazh]
> you have the wrong number vous faites erreur [voo fet eruhr]

phone call l'appel *m* (téléphonique) [apel (taylay-foneek)]
▸ I'd like to make a phone call je voudrais téléphoner [zhuh voodreh taylay-fonay]

phonecard la carte téléphonique/de téléphone [kart taylay-foneek/duh taylay-fon]
▸ where can I buy a phonecard? où est-ce que je peux acheter une carte de téléphone ? [oo eskuh zhuh puh ashtay Un kart duh taylay-fon]

photo la photo [fotoh]
▸ can I take photos in here? est-ce que je peux prendre des photos ici ? [eskuh zhuh puh prONdr day fotoh eesee]
▸ could you take a photo of us? pourriez-vous nous prendre en photo ? [pooryay-voo noo prONdr ON fotoh]
▸ I'd like copies of some photos je voudrais faire des doubles de certaines photos [zhuh voodreh fehr day doobl duh serten fotoh]

photography la photo [fotoh]
▸ photography is strictly forbidden in the museum les photographies sont interdites dans le musée [lay foto-grafee sONt ANter-deet dON luh mUzay]

picnic le pique-nique [peek-neek]
▸ could we go for a picnic by the river? on pourrait faire un pique-nique près de la rivière ? [ON pooreh fehr AN peek-neek preh duh la reevyehr]

piece *(of chocolate, paper, wood)* le morceau [morsoh]; *(of cake)* la part [part]; *(of apple)* le quartier [kartyay]
▸ a piece of cake une part de gâteau [Un par duh gatoh]
▸ a piece of advice un conseil [AN kONsey]
▸ a piece of news une nouvelle [Un noovel]

pill la pilule [peelUl]
▸ a bottle of pills un flacon de pilules [AN flakON duh peelUl]
▸ the pill *(contraceptive)* la pilule [la peelUl]

pillow l'oreiller *m* [o-reray]
▸ could I have another pillow? est-ce que je pourrais avoir un autre oreiller ? [eskuh zhuh poorehz avvar AN ohtr o-reray]

pizza la pizza [peetsa]
▸ I'd like a mushroom pizza j'aimerais une pizza aux champignons [zhemuh-reh Un peetsa oh shONpeen-yON]

place *(area)* l'endroit *m* [ONdrwah]; *(house)* la maison [mehzON]; *(seat)* la place [plas]; *(place setting)* le couvert [koovehr]
▸ can you recommend a nice place to eat? auriez-vous un bon restaurant à recommander ? [ohryay-vooz AN bON resto-rON a ruhko-mONday]
▸ do you want to change places with me? vous voulez changer de place avec moi ? [voo voolay shONzhay duh plas avek mwa]

plain *(simple)* simple [sANpl]; *(clear)* clair(e) [klehr]; *(with nothing added)* nature [natUr]
▸ do you have any plain yogurts? il y a des yaourts nature ? [eel ya day ya-oort natUr]

plan *(strategy)* le plan [plON]; *(intention, idea)* le projet [prozheh] ♦ *(organize)* prévoir [prayvwar]; *(intend)* projeter [prozhtay]
  ▸ I am planning to stay for just one night j'envisage de rester une nuit seulement [zhONvee-zazh duh restay Un nwee suhlmON]

plane l'avion *m* [avyON]
  ▸ which gate does the plane go from? l'avion part de quelle porte ? [lavyON par duh kel port]
  ▸ how much does a plane ticket to Nice cost? combien coûte un billet d'avion pour Nice ? [kONbyAN koot AN beeyeh davyON poor nees]

plate l'assiette *f* [asyet]
  ▸ this plate's got a crack in it cette assiette est fêlée [set asyet eh felay]

platform *(at a station)* le quai [keh], la voie [vwah]
  ▸ which platform does the train leave from? de quelle voie part ce train ? [duh kel vwah par suh trAN]

play *(at a theater)* la pièce (de théâtre) [pyes (duh tay-atr)] ♦ jouer [zhway]
  ▸ do you play tennis? tu joues au tennis ? [tU zhoo oh tenees]
  ▸ I play the cello je joue du violoncelle [zhuh zhoo dU vyolON-sel]

playroom la salle de jeu [sal duh zhuh]
  ▸ is there a children's playroom here? est-ce qu'il y a une salle de jeu pour les enfants ici ? [eskeel ya Un sal duh zhuh poor layz ONfON eesee]

please s'il vous plaît [seel voo play]
  ▸ please sit down asseyez-vous donc [a-seyay-voo dONk]
  ▸ can I come in? – please do puis-je entrer – je vous en prie [pweezh ONtray – zhuh vooz ON pree]

pleased enchanté(e) [ONshON-tay]
  ▸ pleased to meet you enchanté [ONshON-tay]

pleasure le plaisir [playzeer]
  ▸ with pleasure! avec plaisir ! [avek playzeer]
  ▸ it's a pleasure c'est un plaisir [seht AN playzeer]

plug *(on electrical equipment)* la prise (de courant) [preez (duh koorON)]
  ▸ where can I find an adaptor for the plug on my hairdryer? où puis-je trouver un adaptateur pour la prise de mon sèche-cheveux ? [oo pweezh troovay AN adap-tatuhr poor la preez duh mON sesh-shuhvuh]

plug in brancher [brONshay]
  ▸ can I plug my cellphone in here to recharge it? est-ce que je peux brancher mon portable ici pour le recharger ? [eskuh zhuh puh brONshay mON portabl eesee poor luh ruhsharg-zhay]

point *(moment)* le point [pwAN] ♦ *(direct)* indiquer [ANdee-kay]
  ▸ to be on the point of doing... être sur le point de faire... [etr sUr luh pwAN duh fehr]
  ▸ points of the compass points cardinaux [pwAN kardee-noh]

police

The *Police nationale*, the main law-enforcement agency, operates in large towns and cities, where it is responsible for security and can carry out identity checks. It is also the force which carries out criminal investigations. In small towns and villages in France, the *gendarmerie*, which is technically part of the armed forces, is the police. *Gendarmes* are also responsible for patroling the road network, national borders and ports, and for carrying out duties relating to national security, for example at military installations.

▶ can you point me in the direction of the freeway? pourriez-vous m'indiquer la direction de l'autoroute ? [pooryay-voo mANdee-kay la deerek-syON duh lotoh-root]

police la police [polees]
▶ call the police! appelez la police ! [aplay la polees]
▶ what's the number for the police? quel est le numéro de la police ? [kel eh luh nUmay-roh duh la polees]

police station le commissariat (de police) [komee-saryah (duh polees)], le poste (de police) [post (duh polees)]
▶ where is the nearest police station? où est le commissariat le plus proche ? [oo eh luh komee-saryah luh plU prosh]

pool *(for swimming)* la piscine [peeseen], le bassin [basAN]
▶ main pool grand bassin [grON basAN]
▶ children's pool petit bassin [puhtee basAN]
▶ is the pool heated? la piscine est-elle chauffée ? [la peeseen eht-el shohfay]
▶ is there an indoor pool? est-ce qu'il y a une piscine couverte ? [eskeel ya Un peeseen koovehrt]

pork le porc [por]
▶ I don't eat pork je ne mange pas de porc [zhuh nuh mONzh pa duh por]

portable portable [portabl], d'appoint [dapwAN]
▶ do you have a portable heater we could borrow? auriez-vous un chauffage d'appoint à nous prêter ? [ohryay-vooz AN shohfazh dapwAN a noo prehtay]

portion la portion [porsyON]
▶ a portion of fries une portion de frites [Un porsyON duh freet]

possible possible [poseebl]
▶ without sauce, if possible sans sauce, si possible [sON sohs see poseebl]

postcard la carte postale [kart postal]
▶ where can I buy postcards? où puis-je acheter des cartes postales ? [oo pweezh ashtay day kart postal]
▶ how much are stamps for postcards to the States? combien coûte un timbre de carte postale pour les États-Unis ? [kONbyAN koot AN tANbr duh kart postal poor layz aytaz-Unee]

at the post office

▸ how much is it to send a letter/postcard to the Unites States? c'est combien pour envoyer une lettre/une carte postale pour les États-Unis ? [seh kONbyAN poor ONvwa-yay Un letr/Un kart postal poor layz aytaz-Unee]

▸ I'd like ten stamps for Canada je voudrais dix timbres pour le Canada [zhuh voodreh dee tANbr poor luh kana-da]

▸ I'd like to send this parcel by registered post je voudrais envoyer ce paquet en recommandé [zhuh voodreh ON vwa-yay suh pakeh ON ruhko-mONday]

▸ how long will it take for the letter to arrive? combien de temps mettra la lettre ? [kONbyAN duh tON metra la letr]

post office le bureau de poste [bUroh duh post]

▸ where is the nearest post office? où se trouve le bureau de poste le plus proche ? [oo suh troov luh bUroh duh post luh plU prosh]

power *(electricity)* le courant [koorON]

▸ there's no power il n'y a pas de courant [eel nya pa duh koorON]

power failure la panne d'électricité/de courant [pan daylek-treesee-tay/duh koorON]

▸ there's a power failure il y a une panne d'électricité [eel ya Un pan daylek-treesee-tay]

▸ how long is the power failure expected to last? combien de temps va durer la panne de courant ? [kONbyAN duh tON va dUray la pan duh koorON]

prefer préférer [prayfay-ray]

▸ I'd prefer a black tea je préférerais un thé nature [zhuh prayfay-ruhrehz AN tay natUr]

▸ I'd prefer you not smoke j'aimerais mieux que tu ne fumes pas [zhemuh-reh myuh kuh tU nuh fUm pa]

preference la préférence [prayfay-rOns]

expressing a preference

▸ I prefer red wine to white wine j'aime mieux le vin rouge que le vin blanc [zhem myuh luh vAN roozh kuh luh vAN blON]

▸ I'd rather fly than go by train plutôt que d'y aller en train, j'aimerais mieux prendre l'avion [plUtoh kuh dee alay ON trAN zhemuh-reh myuh prONdr lavyON]

▸ Saturday would suit me better samedi me conviendrait davantage [samdee muh kONvyAN-dreh davON-tazh]

prescription *(medicine)* l'ordonnance *f* [ordo-nONs]
- is it only available on prescription? c'est délivrable uniquement sur ordonnance ? [seh dayleev-rabl Uneek-mON sUr ordo-nONs]

present le cadeau [kadoh]
- where can we buy presents around here? où peut-on trouver des cadeaux près d'ici ? [oo puht-ON troovay day kadoh preh deesee]

pretty joli(e) [zholee]
- she's a very pretty girl c'est une très jolie fille [seht Un treh zholee feey]

price *(cost)* le prix [pree]
- what's the price of gas? quel est le prix de l'essence ? [kel eh luh pree duh lesONs]

price list le tarif [tareef], la liste des prix [leest day pree]
- do you have a price list? auriez-vous la liste des prix ? [ohryay-voo la leest day pree]

print *(photograph)* le tirage [teerazh]
- could I have another set of prints? je voudrais un autre tirage [zhuh voodreh AN ohtr teerazh]

private *(not public)* privé(e) [preevay]; *(personal)* personnel(le) [perso-nel]
- is it a private beach? est-ce que c'est une plage privée ? [eskuh seht Un plazh preevay]

problem le problème [problem]
- I've got a problem with the central heating il y a un problème avec le chauffage central [eel ya AN problem avek luh shohfazh sONtral]
- no problem pas de problème [pa duh problem]

program *(in a movie theater)* la séance [say-ONs]
- what time does the program start? à quelle heure est la séance ? [a kel uhr eh la say-ONs]

pronounce *(word)* prononcer [pronON-say]
- how is that pronounced? comment ça se prononce ? [komON sa suh pronONs]

public *(state)* public [pUbleek], publique [pUbleek]; *(open to all)* exposé(e) [ekspo-zay] ◆ le public [pUbleek]
- let's go somewhere less public allons dans un endroit moins exposé [alON dONz AN ON-drwah mwAN ekspo-zay]
- is the castle open to the public? le château est-il ouvert au public ? [luh shatoh eht-eel oovehr oh pUbleek]

public holiday le jour férié [zhoor fayryay]
- is tomorrow a public holiday? c'est un jour férié, demain ? [seht AN zhoor fayryay duhmAN]

public transportation

If you're using public transportation in Paris, it's cheaper to buy a *carnet* or book of ten tickets, rather than buy them individually. You can get them at *métro*, train or bus stations, or in stores displaying the official Paris transportation (*RATP*) sign.

public transportation les transports *m* publics [trONspor pUbleek]
- can you get there by public transportation? est-ce que c'est accessible par les transports en commun ? [eskuh seht akseh-seebl par lay trONspor ON komAN]

pull *(muscle)* déchirer [dayshee-ray]; *(tooth)* arracher [ara-shay]
- I've pulled a muscle je me suis déchiré un muscle [zhuh muh swee dayshee-ray AN mUskl]

puncture la crevaison [kruhveh-zON], le pneu crevé [pnuh kruhvay]
- I've had a puncture j'ai crevé [zhay kruhvay]

purpose *(reason)* la raison [rehzON]; *(aim)* le but [bUt] ◆ **on purpose** exprès [ekspres]
- sorry, I didn't do it on purpose désolé, je ne l'ai pas fait exprès [dayzo-lay zhuh nuh lay pa feh ekspre]

purse *(handbag)* le sac à main [sak a mAN]; *(change purse)* le porte-monnaie [port-moneh]
- I've had my purse stolen on m'a volé mon porte-monnaie [ON ma volay mON port-moneh]

push pousser [poosay]
- can you help us to push the car? pouvez-vous nous aider à pousser la voiture ? [poovay-voo nooz ayday a poosay la vwatUr]

put *(into place, position)* mettre [metr]
- is there somewhere I can put my bags? je peux mettre mes bagages quelque part ? [zhuh puh metr may bagazh kelkuh par]

put down *(set down)* déposer [daypo-zay]
- you can put the bags down over there vous pouvez déposer vos bagages là-bas [voo poovay daypo-zay voh bagazh la-bah]

put on *(clothes, heating)* mettre [metr]; *(TV, radio)* allumer [alU-may]; *(on telephone)* passer [pasay]
- can you put the heating on? tu peux mettre le chauffage ? [tU puh metr luh shohfazh]

put out *(cigarette, fire)* éteindre [aytANdr]
- can you please put your cigarette out? vous pouvez éteindre votre cigarette, s'il vous plaît ? [voo poovay aytANdr votr seega-ret seel voo play]

put up *(erect)* monter [mONtay]; *(provide accommodations for)* loger [lozhay]
▸ can we put up our tent here? pouvons-nous monter notre tente ici ? [poovON-noo mONtay notr tONt eesee]

q

quarter *(fourth)* le quart [kar]
▸ I'll be back in a quarter of an hour je serai de retour d'ici un quart d'heure [zhuh suhray duh ruhtoor deesee AN kar duhr]
▸ a quarter past or after one une heure et quart [Un uhr ay kar]
▸ a quarter to or of one une heure moins le quart [Un uhr mwAN luh kar]

quay le quai [keh]
▸ is the boat at the quay? est-ce que le bateau est à quai ? [eskuh luh batoh eht a keh]

question la question [kestyON]
▸ can I ask you a question? puis-je vous poser une question ? [pweezh voo pozay Un kestyON]

quickly vite [veet]
▸ everyone speaks so quickly les gens parlent tellement vite [lay zhON parl telmON veet]

quiet tranquille [trONkeel]
▸ is it a quiet beach? est-ce que c'est une plage tranquille ? [eskuh seht Un plazh trONkeel]
▸ do you have anything quieter? avez-vous quelque chose de plus calme ? [avay-voo kelkuh shohz duh plU kalm]

quite *(rather)* assez [asay]
▸ it's quite expensive around here c'est assez cher par ici [seht asay shehr par eesee]

r

racket *(for tennis)* la raquette [raket]
▸ can you rent rackets? peut-on louer des raquettes de tennis ? [puht-ON lway day raket duh tenees]

radiator le radiateur [radya-tuhr]
▸ the radiator's leaking il y a une fuite dans le radiateur [eel ya Un fweet dON luh radya-tuhr]

radio *(set)* la radio [radyoh]
▸ the radio doesn't work la radio ne fonctionne pas [la radyoh nuh fONksyon pa]

radio station la station de radio [stasyON duh radyoh]
▸ can you get any English radio stations here? on capte des stations de radio anglaises, ici ? [ON kapt day stasyON duh radyoh ONglez eesee]

railroad le chemin de fer [shuhmAN duh fehr]; *(track)* la voie ferrée [vwah feray]
▸ is the town on the railroad? est-ce que la ville est accessible en train ? [eskuh la veel eht aksseh-seebl ON trAN]

rain pleuvoir [pluhvwar]
▸ it's raining il pleut [eel pluh]

random
▸ at random au hasard [oh azar]

rare *(meat)* saignant(e) [saynyON(saynyONt)]
▸ rare, please saignant, s'il vous plaît! [saynyON seel voo play]

rate *(price)* le tarif [tareef]
▸ what's your daily rate? quels sont vos tarifs par jour ? [kel sON voh tareef par zhoor]

rate of exchange le taux de change [toh duh shONzh]
▸ they offer a good rate of exchange ils ont un taux de change intéressant [eelz ON AN toh duh shONzh ANtay-resON]

razor le rasoir (électrique) [razwar (aylek-treek)]
▸ where can I buy a new razor? où puis-je trouver un rasoir ? [oo pweezh troovay AN razwar]

razor blade la lame de rasoir [lam duh razwar]
▸ I need to buy some razor blades je dois acheter des lames de rasoir [zhuh dwaz ashtay day lam duh razwar]

ready prêt(e) [preh(pret)]
▸ when will it be ready? ça sera prêt quand ? [sa suhra preh kON]

really vraiment [vrehmON]
▸ it really doesn't matter ce n'est vraiment pas important [suh neh vrehmON paz ANpor-tON]
▸ really? ah, bon ? [ah bON]

rear *(of a train)* la queue [kuh]
▸ our seats are in the rear of the train nos places sont en queue du train [noh plas sONt ON kuh dU trAN]

rec center, recreation center la base de loisirs [baz duh lwazeer]
▸ what facilities does the recreation center have? quels sont les équipements de la base de loisirs ? [kel sON layz aykeep-mON duh la baz duh lwazeer]

receipt le reçu [ruhsU]; *(for a bill)* l'acquit *m* [akee]; *(for rent)* la quittance [keetONs]

▸ can I have a receipt, please? puis-je avoir un reçu, s'il vous plaît ? [pweezh avwar AN ruhsU seel voo play]

receive *(package, letter)* recevoir [ruhsuh-vwar]

▸ I should have received the package this morning j'aurais dû recevoir le paquet ce matin [zhohreh dU ruhsuh-vwar luh pakeh suh matAN]

reception la réception [raysep-syON]; *(in an office)* l'accueil *m* [akoy]

▸ can you ask reception to call me a taxi? vous pouvez demander à l'accueil de m'appeler un taxi ? [voo poovay duhmON-day a lakoy duh maplay AN taksee]

▸ there's no reception il n'y a pas de réseau [eel nya pa duh rayzoh]

reception desk la réception [raysep-syON]

▸ can I leave my backpack at the reception desk? est-ce que je peux laisser mon sac à dos à la réception ? [eskuh zhuh puh laysay mON sak a doh a la raysep-syON]

recline reculer [ruhkU-lay]

▸ do you mind if I recline my seat? ça vous ennuie si je recule mon siège ? [sa vooz ONnwee see zhuh ruhkUl mON syezh]

recommend recommander [ruhko-mONday]

▸ could you recommend another hotel? pourriez-vous me recommander un autre hôtel ? [pooryay-voo muh ruhko-mONday AN ohtr otel]

▸ could you recommend a restaurant? pourriez-vous me conseiller un restaurant ? [pooryay-voo muh kON-seyay AN resto-rON]

▸ what do you recommend? que nous recommandez-vous ? [kuh noo ruhko-mONday-voo]

▸ can you recommend anything on the menu? avez-vous des plats à me recommander ? [avay-voo day plah a muh ruhko-mONday]

record store le magasin de disques [maga-zAN duh deesk]

▸ I'm looking for a record store je cherche un magasin de disques [zhuh shersh AN maga-zAN duh deesk]

red rouge [roozh]; *(hair)* roux [roo], rousse [roos]

▸ dressed in red habillé en rouge [abee-yay ON roozh]

redhead roux [roo], rousse [roos]

▸ a tall redhead wearing glasses une grande rousse avec des lunettes [Un grONd roos avek day lUnet]

reduced *(price, rate)* réduit(e) [raydwee(raydweet)]

▸ is there a reduced rate for students? est-ce qu'il y a un tarif réduit pour les étudiants ? [eskeel ya AN tareef raydwee poor layz aytU-dyON]

reduced-price *(ticket)* à tarif réduit [a tareef raydwee]

▸ two reduced-price tickets and one full-price deux tarifs réduits et un plein tarif [duh tareef raydwee ay AN plAN tareef]

reduction la réduction [raydUk-syON]
- do you have reductions for groups? vous avez des tarifs réduits pour les groupes ? [vooz avay day tareef raydwee poor lay groop]

red wine le vin rouge [vAN roozh]
- a bottle of red wine une bouteille de vin rouge [UN bootey duh vAN roozh]

refresher course le cours de remise à niveau [koor duh ruhmeez a neevoh]
- I need a refresher course j'ai besoin d'un cours de remise à niveau [zhay buhzwAN dAN koor duh ruhmeez a neevoh]

refundable
- are the tickets refundable? les billets peuvent-ils être remboursés ? [lay beeyeh puhvt-eel etr rONboor-say]

regard *(respect)* la considération [kONsee-dayra-syON] • **regards** les amitiés *f* [amee-tyay] • **with regard to** au sujet de [oh sUzheh duh]
- give my regards to your parents! mes amitiés à vos parents ! [mayz amee-tyay a voh parON]
- I'm calling you with regard to... je vous appelle au sujet de... [zhuh vooz apel oh sUzheh duh]

region la région [rayzhyON]
- in the Basque region of France dans le pays Basque [dON luh peyee bask]

registered mail le (courrier) recommandé [kooryay ruhko-mONday]
- I would like to send a letter by registered mail je voudrais envoyer une lettre en recommandé [zhuh voodreh ONvwa-yay Un letr ON ruhko-mONday]

registration *(of vehicle)* les papiers *m* du véhicule [papyay dU vay-eekUl]
- here's the vehicle's registration voici les papiers du véhicule [vwasee lay papyay dU vay-eekUl]

relative le parent [parON], la parente [parONt], la famille [fameey]
- I have relatives in Paris j'ai de la famille à Paris [zhay duh la fameey a paree]

remember se souvenir de [suh soovneer duh]
- do you remember me? vous vous souvenez de moi ? [voo voo soovnay duh mwa]
- I can't remember his name je ne me souviens plus de son nom [zhuh nuh muh soovyAN plU duh sON nON]

remote (control) la télécommande [taylay-komONd]
- I can't find the remote for the TV je ne trouve pas la télécommande de la télé [zhuh nuh troov pa la taylay-komONd duh la taylay]

rent la location [loka-syON] • louer [lway]
- how much is the rent per week? quel est le prix de la location à la semaine ? [kel eh luh pree duh la loka-syON a la suhmen]

> ▸ I'd like to rent a car for a week je voudrais louer une voiture pour une semaine [zhuh voodreh lway Un vwatUr poor Un suhmen]

> ▸ I'd like to rent a boat j'aimerais louer un bateau [zhemuh-reh lway AN batoh]

> ▸ is it cheaper to rent the equipment by the week? c'est moins cher de louer le matériel à la semaine ? [seh mwAN sher duh lway luh matay-ryel a la suhmen]

rental *(renting)* la location [loka-syON]; *(apartment)* l'appartement *m* en location [apar-tuhmON ON loka-syON]; *(house)* la maison en location [mehzON ON loka-syON]; *(car)* la voiture de location [vwatUr ON loka-syON]

> ▸ the car is a rental c'est une voiture de location [seht Un vwatUr duh loka-syON]

repair la réparation [raypa-rasyON] ◆ réparer [raypa-ray]

> ▸ will you be able to carry out the repairs today? pourrez-vous faire les réparations aujourd'hui ? [pooray-voo fehr lay raypa-rasyON ohzhoor-dwee]

> ▸ how long will it take to repair? ça va prendre combien de temps à réparer ? [sa va prONdr kONbyAN duh tON a raypa-ray]

repeat répéter [raypay-tay]

> ▸ can you repeat that, please? vous pouvez répéter, s'il vous plaît ? [voo poovay raypay-tay seel voo play]

report *(theft)* déclarer [daykla-ray]

> ▸ I'd like to report something stolen je dois faire une déclaration de vol [zhuh dwah fehr Un daykla-rasyON duh vol]

> ▸ I'd like to report the loss of my credit cards je voudrais signaler la perte de mes cartes de crédit [zhuh voodreh seenya-lay la pert duh may kart duh kraydee]

reservation la réservation [rayzer-vasyON]

> ▸ do you have to make a reservation? faut-il faire une réservation ? [foht-eel fehr Un rayzer-vasyON]

> ▸ I have a reservation in the name of Jones j'ai une réservation au nom de Jones [zhay Un rayzer-vasyON oh nON duh Jones]

> ▸ can I change my reservation? puis-je changer ma réservation ? [pweezh shONzhay ma rayzer-vasyON]

reserve *(ticket, room)* réserver [rayzer-vay]

> ▸ hello, I'd like to reserve a table for two for tomorrow night bonjour, je voudrais réserver une table pour deux pour demain soir [bONzhoor zhuh voodreh rayzer-vay Un tabl poor duh poor duhmAN swar]

reserved *(booked)* réservé(e) [rayzer-vay]

> ▸ is this table reserved? est-ce que cette table est réservée ? [eskuh set tabl eh rayzer-vay]

rest *(relaxation)* le repos [ruhpoh] ◆ *(relax)* se reposer [suh ruhpo-zay]

> ▸ I've come here to get some rest je suis venu pour me reposer [zhuh swee vuhnu poor muh ruhpo-zay]

restaurants

Eating and drinking play a big part in French life and the number and the variety of *restaurants* on offer illustrate this. Whether you choose to eat in a *restaurant* or a more modest *brasserie* or *bistrot*, as well as the *à la carte* menu there will usually also be a good-value set-price *menu* involving the *plat du jour* (day's specialty).

restaurant restaurant [resto-rON]

▸ are there any good restaurants around here? est-ce qu'il y a de bons restaurants par ici ? [eskeel ya duh bON resto-rON par eesee]

restriction la limitation [leemee-tasyON]

▸ are there restrictions on how much luggage you can take? y a-t-il une limitation sur le nombre de bagages autorisé ? [ee ateel Un leemee-tasyON sUr luh nONbr duh bagazh otoh-reezay]

restroom les toilettes *f* [twalet]

▸ is there a restroom on the bus? y a-t-il des toilettes dans le car ? [ee ateel day twalet dON luh kar]

retired à la retraite [a la ruhtret]

▸ I'm retired now je suis à la retraite maintenant [zhuh sweez a la ruhtret mANt-nON]

return *(arrival back)* le retour [ruhtoor] ◆ rendre [rONdr]

▸ we have to return the car by noon Friday nous devons rendre la voiture vendredi à midi [noo duhvON rONdr la vwatUr vONdruh-dee a meedee]

return trip le retour [ruhtoor]

▸ the return trip is scheduled for 6 o'clock le retour est prévu à dix-huit heures [luh rhutoor eh prayvU a deez-weet uhr]

at a restaurant

▸ I'd like to reserve a table for tonight je voudrais réserver une table pour ce soir [zhuh voodreh rayzer-vay Un tabl poor suh swar]

▸ can we see the menu? pouvons-nous voir la carte ? [poovON-noo vwar la kart]

▸ do you have a set menu? avez-vous un menu à prix fixe ? [avay-voo AN muhnU a pree feeks]

▸ rare/medium/well done, please saignant/à point/bien cuit, s'il vous plaît [saynyON/a pwAN/byAN kwee seel voo play]

▸ can I have the check, please? l'addition, s'il vous plaît [ladee-syON seel voo play]

rice le riz [ree]
▸ I'd like some rice, please je voudrais du riz, s'il vous plaît [zhuh voodreh dU ree seel voo play]

ride *(trip in a car)* le tour (en voiture) [luh toor (ON vwatUr)]; *(lift)* l'accompagnement *m* [akON-panyuh-mON]; *(on a bike)* la promenade [promnad]; *(on a motorcycle)* le tour (en moto) [toor (ON motoh)]
▸ could you give me a ride to the airport? pourrais-tu me raccompagner à l'aéroport? [pooreh-tU muh rakON-panyay a la-ayro-por]
▸ where can we go for a ride around here? où peut-on faire une promenade dans le coin? [oo puht-ON fehr Un promnad dON luh kwAN]

riding l'équitation *f* [aykee-tasyON]
▸ to go riding faire du cheval [fehr dU shuhval]

right *(correct)* bon(ne) [bON(bon)], juste [zhUst]; *(not left)* droit(e) [drwah(drwat)]
▸ on the right (of) à droite (de) [a drwat (duh)]
▸ that's right c'est vrai [seh vreh]
▸ I don't think the check's right je crois que l'addition n'est pas juste [zhuh krwah kuh ladee-syON neh pa zhUst]
▸ is this the right train for Brussels? ce train est-il bien celui de Bruxelles? [suh trAN eht-eel byAN suhlwee duh brUsel]
▸ is this the right number? est-ce le bon numéro? [es luh bON nUmay-roh]
▸ take the next right prenez la première à droite [pruhnay la pruhmyehr a drwat]
▸ you have to turn right il faut aller à droite [eel foht alay a drwat]

right-hand (de) droite [(duh) drwat]
▸ on your right-hand side à votre droite [a votr drwat]

right of way la priorité [pree-oree-tay]
▸ who has right of way here? qui a la priorité, ici? [kee a la pree-oree-tay eesee]

road la route [root]
▸ which road do I take for Nantes? quelle route dois-je prendre pour aller à Nantes? [kel root dwazh prONdr poor alay a nONt]
▸ what is the speed limit on this road? quelle est la limitation de vitesse sur cette route? [kel eh la leemee-tasyON duh veetes sUr set root]

rob *(person)* voler [volay]
▸ I've been robbed! au voleur! [oh voluhr]

rock climbing la varappe [varap]
▸ can you go rock climbing here? est-ce qu'on peut faire de la varappe ici? [eskON puh fehr duh la varap eesee]

roller skate le roller [roluhr], le patin à roulettes [patAN a roolet]
▸ where can we rent roller skates? où peut-on louer des rollers? [oo puht-ON lway day roluhr]

room *(bedroom)* la chambre [shONbr]; *(in a house)* la pièce [pyes]; *(in a building)* la salle [sal]; *(space)* la place [plas]

- do you have any rooms available? est-ce qu'il vous reste des chambres libres ? [eskeel voo rest day shONbr leebr]
- how much is a room with en-suite bathroom? combien coûte une chambre avec salle de bains ? [kONbyAN koot Un shONbr avek sal duh bAN]
- I've reserved a room for tonight under the name of Pearson j'ai réservé une chambre pour ce soir au nom de Pearson [zhay ruhzer-vay Un shONbr poor suh swar oh nON duh Pearson]
- can I see the room? est-ce que je peux voir la chambre ? [eskuh zhuh puh vwar la shONbr]

rosé le rosé [rozay]

- could you recommend a good rosé? pouvez-vous me recommander un bon rosé ? [poovay-voo muh ruhko-mONday AN bON rosay]

round trip l'aller-retour m [alay-ruhtoor]

- how long does the round trip take? combien de temps dure l'aller-retour ? [kONbyAN duh tON dUr lalay-ruhtoor]

round-trip ticket le billet aller-retour [beeyeh alay-ruhtoor]

- two round-trip tickets to Paris, please deux billets aller et retour pour Paris, s'il vous plaît [duh beeyeh alay ay ruhtoor poor paree seel voo play]
- I'd like a round-trip ticket to Cannes, leaving on the 3rd and coming back on the 9th je voudrais un aller-retour pour Cannes, départ le trois, retour le neuf [zhuh voodreh AN alay-ruhtoor poor kan daypar luh trwah ruhtoor luh nuhf]
- a round-trip ticket for one car, two adults and two children, please un aller-retour pour une voiture, deux adultes et deux enfants, s'il vous plaît [AN alay-ruhtoor poor Un vwatUr duhz adUlt ay duhz ONfON seel voo play]

route (itinerary) la route [root], l'itinéraire m [eetee-nayrehr]; (of bus, train, plane) la route [root], le chemin [shuhmAN]

- is there an alternative route we could take est-ce qu'il y a un itinéraire bis ? [eskeel ya AN eetee-nayrehr bees]
- isn't there a more direct route? il n'y a pas de route plus directe ? [eel nya pa duh root plU deerekt]

row (of seats) le rang [rON]

- can we have seats in the front row? peut-on avoir des places au premier rang ? [puht-ON avwar day plas oh pruhmyay rON]
- sometimes there are two buses in a row il y a parfois deux bus de suite [eel ya parfwah duh bUs duh sweet]

rowboat le canot à rames [kanoh a ram]

- can we rent a rowboat? pouvons-nous louer un canot à rames ? [poovON-noo lway AN kanoh a ram]

rubber ring la bouée [bway]

- where can I buy a rubber ring? où puis-je acheter une bouée ? [oo pweezh ashtay Un bway]

run *(on foot)* la course [koors]; *(in a car)* l'excursion *f* [ekskUr-syON], la promenade [promnad]; *(for skiing)* la piste [peest] ♦ *(on foot)* courir [kooreer]; *(bus, train)* passer [pasay]; *(engine)* tourner [toornay] ♦ *(traffic light)* brûler [brUlay]

▶ I'm going for a run je vais courir [zhuh veh kooreer]

▶ the bus runs every half hour le bus passe toutes les demi-heures [luh bUs pas toot lay duhmee uhr]

running le jogging [dzhogeeng]

▶ where can you go running here? où peut-on courir ici ? [oo puht-ON kooreer eesee]

run out of être en panne de [etr ON pan duh]

▶ I've run out of gas je suis en panne d'essence [zhuh sweez ON pan desOns]

S

safe sûr(e) [sUr] ♦ *(for valuables)* le coffre-fort [kofr-for]

▶ is it safe to swim here? est-ce que l'on peut se baigner ici sans danger ? [eskuh lON puh suh baynyay eesee sON dANzhay]

▶ is it safe to camp here? est-ce que c'est dangereux de camper ici ? [eskuh seh dONzhuh-ruh duh kONpay eesee]

▶ is there a safe in the room? est-ce qu'il y a un coffre-fort dans la chambre ? [eskeel ya AN kofr-for dON la shONbr]

sail *(of a boat)* la voile [vwal]

▶ we need to adjust the sail il faut régler la voile [eel foh rayglay la vwal]

sailboat le bateau à voiles [batoh a vwal]

▶ can we rent a sailboat? pouvons-nous louer un bateau à voiles ? [poovON-noo lway AN batoh a vwal]

sailing la voile [vwal]

▶ to go sailing faire de la voile [fehr duh la vwal]

▶ I'd like to take beginners' sailing classes je voudrais prendre des cours de voile pour débutants [zhuh voodreh prONdr day koor duh vwal poor daybU-tON]

salad la salade [salad]

▶ can I just have a salad? puis-je avoir juste une salade ? [pweezh avwar zhUst Un salad]

sale *(selling)* la vente [vONt]; *(at reduced prices)* les soldes *m* [sold]

▶ is it for sale? c'est à vendre ? [seht a vONdr]

▶ can you get your money back on sale items? est-ce que les soldes sont remboursables ? [eskuh lay sold sON rONboor-sabl]

sales tax la TVA [tayvay-ah]
- is sales tax included? est-ce que la TVA est comprise ? [eskuh la tayvay-ah eh kONpreez]
- can you deduct the sales tax? pouvez-vous déduire la TVA ? [poovay-voo daydweer la tayvay-ah]

salt le sel [sel] ◆ saler [salay]
- can you pass me the salt? tu peux me passer le sel ? [tU puh muh pasay luh sel]
- it doesn't have enough salt ce n'est pas assez salé [suh neh paz asay salay]

salty salé(e) [salay]
- it's too salty c'est trop salé [seh troh salay]

same même [mem]
- I'll have the same la même chose pour moi [la mem shohz poor mwa]
- the same (as) le même (que) [luh mem (kuh)]
- it's the same as yours c'est le même que le vôtre [seh luh mem kuh luh vohtr]

sandwich le sandwich [sONdweesh]
- a chicken sandwich, please un sandwich au poulet, s'il vous plaît [AN sONdweesh oh pooleh seel voo play]

Saturday samedi *m* [samdee]
- Saturday September 13th samedi treize septembre [samdee trehz septONbr]
- it's closed on Saturdays c'est fermé le samedi [seh fehrmay luh samdee]
- I've been here since Saturday je suis là depuis samedi [zhuh swee la duhpwee samdee]

sauce la sauce [sohs]
- do you have a sauce that isn't too strong? est-ce que vous avez une sauce qui ne soit pas trop forte ? [eskuh vooz avay Un sohs kee nuh swah pa troh fort]

sauna le sauna [sohna]
- is there a sauna? y a-t-il un sauna ? [ee ateel AN sohna]

sausage la saucisse [sohsees]
- I'd like a grilled sausage with mustard j'aimerais une saucisse grillée avec de la moutarde [zhemuh-rehz Un sohsees greeyay avek duh la mootard]

say dire [deer]
- how do you say 'good luck' in French? comment dit-on 'good luck' en français ? [komON deet-ON good luck ON frONsay]

scared
- to be scared avoir peur [avwar puhr]
- I'm scared of spiders j'ai peur des araignées [zhay puhr dayz arayn-yay]

scheduled flight le vol régulier [vol raygUl-yay]
- is yours a scheduled flight or a charter? c'est un vol régulier ou un charter que vous avez ? [seht AN vol raygUl-yay oo AN shartehr kuh vooz avay]

school *(for children)* l'école *f* [aykol]; *(college, university)* l'université *f* [Unee-versee-tay]

▸ are you still in school? tu vas encore à la fac ? [tU va ONkor a la fak]

scoop la boule [bool]

▸ I'd like a cone with two scoops j'aimerais un cornet avec deux boules [zhemuh-reh AN corneh avek duh bool]

scooter le scooter [skootuhr]

▸ I'd like to rent a scooter j'aimerais louer un scooter [zhemuh-reh lway AN skootuhr]

Scotch *(whiskey)* le scotch [skotsh]

▸ a Scotch on the rocks, please un scotch avec glaçons, s'il vous plaît [AN skotsh avek glasON seel voo play]

Scotch tape® le Scotch® [skotsh]

▸ do you have any Scotch tape®? est-ce que vous avez du Scotch® ? [eskuh vooz avay dU skotsh]

scrambled eggs les œufs *m* brouillés [uh broo-yay]

▸ I'd like scrambled eggs for breakfast je voudrais des œufs brouillés pour le petit déjeuner [zhuh voodreh days uh broo-yay poor luh puhtee dayzhuh-nay]

screen *(room in a movie theater)* la salle [sal]

▸ how many screens does the movie theater have? combien de salles comprend le cinéma ? [kONbyAN duh sal kONprON luh seenay-ma]

scuba diving la plongée avec bouteilles [plONzhay avek bootey]

▸ can we go scuba diving? peut-on faire de la plongée avec bouteilles ? [puht-ON fehr duh la plONzhay avek bootey]

sea la mer [mehr]

▸ the sea is rough la mer est agitée [le mehr eht azhee-tay]

▸ how long does it take to walk to the sea? la mer est à combien de temps à pied ? [la mehr eht a kONbyAN duh tON a pyay]

seasick

▸ I feel seasick j'ai le mal de mer [zhay luh mal duh mehr]

seasickness le mal de mer [mal duh mehr]

▸ can you give me something for seasickness, please? auriez-vous quelque chose contre le mal de mer ? [ohryay-voo kelkuh shohz kONtr luh mal duh mehr]

seaside resort la station balnéaire [stasyON balnay-ehr]

▸ what's the nearest seaside resort to here? quelle est la station balnéaire la plus proche d'ici ? [kel eh la stasyON balnay-ehr la plU prosh deesee]

season *(of the year)* la saison [sehzON]

▸ which is the best season to come here? quelle est la meilleure saison pour venir ici ? [kel eh la meyuhr sehzON poor vuhneer eesee]

season ticket le forfait [forfeh]

▸ how much is a season ticket? combien coûte un forfait ? [kONbyAN koot AN forfeh]

seat le siège [syezh]; *(in a bus, a train)* la place [plas]; *(in a car)* le siège [syezh], la banquette [bONket]; *(in a theater, a movie theater)* la place [plas]

▸ is this seat taken? cette place est-elle prise ? [set plas eht-el preez]

▸ excuse me, I think you're (sitting) in my seat excusez-moi, je crois que vous êtes assis à ma place [ekskU-zay-mwa zhuh krwah kuh vooz et asee a ma plas]

second *(unit of time, gear)* la seconde [suhgONd] ♦ second(e) [suhgON(suhgONd)]

▸ wait a second! attends une seconde ! [atONz Un suhgONd]

▸ is it in second? c'est bien en seconde ? [seh byAN ON suhgONd]

▸ it's the second street on your right c'est la deuxième rue à droite [seh la duhzyem rU a drwat]

second class la seconde (classe) [suhgONd (klas)] ♦ en tarif lent [ON tareef lON]

▸ your seat's in second class votre place est en seconde (classe) [votr plas eht ON suhgONd (klas)]

▸ to travel second class voyager en seconde [vwa-yazhay ON suhgONd]

see voir [vwar]

▸ I'm here to see Dr. Jacot je voudrais voir le Dr Jacot [zhuh voodreh vwar luh doktuhr zhakoh]

▸ can I see the room? est-ce que je peux voir la chambre ? [eskuh zhuh puh vwar la shONbr]

▸ I'd like to see the dress in the window j'aimerais voir la robe qui est en vitrine [zhemuh-reh vwar la rob kee eht ON veetreen]

▸ see you à plus [a plUs]

▸ see you soon à bientôt [a byANtoh], à tout à l'heure [a toot a luhr]

▸ see you later à plus tard [a plU tar]

▸ see you (on) Thursday à jeudi [a zhuhdee]

self-service *(restaurant, gas station)* le self-service [self-servees], le libre-service [leebr-servees]

▸ is it self-service? est-ce que c'est un self-service ? [eskuh seht AN self-servees]

sell vendre [vONdr]

▸ do you sell stamps? est-ce que vous vendez des timbres ? [eskuh voo vONday day tANbr]

send envoyer [ONvwa-yay]

▸ I'd like to send this package to New York by airmail je voudrais envoyer ce colis à New York par avion [zhuh voodreh ONvwa-yay suh kolee a new york par avyON]

▸ could you send a breakdown lorry? est-ce que vous pourriez envoyer une dépanneuse ? [eskuh voo pooryay ONvwa-yay Un daypa-nuhz]

separately *(individually)* séparément [saypa-raymON], à l'unité [a lUnee-tay]

▸ is it sold separately? est-ce vendu à l'unité ? [es vONdU a lUnee-tay]

September septembre [septONbr]

▸ September 9th le neuf septembre [luh nuhf septONbr]

serve *(meal, drink, customer)* servir [serveer]; *(town, station)* desservir [day-serveer]

- what time is breakfast served from? le petit déjeuner est servi à partir de quelle heure ? [luh puhtee dayzhuh-nay eh servee a parteer duh kel uhr]
- do you still serve lunch at this time? est-ce que vous servez encore à déjeuner à cette heure-ci ? [eskuh voo servay ONkor a dayzhu-nay a set uhr-see]

service (in a restaurant) le service [servees] ◆ (car) réviser [rayvee-zay]
- the service was terrible le service était lamentable [luh servees ayteh lamON-tabl]
- we have to have the car serviced il faut faire réviser la voiture [eel foh fehr rayvee-zay la vwatUr]

service charge le service [servees]
- is service charge included? le service est-il compris ? [luh servees eht-eel kONpree]

set (of crockery) le service [servees]; (of keys) le jeu [zhuh], le trousseau [troosoh]; (of clothes) l'ensemble m [ONsONbl] ◆ (sun) se coucher [suh kooshay]
- do you have a spare set of keys? avez-vous un double du trousseau de clés ? [avay-vooz AN doobl dU troosoh duh klay]
- do you have a clean set of clothes? vous avez des vêtements propres ? [vooz avay day vetmON propr]
- what time does the sun set? à quelle heure le soleil se couche-t-il ? [a kel uhr luh soley suh koosh-teel]

seven sept [set]
- there are seven of us nous sommes sept [noo som set]

several plusieurs [plUzyuhr]
- I've been before, several years ago je suis déjà venu il y a plusieurs années [zhuh swee dayzha vuhnU eel ya plUzyuhrz anay]

shade (shadow) l'ombre f [ONbr]
- can we have a table in the shade? est-ce qu'on peut avoir une table à l'ombre ? [eskON puht avwar Un tabl a lONbr]
- let's go and sit in the shade of that tree allons nous installer à l'ombre de cet arbre [alON nooz ANsta-lay a lONbr duh set arbr]

shake (bottle) secouer [suhkway] ◆ (in agreement) se serrer la main [suh seray la mAN]
- shake the bottle well before use bien secouer la bouteille avant usage [byAN suhkway la bootey avONt Uzazh]
- to shake hands se serrer la main [suh seray la mAN]

shame (remorse, humiliation) la honte [ONt]; (pity) le dommage [domazh]
- (what a) shame! (quel) dommage ! [(kel) domazh]

shampoo le shampo(o)ing [shONpwAN]
- do you have any shampoo? auriez-vous du shampooing ? [ohryay-voo dU shONpwAN]

share partager [parta-zhay]
- we're going to share it: can you bring us two plates? on va partager, pouvez-vous nous apporter deux assiettes ? [ON va parta-zhay poovay-voo nooz apor-tay duhz asyet]

shared *(bathroom, kitchen)* commun(e) [komAN(komUn)]
- is the bathroom shared? la salle de bains est commune ? [la sal duh bAN eh komUn]

shaver le rasoir [razwar]
- where can I buy a new shaver? où puis-je trouver un rasoir ? [oo pwezh troovay AN razwar]

sheet *(for a bed)* le drap [drah]; *(of paper)* la feuille [foy]
- are there more sheets? y a-t-il d'autres draps ? [ee ateel dohtr drah]

ship le bateau [batoh]
- when does the ship dock? quand est-ce que le bateau se met à quai ? [kONt eskuh luh batoh suh met a keh]

shoe la chaussure [shohsUr]
- what sort of shoes should you wear? quelle genre de chaussures faut-il mettre ? [kel zhONr duh shohsUr foht-eel metr]

shoe size la pointure [pwANtUr]
- what's your shoe size? quelle est ta pointure ? [kel eh ta pwANtUr]

shop *(store)* le magasin [maga-zAN], la boutique [booteek]
- what time do the shops close? à quelle heure ferment les magasins ? [a kel uhr ferm lay maga-zAN]

shopping les courses *f* [koors]
- I'm going shopping je vais faire les courses [zhuh veh fehr lay koors]
- where can you go shopping around here? où peut-on faire des courses dans le coin ? [oo puht-ON fehr day koors dON luh kwAN]

shopping bag le sac (de course) [sak (duh koors)], le cabas [kabah]
- can I have a plastic shopping bag, please? puis-je avoir un sac en plastique, s'il vous plaît ? [pweezh avvar AN sak ON plasteek seel voo play]

shopping center le centre commercial [sONtr komer-syal]
- I'm looking for a shopping center je cherche un centre commercial [zhuh shersh AN sONtr komer-syal]

shop window la vitrine [veetreen]
- we've just been looking in shop windows on vient de regarder les vitrines [ON vyAN duh ruhgar-day lay veetreen]

short court(e) [koor(koort)], bref [bref], brève [brev]; *(in height)* petit(e) [puhtee (puhteet)]
- we're only here for a short time nous sommes ici pour peu de temps [noo somz eesee poor puh duh tON]
- I'm two euros short il me manque deux euros [eel muh mONk duhz uhroh]

shortcut le raccourci [rakoor-see]
- is there a shortcut? y a-t-il un raccourci ? [ee ateel AN rakoor-see]

short wave les petites ondes *f* [puhteet ONd]
- can you get any English stations on short wave? on capte des stations anglaises sur les petites ondes ? [ON kapt day stasyONz ONglez sUr lay puhteet Ond]

should
- what should I do? qu'est-ce que je dois faire ? [keskuh zhuh dwah fehr]

show *(at the theater, movies)* le spectacle [spektakl] • *(let see)* montrer [mONtray]
- what time does the show begin at? à quelle heure commence le spectacle ? [a kel uhr komONs luh spektakl]
- could you show me where that is on the map? pourriez-vous me montrer où ça se trouve sur la carte ? [pooryay-voo muh mONtray oo sa suh troov sUr la kart]
- could you show me the room? pourriez-vous me montrer ma chambre ? [pooryay-voo muh mONtray ma shONbr]

shower *(device, act)* la douche [doosh]; *(of rain)* l'averse *f* [avehrs]
- I'd like a room with a shower, please je voudrais une chambre avec douche, s'il vous plaît [zhuh voodreh Un shONbr avek doosh seel voo play]
- how does the shower work? comment marche la douche ? [komON marsh la doosh]
- the shower is leaking la douche fuit [la doosh fwee]

shower head la pomme de douche [pom duh doosh]
- there's no shower head il n'y a pas de pomme de douche [eel nya pa duh pom duh doosh]

shut fermer [fermay]
- it won't shut ça ne ferme pas [sa nuh ferm pa]

shutter *(on a window)* le volet [voleh]; *(on a camera)* l'obturateur *m* [obtUratuhr]
- are there shutters? est-ce qu'il y a des volets ? [eskeel ya day voleh]

shuttle *(vehicle)* la navette [navet]
- is there a shuttle? est-ce qu'il y a une navette ? [eskeel ya Un navet]

sick *(unwell)* malade [malad]
- I feel sick j'ai envie de vomir [zhay ONvee duh vomeer], j'ai mal au cœur [zhay mal oh kuhr]
- to be sick *(be unwell)* être malade [etr malad]; *(vomit)* vomir [vomeer], rendre [rONdr]
- she's been sick elle a vomi [el a vomee]

side le côté [kotay]
- I have a pain in my right side j'ai une douleur au côté droit [zhay Un dooluhr oh kotay drwah]
- could we have a table on the other side of the room? pourrions-nous avoir une table de l'autre côté de la salle ? [pooryON-nooz avwar Un tabl duh lohtr kotay duh la sal]

sidewalk le trottoir [trotwar]

> the sidewalks are very clean here les trottoirs sont très propres ici [lay trotwar sON treh propr eesee]

sight *(seeing)* la vue [vU] ◆ **sights** *(of a place)* les attractions *f* touristiques [atrak-syON tooreez-teek]

> I'm experiencing problems with my sight j'ai des problèmes de vue [zhay day problem duh vU]
> what are the sights that are most worth seeing? quels sont les monuments les plus dignes d'intérêt ? [kel sON lay monU-mON lay plU deenyuh dANtay-reh]

sign signer [seenyay]

> do I sign here? je dois signer ici ? [zhuh dwah seenyay eesee]

signpost signaler [seenya-lay], indiquer [ANdee-kay]

> is the route well signposted? est-ce que la route est bien indiquée ? [eskuh la root eh byAN ANdee-kay]

silver *(metal)* l'argent *m* [arzhON]

> is it made of silver? c'est de l'argent ? [seh duh larzhON]

since depuis (que) [duhpwee (kuh)] ◆ *(because)* puisque [pweesk]

> I've been here since Tuesday je suis là depuis mardi [zhuh swee la duhpwee mardee]
> it hasn't rained once since we've been here depuis que nous sommes ici, il n'a pas plu une seule fois [duhpwee kuh noo somz eesee eel na pa plU Un suhl fwah]

single *(only one)* seul(e) [suhl]; *(unmarried)* célibataire [saylee-batehr]

> not a single one pas un seul [paz AN suhl]
> I'm single je suis célibataire [zhuh swee saylee-batehr]
> she's a single woman in her thirties c'est une célibataire d'une trentaine d'années [seht Un saylee-batehr dUn trONten danay]

single bed le lit simple [lee sANpl]

> we'd prefer two single beds nous préférerions deux lits à une place [noo prayfay-ruhryON duh lee a Un plas]

single room la chambre simple [shONbr sANpl]

> I'd like to book a single room for 5 nights, please je voudrais réserver une chambre simple pour cinq nuits, s'il vous plaît [zhuh voodreh rayzer-vay Un shONbr sANpl poor sANk nwee seel voo play]

sister la sœur [suhr]

> I have two sisters j'ai deux sœurs [zhay duh suhr]

sit s'asseoir [saswar]

> may I sit at your table? puis-je m'asseoir à votre table ? [pweezh maswar a votr tabl]
> is anyone sitting here? cette place est-elle prise ? [set plas eht-el preez]

site *(of a town, a building)* l'emplacement *m* [ONplas-mON]; *(archaeological)* le site [seet]

▸ can we visit the site? peut-on visiter le site ? [puht-ON veezee-tay luh seet]

sitting *(for a meal)* le service [servees]
▸ is there more than one sitting for lunch? est-ce qu'il y a plusieurs services au déjeuner ? [eskeel ya plUzyuhr servees oh dayzhuh-nay]

six six [sees]
▸ there are six of us nous sommes six [noo som sees]

sixth sixième [seezyem]
▸ this is the sixth time I've asked you c'est la sixième fois que je vous le demande [seh la seezyem fwah kuh zhuh voo luh duhmONd]
▸ our room is on the sixth floor notre chambre est au sixième [notr shONbr eht oh seezyem]

size *(of a person, clothes)* la taille [ta-yuh]
▸ do you have another size? avez-vous une autre taille ? [avay-vooz Un ohtr ta-yuh]
▸ do you have it in a smaller size? avez-vous une plus petite taille ? [avay-vooz Un plU puhteet ta-yuh]
▸ I take a/I'm a size 38 je fais du trente-huit (comme taille) [zhuh feh dU trONt-weet (kom ta-yuh)]

skate *(for skating)* le patin [patAN] ◆ faire du patin [fehr dU patAN], patiner [patee-nay]
▸ how much is it to rent skates? combien coûte la location de patins ? [kONbyAN koot la loka-syON duh patAN]
▸ can you skate? tu sais faire du patin ? [tU seh fehr dU patAN]

skating faire du patin [fehr dU patAN]
▸ where can we go skating? où peut-on faire du patin ? [oo puht-ON fehr dU patAN]

ski le ski [skee]
▸ I'd like to rent a pair of skis for the week, please je voudrais louer une paire de skis pour la semaine, s'il vous plaît [zhuh voodreh lway Un pehr duh skee poor la suhmen seel voo play]

ski boots les chaussures *f* de ski [shohsUr duh skee]
▸ I'd like to rent ski boots je voudrais louer des chaussures de ski [zhuh voodreh lway day shohsUr duh skee]

skiing le ski [skee]
▸ where can we go skiing near here? où peut-on aller skier par ici ? [oo puht-ON alay skee-ay par eesee]

sleep *(be asleep)* dormir [dormeer]; *(spend night)* coucher [kooshay]
▸ I slept well j'ai bien dormi [zhay byAN dormee]
▸ I can't sleep je ne peux pas dormir [zhuh nuh puh pa dormeer]

sleeping bag le sac de couchage [sak duh kooshazh]
▸ where can I buy a new sleeping bag? où est-ce que je peux acheter un sac de couchage ? [oo eskuh zhuh puh ashtay AN sak duh kooshazh]

sleeping pill le somnifère [somnee-fehr]
> I'd like a sleeping pill j'aimerais un somnifère [zhemuh-rehz AN somnee-fehr]

slice *(of bread, ham)* la tranche [trONsh] ◆ couper en tranches [koopay ON trONsh]
> a thin slice of ham une fine tranche de jambon [Un feen trONsh duh zhONbON]

slim *(person)* mince [mANs]
> she's slim elle est mince [el eh mANs]

slow lent(e) [lONt(lONt)]; *(clock, watch)* en retard [ON ruhtar]
> the fog was slow to clear le brouillard a mis du temps à se dissiper [luh broo-yar a mee dU tON a suh deesee-pay]
> is that clock slow? est-ce que cette horloge est en retard ? [eskuh set orlozh eht ON ruhtar]

slowly lentement [lONtmON]
> could you speak more slowly, please? pourriez-vous parler plus lentement, s'il vous plaît ? [pooryay-voo parlay plU lONtmON seel voo play]

small petit(e) [puhtee(puhteet)]
> have you anything smaller? avez-vous quelque chose de plus petit ? [avay-voo kelkuh shohz duh plU puhtee]

smell sentir [sONteer]; *(have a bad smell)* sentir mauvais [sONteer mohveh]
> can you smell something burning? vous ne trouvez pas que ça sent le brûlé ? [voo nuh troovay pa kuh sa sON luh brUlay]
> it smells in here ça sent mauvais, ici [sa sON mohvehz eesee]
> it smells of coffee ça sent le café [sa sON luh kafay]

smoke la fumée [fUmay] ◆ *(person)* fumer [fUmay]
> do you mind if I smoke? est-ce que ça vous dérange si je fume ? [eskuh sa voo dayrONzh see zhuh fUm]
> no thanks, I don't smoke non merci, je ne fume pas [nON mersee zhuh nuh fUm pa]

smoker fumeur [fUmuhr], fumeuse [fUmuhz]
> are you smokers or nonsmokers? êtes-vous fumeurs ou non-fumeurs ? [et-voo fUmuhr oo nON-fUmuhr]

smoking
> is smoking allowed here? on a le droit de fumer ici ? [ON a luh drwah duh fUmay eesee]
> I can't stand smoking je ne supporte pas la fumée [zhuh nuh sUport pa la fUmay]

smoking compartment le compartiment fumeur [kONpar-teemON fUmuhr]
> I'd like a seat in a smoking compartment je voudrais une place en compartiment fumeur [zhuh voodreh Un plas ON kONpar-teemON fUmuhr]
> is there a smoking compartment? y a-t-il un compartiment fumeur ? [ee ateel AN kONpar-teemON fUmuhr]

smoking section la zone fumeur [zon fUmuhr]
> I'd like a table in the smoking section je voudrais une table en zone fumeur [zhuh voodreh Un tabl ON zon fUmuhr]

sneaker la tennis [tenees]

> your sneakers are really trendy! elles sont tendance, tes tennis ! [el sOn tONdONs tay tenees]

snorkel le tuba [tUba]

> I'd like to rent a snorkel and mask, please je voudrais louer un tuba et un masque, s'il vous plaît [zhuh voodreh lway AN tUba ay AN mask seel voo play]

snow neiger [nayzhay]

> it's snowing il neige [eel nezh]

snowboard le surf (des neiges) [suhrf (day nehzh)]

> I'd like to rent a snowboard je voudrais louer un surf [zhuh voodreh lway AN suhrf]

snowboarding le surf (des neiges) [suhrf (day nehzh)]

> where can we go snowboarding near here? où peut-on faire du surf par ici ? [oo puht-ON fehr dU suhrf par eesee]

snow tire le pneu neige [pnuh nezh]

> do I need snow tires? est-ce que j'ai besoin de pneus neige ? [eskuh zhay buhzwAN duh pnuh nezh]

so *(to such a degree)* si [see]; *(also)* aussi [ohsee]; *(consequently)* du coup [dU koo]

> I've never seen anything so beautiful je n'ai jamais rien vu d'aussi beau [zhuh nay zhameh ryAN vU dohsee boh]

> it's so big! comme c'est grand ! [kom seh grON]

> I'm hungry – so am I! j'ai faim – moi aussi ! [zhay fAN – mwa ohsee]

soap le savon [savON]

> there's no soap il n'y a pas de savon [eel nya pa duh savON]

socket *(in a wall)* la prise (de courant) [preez duh koorON]

> is there a socket so that I can use to recharge my cell? y a-t-il une prise pour que je recharge mon portable ? [ee ateel Un preez poor kuh zhuh ruhsharzh mON portabl]

solution la solution [solU-syON]

> that seems to be the best solution ça me paraît être la bonne solution [sa muh paret etr la bon solU-syON]

> I'd like some rinsing solution for soft lenses je voudrais une solution de rinçage pour lentilles souples [zhuh voodreh Un solU-syON duh rANsazh poor lONteey soopl]

some *(an amount of)* de [duh], du [dU], des [day]; *(a number of)* quelques [kelkuh]

+ *(an amount)* quelques-uns [kelkuhz-AN], quelques-unes [kelkuhz-Un], en [ON]; *(a number)* certains [sertAN], certaines [serten]

> I'd like some coffee je voudrais du café [zhuh voodreh dU kafay]

> some friends recommended this place des amis m'ont recommandé cet endroit [dayz amee mON ruhko-mONday set ONdrwah]

> can I have some? est-ce que je peux en avoir ? [eskuh zhu puh ON avwar]

somebody, someone quelqu'un [kelkAN]
- somebody left this for you quelqu'un a laissé ceci pour vous [kelkAN a laysay suhsee poor voo]

something quelque chose [kelkuh shohz]
- is something wrong? quelque chose ne va pas ? [kelkuh shohz nuh va pa]

somewhere quelque part [kelkuh par]
- I'm looking for somewhere to stay je cherche un endroit où loger [zhuh shersh AN ONdrwah oo lozhay]
- somewhere near here quelque part près d'ici [kelkuh par preh deesee]
- somewhere else autre part [ohtr par]

son le fils [fees]
- this is my son voici mon fils [vwasee mON fees]

soon bientôt [byANtoh]
- see you soon! à tout à l'heure ! [a toot a luhr]
- as soon as possible le plus tôt possible [luh plU toh poseebl]

sore throat le mal de gorge [mal duh gorzh], l'angine f [ONzheen]
- I have a sore throat j'ai mal à la gorge [zhay mal a la gorzh]

sorry désolé(e) [dayzo-lay]
- I'm sorry je suis désolé [zhuh swee dayzo-lay], excusez-moi [ekskU-zay-mwa], pardon ! [pardON]
- sorry I'm late désolé d'être en retard [dayzo-lay detr ON ruhtar]
- I'm sorry, but this seat is taken désolé, il y a déjà quelqu'un [dayzo-lay eel ya dayzha kelkAN]
- sorry to bother you excusez-moi de vous déranger [ekskU-zay-mwa duh voo dayrON-zhay]
- sorry? *(asking for repetition)* comment ? [komON]
- no, sorry non, je regrette [nON zhuh ruhgret]

sound le son [sON]
- can you turn the sound down? vous pouvez baisser le son ? [voo poovay baysay luh sON]

souvenir le souvenir [soovneer]
- where can I buy souvenirs? où puis-je acheter des souvenirs ? [oo pweezh ashtay day soovneer]

souvenir shop la boutique de souvenirs [booteek duh soovneer]
- I'm looking for a souvenir shop je cherche une boutique de souvenirs [zhuh shersh Un booteek duh soovneer]

spa le spa [spa]; *(town)* la station thermale [stasyON termal]
- the spa's not working le spa ne fonctionne pas [luh spa nuh fONksyon pa]

space la place [plas]; *(for a tent, a trailer)* l'emplacement *m* [ONplas-mON]
- is there space for another bed in the room? est-ce qu'il y a de la place pour un

autre lit dans la chambre ? [eskeel ya duh la plas poor AN ohtr lee dON la shONbr]

▶ I'd like a space for one tent for two days je voudrais un emplacement pour une tente pour deux jours [zhuh voodreh AN ONplas-mON poor Un tONt poor duh zhoor]

▶ do you have any spaces farther from the road? est-ce qu'il vous reste des emplacements plus éloignés de la route ? [eskeel voo rest dayz ONplas-mON plUz aylwan-yay duh la root]

spare *(clothes, battery)* de rechange [duh ruhshONzh] ◆ *(tire)* le pneu de rechange [pnuh duh ruhshONzh]; *(part)* la pièce de rechange [pyes duh ruhshONzh]

▶ take some spare clothes prenez des vêtements de rechange [pruhnay day vetmON duh ruhshONzh]

▶ I don't have any spare cash je n'ai plus d'argent [zhuh nay plU darzhON]

▶ I've got a spare ticket for the game j'ai un billet en plus pour le match [zhay AN beeyeh ON plUs poor luh matsh]

spare part la pièce de rechange [pyes duh ruhshONzh]

▶ where can I get spare parts? où puis-je trouver des pièces de rechange ? [oo pweezh troovay day pyes duh ruhshONzh]

spare tire le pneu de rechange [pnuh duh ruhshONzh]

▶ the spare tire's flat too le pneu de rechange aussi est à plat [luh pnuh duh ruhshONzh ohsee eht a plah]

spare wheel la roue de secours [roo duh suhkoor]

▶ there's no spare wheel il n'y a pas de roue de secours [eel nya pa duh roo duh suhkoor]

sparkling *(water)* gazeux [gazuh], gazeuse [gazuhz]; *(wine)* pétillant(e) [paytee-yON(-yONt)]

▶ could I have a bottle of sparkling water, please? pourriez-vous m'apporter une bouteille d'eau gazeuse, s'il vous plaît ? [pooryay-voo mapor-tay Un bootey doh gazuhz seel voo play]

speak parler [parlay]

▶ I speak hardly any French je parle à peine le français [zhuh parl a pehn luh frONsay]

▶ is there anyone here who speaks English? y a-t-il quelqu'un qui parle anglais ? [ee ateel kelkAN kee parl ONglay]

▶ could you speak more slowly? est-ce que vous pourriez parler plus lentement ? [eskuh voo pooryay parlay plU lONtmON]

▶ hello, I'd like to speak to Mr...; this is... allô, bonjour, je voudrais parler à M....., de la part de... [alloh bONzhoor zhuh voodreh parlay a muhsyuh... duh la par duh]

▶ who's speaking please? qui est à l'appareil ? [kee eht a lapa-rey]

special *(on menu)* le plat du jour [plah dU zhoor]

▶ what's today's special? quel est le plat du jour ? [kel eh luh plah dU zhoor]

specialist spécialiste [spaysya-leest]

▸ could you refer me to a specialist? pourriez-vous m'envoyer chez un spécialiste ? [pooray-voo mONvwa-yay shayz AN spaysya-leest]

specialty la spécialité [spaysya-leetay]

▸ what are the local specialties? quelles sont les spécialités régionales ? [kel sON lay spaysya-leetay rayzhyo-nal]

speed limit la limitation de vitesse [leemeta-tasyON duh veetes]

▸ what's the speed limit on this road? quelle est la limitation de vitesse sur cette route ? [kel eh la leemeta-tasyON duh veetes sUr set root]

▸ what's the speed limit in town? à combien la vitesse est-elle limitée en ville ? [a kONbyAN la veetes eht-el leemee-tay ON veel]

spell écrire [aykreer], épeler [ayplay]

▸ you've spelled my name wrong vous avez mal écrit mon nom [vooz avay mal aykree mON nON]

▸ how do you spell your name? comment s'écrit votre nom ? [komON saykree votr nON]

spend *(money)* dépenser [daypON-say]; *(time, vacation)* passer [pasay]

▸ how much are you prepared to spend? combien comptez-vous dépenser ? [kONbyAN kONtay-voo daypON-say]

▸ I spent a month in France a few years ago j'ai passé un mois en France il y a quelques années [zhay pasay AN mwah ON frONs eel ya kelkuhz anay]

spicy épicé(e) [aypee-say]

▸ is it spicy? est-ce que c'est épicé ? [eskuh seht aypee-say]

spoon la cuillère [kweeyehr]

▸ could I have a spoon? pourriez-vous m'apporter une cuillère ? [pooray-voo mapor-tay Un kweeyehr]

sport le sport [spor]

▸ do you play any sports? pratiques-tu un sport ? [prateek-tU AN spor]

▸ I do a lot of sport je fais beaucoup de sport [zhuh feh bohkoo duh spor]

sporty *(person)* sportif [sporteef], sportive [sporteev]

▸ I'm not very sporty je ne suis pas très sportif [zhuh nuh swee pa treh sporteef]

sprain se fouler [suh foolay]

▸ I've sprained my ankle je me suis foulé la cheville [zhuh muh swee foolay la shuhveey]

▸ my wrist is sprained mon poignet est foulé [mON pwanyeh eh foolay]

square *(in a town)* la place [plas]

▸ where is the main square? où est la place principale ? [oo eh la plas prANsee-pal]

stain la tache [tash]

▶ can you remove this stain? est-ce que vous pouvez enlever cette tache ? [eskuh voo poovay ONluh-vay set tash]

stairs les escaliers *m* [eskal-yay]

▶ where are the stairs? où sont les escaliers ? [oo sON layz eskal-yay]

stamp *(for letter, postcard)* le timbre [tANbr]

▶ do you sell stamps? est-ce que vous vendez des timbres ? [eskuh voo vONday day tANbr]

stand *(stall, booth)* le stand [stONd]; *(in a stadium)* la tribune [treebUn] ◆ *(tolerate)* supporter [sUpor-tay] ◆ *(be upright)* se tenir debout [suh tuhneer duhboo]; *(get up)* se mettre debout [suh metr duhboot]

▶ where's stand number five? où se trouve le stand numéro cinq ? [oo suh troov luh stONd nUmay-roh sANk]

▶ I can't stand him je ne peux pas le supporter [zhuh nuh puh pa luh sUpor-tay]

start *(begin)* commencer [komON-say]; *(function)* démarrer [dayma-ray]

▶ when does the concert start? à quelle heure commence le concert ? [a kel uhr komONs luh kONsehr]

▶ the car won't start la voiture ne veut pas démarrer [la vwatUr nuh vuh pa dayma-ray]

starving

▶ I'm absolutely starving je suis morte de faim [zhuh swee mort duh fAN]

States

▶ the States les États-Unis [layz aytaz-Unee]

▶ I'm from the States je viens des États-Unis [zhuh vyAN dayz aytaz-Unee]

▶ I live in the States j'habite aux États-Unis [zhabeet ohz aytaz-Unee]

▶ have you ever been to the States? êtes-vous déjà allé aux États-Unis ? [et-voo dayzha alay ohz aytaz-Unee]

station *(railroad, bus)* la gare [gar]; *(subway, TV, radio)* la station [stasyON]; *(police)* le commissariat [komee-saryah]

▶ to the station, please! à la gare, s'il vous plaît ! [a la gar seel voo play]

▶ where is the station? où est la gare ? [oo eh la gar]

stay *(in a place)* rester [restay] ◆ *(visit)* le séjour [sayzhoor]

▶ we're planning to stay for two nights nous pensons rester deux nuits [noo pONsON restay duh nwee]

▶ I'm staying with her for a few days je loge chez elle pendant quelques jours [zhuh lozh shayz el pONdON kelkuh zhoor]

▶ a two-week stay un séjour de deux semaines [AN sayzhoor duh duh suhmen]

steak le steak [stek]

▶ I'd like a steak and fries je voudrais un steak avec des frites [zhuh voodreh AN stek avek day freet]

steal *(money, wallet, necklace)* voler [volay]

▶ my passport's been stolen on m'a volé mon passeport [ON ma volay mON paspor]

- our car has been stolen on nous a volé notre voiture [ON nooz a volay notr vwatUr]

still encore [ONkor]

- how many kilometers are there still to go? combien de kilomètres reste-t-il encore ? [kONbyAN duh keelo-metr restuh-teel ONkor]
- we're still waiting to be served on ne nous a pas encore servis [ON nuh nooz a paz ONkor servee]

sting *(wasp, nettle)* piquer [peekay]

- I've been stung by a wasp je me suis fait piquer par une guêpe [zhuh muh swee feh peekay par Un gep]

stomach l'estomac *m* [estomah], le ventre [vONtr]

- I've got a sore stomach j'ai mal au ventre [zhay mal oh vONtr]

stomachache le mal de ventre [mal duh vONtr]

- I have a really bad stomachache j'ai très mal au ventre [zhay treh mal oh vONtr]

stop *(for buses)* l'arrêt *m* [areh]; *(for trains)* la station [stasyON]; *(on a journey, a flight)* l'escale *f* [eskal] ◆ (s')arrêter [(s)areh-tay]

- is this the right stop for...? c'est bien l'arrêt pour... ? [seh byAN lareh poor]
- stop it! arrête ! [aret]
- please stop here arrêtez-vous ici [areh-tay-vooz eesee]
- which stations does this train stop at? quelles gares dessert ce train ? [kel gar dayserhr suh trAN]
- do we stop at Laval ? est-ce que nous nous arrêtons à Laval ? [eskuh noo nooz areh-tONz a laval]

store *(place selling goods)* le magasin [maga-zAN]

- are there any bigger stores in the neighborhood? y a-t-il de plus grands magasins dans le coin ? [ee ateel duh plU grON maga-zAN dON luh kwAN]

---

in a store

- no, thanks. I'm just looking non, merci. Je ne fais que regarder [nON mersee zhuh nuh feh kuh ruhgar-day]
- how much is this? combien ça coûte ? [kONbyAN sa koot]
- I take a/I'm a size 38 je fais du trente-huit [zhuh feh dU trONt-weet]
- can I try this coat on? est-ce que je peux essayer ce manteau ? [eskuh zhuh puh e-seyay suh mONtoh]
- can it be exchanged? est-il possible de l'échanger ? [eht-eel poseebl duh layshON-zhay]

store window la vitrine [veetreen]
- we've just been looking in store windows on vient de regarder les vitrines [ON vyAN duh ruhgar-day lay veetreen]

storm l'orage *m* [orazh]
- is there going to be a storm? est-ce qu'il va y avoir de l'orage ? [eskeel va ee avwar duh lorazh]

straight *(line, road)* droit(e) [drwah(drwat)]; *(hair)* raide [rehd]
- you have to keep going straight on il faut aller tout droit [eel foht alay too drwah]

street la rue [rU]
- will this street take me to the station? est-ce que cette rue mène à la gare ? [eskuh set rU men a la gar]

streetcar le tramway [tramweh]
- can you buy tickets on the streetcar? est-ce qu'on peut acheter les billets dans le tramway ? [eskON puht ashtay lay beeyeh dON luh tramweh]
- which streetcar line do we have to take? il faut prendre quelle ligne de tramway ? [eel foh prONdr kel leen-yuh duh tramway]
- where is the nearest streetcar stop? où se trouve l'arrêt de tramway le plus proche ? [oo suh troov lareh duh tramweh luh plU prosh]

street map le plan de la ville [plON duh la veel]
- where can I buy a street map? où puis-je acheter un plan de la ville ? [oo pweezh ashtay AN plON duh la veel]

strong fort(e) [for(fort)]
- is the current very strong here? est-ce que le courant est fort ici ? [eskuh luh koorON eh for eesee]

stuck
- to be stuck *(jammed)* être coincé [etr kwANsay]; *(trapped)* être bloqué [etr blokay]
- someone is stuck in the elevator quelqu'un est bloqué dans l'ascenseur [kelkAN eh blokay dON lasON-suhr]

student étudiant(e) [aytU-dyON(-dyONt)]
- I'm a student je suis étudiant [zhuh sweez aytU-dyON]

student discount la réduction pour les étudiants [raydUk-syON poor layz aytU-dyON]
- do you do student discounts? faites-vous des réductions pour les étudiants ? [fet-voo day raydUk-syON poor layz aytU-dyON]

studio (apartment) le studio [stUdyoh]
- I'm renting a studio apartment je loue un studio [zhuh loo AN stUdyoh]

style *(manner)* le style [steel]; *(design)* le modèle [model]; *(elegance)* l'allure *f* [alUr]
- she's got style elle a vraiment de l'allure [el a vrehmON duh lalUr]

the subway

The Paris subway system (*le métro*) is very extensive and highly efficient. Trains run from 5:30 a.m. to 1 a.m., serving 301 stations along 208 kilometers of track. The first line was opened in 1900 and the latest one, the fourteenth, which is driverless and operated by computer, in 1998. Tickets are not expensive and there are several special deals for tourists and visitors, such as the *Paris Visite* card.

subway le métro [maytroh]
▸ can I have a map of the subway? est-ce que je peux avoir un plan du métro ? [eskuh zhuh puh avwar AN plON dU maytroh]

subway train la rame [ram]
▸ when's the last subway train from this station? quand passe la dernière rame à cette station ? [kON pas la demyehr ram a set stasyON]

sudden soudain(e) [soodAN(sooden)]
▸ all of a sudden d'un (seul) coup [dAn (suhl) koo]

sugar le sucre [sUkr]
▸ can you pass me the sugar? tu peux me passer le sucre ? [tU puh muh pasay luh sUkr]

suggest *(propose)* proposer [propo-zay]
▸ do you have anything else you can suggest? auriez-vous autre chose à me proposer ? [ohryay-vooz ohtr shohz a muh propo-zay]

suit *(be convenient for)* convenir à [kONvneer a]
▸ that suits me perfectly cela me convient parfaitement [suhla muh kONvyAN parfet-mON]
▸ it doesn't suit me cela ne me va pas [suhla nuh muh va pa]

suitcase la valise [valeez]
▸ one of my suitcases is missing il me manque une valise [eel muh mONk Un valeez]
▸ my suitcase was damaged in transit ma valise a été abîmée pendant le transport [ma valeez a aytay abee-may pONdON luh trONspor]

summer l'été *m* [aytay]
▸ in (the) summer en été [ON aytay]

summer vacation les grandes vacances *f* [grOnd vakONs]
▸ we've come here for our summer vacation nous sommes venus ici pour les grandes vacances [noo som vuhnU eesee poor lay grONd vakONs]

sun le soleil [soley]
▸ the sun's very strong at this time of day le soleil tape dur à cette heure de la journée [luh soley tap dUr a set uhr duh la zhoornay]

sunburn le coup de soleil [koo duh soley]

- I've got a bad sunburn j'ai des gros coups de soleil [zhay day groh koo duh soley]
- do you have a cream for a sunburn? vous avez de la crème contre les coups de soleil ? [vooz avay duh la krem kONtr lay koo duh soley]

Sunday dimanche *m* [deemONsh]

- where can I find a doctor on a Sunday? où est-ce que je peux trouver un médecin un dimanche ? [oo eskuh zhuh puh troovay AN maydsAN AN deemONsh]
- are the stores open on Sunday? les magasins sont-ils ouverts le dimanche ? [lay maga-zAN sONt-eel oovehr luh deemONsh]

sun deck le pont extérieur [pONt ekstayr-yuhr]

- how do I get onto the sun deck? comment se rend-on sur le pont extérieur ? [komON suh rONd-ON sUr luh pONt ekstayr-yuhr]

sunglasses les lunettes *f* de soleil [lUnet duh soley]

- I've lost my sunglasses j'ai perdu mes lunettes de soleil [zhay perdU may lUnet duh soley]

sunny *(day, weather)* ensoleillé(e) [ONso-leyay]

- it's sunny il y a du soleil [eel ya dU soley]

sunrise le lever du soleil [luhvay dU soley]

- what time's sunrise? à quelle heure est le lever du soleil ? [a kel uhr eh luh luhvay dU soley]

sunset le coucher du soleil [kooshay dU soley]

- isn't the sunset beautiful? le coucher de soleil est superbe [luh kooshay dU soley eh sUperb]

suntan lotion la crème solaire [krem solehr]

- I'd like SPF 30 suntan lotion j'aimerais de la crème solaire indice trente [zhemuh-reh duh la krem solehr ANdees trONt]

supermarket le supermarché [sUper-marshay]

- is there a supermarket nearby? est-ce qu'il y a un supermarché dans le quartier ? [eskeel ya AN sUper-marshay dON luh kartyay]

surcharge le supplément [sUplay-mON]

- do I have to pay a surcharge? y a-t-il un supplément à payer ? [ee ateel AN sUplay-mON a peyay]

sure sûr(e) [sUr]

- are you sure that's how you say it? tu es sûr que ça se dit comme ça ? [tU eh sUr kuh sa suh dee kom sa]

surfboard la planche de surf [plONsh du suhrf]

- is there somewhere we can rent surfboards? y a-t-il un endroit où louer des planches de surf quelque part ? [ee ateel AN ONdrwah oo lway day plONsh duh suhrf kelkuh par]

Swiss cantons

Switzerland is a confederation of 26 *cantons*, each with its own constitution, parliament, government and courts of law. Each *canton* is divided into smaller districts called *communes*, which are responsible for education, social services, town and country planning and taxation.

surfing le surf [suhrf]
- can we go surfing around here? peut-on faire du surf par ici ? [puht-ON fehr dU suhrf par eesee]

surprise la surprise [sUrpreez]
- what a nice surprise! quelle bonne surprise ! [kel bon sUrpreez]

surrounding area les environs *m* [ONvee-rOn]
- Grenoble and the surrounding area Grenoble et ses environs [gruhnobl ay sayz ONvee-rON]

swallow avaler [ava-lay]
- the ATM outside has swallowed my credit card le distributeur automatique dehors a avalé ma carte de crédit [luh deestree-bUtuhr otoh-mateek duhor a ava-lay ma kart duh kraydee]
- I can't swallow je ne peux rien avaler [zhuh nuh puh ryAN ava-lay]
- it hurts when I swallow j'ai mal quand j'avale [zhay mal kON zhaval]

swim nager [nazhay] ◆ la baignade [benyad]
- is it safe to swim here? est-ce que l'on peut se baigner ici sans danger ? [eskuh lON puh suh baynyay eesee sON dONzhay]
- to go for a swim aller se baigner [alay suh baynyay]

swimming pool la piscine [peeseen]
- is there an open-air swimming pool? y a-t-il une piscine en plein air ? [ee ateel Un peeseen ON plAN ehr]

Swiss suisse [swees] ◆ Suisse [swees]
- I'm Swiss je suis suisse [zhuh swee swees]
- the Swiss les Suisses [lay swees]

switch *(for a light)* l'interrupteur *m* [ANteh-rUptuhr]; *(on a TV, radio)* le bouton [bootON]
- the switch doesn't work l'interrupteur ne marche pas [lANteh-rUptuhr nuh marsh pa]

switch off éteindre [aytANdr]
- where do you switch the light off? où est-ce qu'on éteint la lumière ? [oo eskON aytAN la lUmyehr]
- my cell was switched off mon portable était éteint [mON portabl ayteht aytAN]

switch on *(light, heating, TV)* allumer [alU-may]; *(engine)* mettre en marche [metr ON marsh]

- where do I switch this light on? où est-ce qu'on allume la lumière ? [oo eskON alUm la lUmyehr]
- have you switched on the ignition? as-tu mis le contact ? [a-tU mee luh kONtakt]

Switzerland la Suisse [swees]

- are you from Switzerland? est-ce que vous venez de Suisse ? [eskuh voo vuhnay duh swees]
- do you live in Switzerland? vous habitez en Suisse ? [vooz abee-tay ON swees]
- I've never been to Switzerland je ne suis jamais allé en Suisse [zhuh nuh swee zhamehz alay ON swees]

synagogue la synagogue [seena-gog]

- where's the nearest synagogue? où est la synagogue la plus proche ? [oo eh la seena-gog la plU prosh]

table la table [tabl]

- I've reserved a table in the name of... j'ai réservé une table au nom de... [zhay rayzer-vay Un tabl oh nON duh]
- a table for four, please une table pour quatre, s'il vous plaît [Un tabl poor katr seel voo play]

table tennis le ping-pong [peeng-pONg]

- are there tables for table tennis? il y a des tables de ping-pong ? [ee atee day tabl duh peeng-pONg]

table wine le vin de table [vAN duh tabl]

- a bottle of table wine une bouteille de vin de table [Un bootey duh vAN duh tabl]

take prendre [prONdr]; *(carry)* porter [portay]; *(lead)* conduire [kONdweer]; *(accompany)* accompagner [akON-panyay]; *(transport)* conduire [kONdweer]; *(require)* durer [dUray], prendre [prONdr]; *(time)* mettre [metr]

- someone's taken my bag on m'a pris mon sac [ON ma pree mON sak]
- can you take me to this address? pouvez-vous me conduire à cette adresse ? [poovay-voo muh kONdweer a set adres]
- are you taking the plane or the train to Paris? vous prenez l'avion ou le train pour aller à Paris ? [voo pruhnay lavyON oo luh trAN poor alay a paree]
- which road should I take? quelle route dois-je prendre ? [kel root dwazh prONdr]
- I take a size 40 je fais du quarante [zhu feh dU karONt]
- how long does it take to get to Calais? combien de temps met-on pour aller à Calais ? [kONyAN duh tON met-ON poor alay a kaleh]

▸ could you take a photo of us? est-ce que vous pourriez nous prendre en photo ? [eskuh voo pooray noo prONdr ON fotoh]

take down *(bags, luggage)* descendre [desOndr]

▸ could you get take these bags down, please? pourriez-vous descendre ces bagages, s'il vous plaît ? [pooray-voo desOndr say bagazh seel voo play]

take in *(bags, luggage)* rentrer [rONtray]

▸ can you have someone take in my bags, please? est-ce que quelqu'un pourrait rentrer mes bagages ? [eskuh kelkAN pooreh rONtray may bagazh]

taken *(seat)* occupé(e) [okU-pay]

▸ sorry, this seat is taken excusez-moi, cette place est occupée [ekskU-zay-mwa set plas eht okU-pay]

take up *(bags, luggage)* monter [mONtay]

▸ can someone take our bags up to our room? est-ce que quelqu'un peut monter nos bagages dans la chambre ? [eskuh kelkAN puh mONtay noh bagazh dON la shONbr]

talk parler [parlay]

▸ could I talk to you for a moment? puis-je vous parler un instant ? [pweezh voo parlay AN ANstON]

▸ you've no right talking to me like that vous n'avez pas à me parler sur ce ton [voo navay paz a muh parlay sUr suh tON]

tall *(person, tree)* grand(e) [grON(grONd)]

▸ what's that tall building over there? c'est quoi, ce grand bâtiment là-bas ? [seh kwa suh grON batee-mON la-bah]

tank *(in a vehicle)* le réservoir [rayzer-vwar]

▸ is the tank full? est-ce que le réservoir est plein ? [eskuh luh rayzer-vwar eh plAN]

tap water l'eau *f* du robinet [robee-neh]

▸ just some tap water, please juste de l'eau du robinet, s'il vous plaît [zhUst duh loh dU robee-neh seel voo play]

taste le goût [goo] ◆ *(sense)* sentir [sONteer]; *(try)* goûter [gootay] ◆ avoir un goût [avwar AN goo]

▸ I can't taste anything je ne sens aucun goût [zhuh nuh sONz ohkAN goo]

▸ would you like to taste the wine? voulez-vous goûter le vin ? [voolay-voo gootay luh vAN]

▸ it tastes funny ça a un drôle de goût [sa a AN drol duh goo]

tax la taxe [taks]

▸ is this price inclusive of tax? le prix est-il toutes taxes comprises ? [luh pree eht-eel toot taks kONpreez]

taxi le taxi [taksee]

▸ how much does a taxi cost from here to the station? combien coûte un taxi d'ici à la gare ? [kONbyAN koot AN taksee deesee a la gar]

▸ I'd like to book a taxi to take me to the airport, please je voudrais réserver un taxi pour m'emmener à l'aéroport, s'il vous plaît [zhuh voodreh rayzer-vay AN taksee poor mONmuh-nay a la-ayro-por seel voo play]

taxi driver le chauffeur de taxi [shohfuhr duh taksee]

▸ can you ask the taxi driver to wait? pouvez-vous demander au chauffeur de taxi d'attendre ? [poovay-voo duhmON-day oh shohfuhr duh taksee datONdr]

taxi stand la station de taxi [stasyON duh taksee]

▸ can you tell me where I can find a taxi stand? pouvez-vous m'indiquer une station de taxi ? [poovay-voo mANdee-kay Un stasyON duh taksee]

tea *(drink)* le thé [tay]

▸ a tea with milk un thé au lait [AN tay oh leh]

▸ a tea without milk un thé nature [AN tay natUr]

teach apprendre [aprONdr]

▸ can you teach me to speak French? peux-tu m'apprendre à parler le français ? [puh-tU maprONdr a parlay luh frONsay]

teacher le professeur [profeh-suhr]

▸ I'm a teacher je suis professeur [zhuh swee profeh-suhr]

telephone le téléphone [taylay-fon] ◆ appeler [aplay] ◆ téléphoner [taylay-fonay]

▸ can I use the telephone? puis-je appeler quelqu'un ? [pweezh aplay kelkAN]

telephone booth la cabine (téléphonique) [kabeen (taylay-foneek)]

▸ is there a telephone booth near here? y a-t-il une cabine téléphonique près d'ici ? [ee ateel Un kabeen taylay-foneek preh deesee]

telephone call l'appel [apel], le coup de téléphone [koo duh taylay-fon]

▸ I'd like to make a telephone call je voudrais téléphoner [zhuh voodreh taylay-fonay]

television la télévision [taylay-veezyON]

▸ what's on television? qu'est-ce qu'il y a à la télévision ? [keskeel ya a la taylay-veezyON]

---

taking a taxi

▸ could you order me a taxi, please? pourriez-vous m'appeler un taxi, s'il vous plaît ? [pooryay-voo maplay AN taksee seel voo play]

▸ to the station/airport, please à la gare/à l'aéroport, s'il vous plaît [a la gar/a la-ayro-por seel voo play]

▸ stop here/at the lights/at the corner, please arrêtez-vous ici/au feu/au coin de la rue [areh-tay-voo eesee/oh fuh/oh kwAN duh la rU]

▸ can you wait for me? pourriez-vous m'attendre ? [pooryay-voo matONdr]

▸ how much is it? combien vous dois-je ? [kONbyAN voo dwazh]

▸ keep the change gardez la monnaie [garday la moneh]

tell dire [deer], indiquer [ANdee-kay]
- can you tell me the way to the museum? pouvez-vous m'indiquer le chemin pour aller au musée ? [poovay-voo mANdee-kay luh shuhmAN poor alay oh mUzay]
- can you tell me when we get to my station? pourriez-vous me prévenir quand on arrivera à la bonne station ? [pooryay-voo muh prayvneer kONd ON aree-vuhra a la bon stasyON]

temperature *(meteorological)* la température [tONpay-ratUr]; *(fever)* la fièvre [fyehvr]
- what's the temperature? quelle est la température ? [kel eh la tONpay-ratUr]
- I've got a temperature j'ai de la fièvre [zhay duh la fyehvr]

ten dix [dees]
- there are ten of us nous sommes dix [noo som dees]

tennis le tennis [tenees]
- where can we play tennis? où est-ce que l'on peut faire du tennis ? [oo eskuh lON puh fehr dU tenees]

tennis racket la raquette de tennis [raket duh tenees]
- can you rent tennis rackets? peut-on louer des raquettes de tennis ? [puht-ON lway day raket duh tenees]

tent la tente [tONt]
- I'd like to book a space for a tent, please j'aimerais réserver une place pour une tente, s'il vous plaît [zhemuh-reh rayzer-vay Un plas poor Un tONt seel voo play]
- can you put up your tent anywhere? peut-on monter sa tente n'importe où ? [puht-ON mONtay sa tONt nANport oo]

tent peg le piquet [peekeh], la sardine [sardeen]
- we're short of tent pegs il manque des piquets [eel mONk day peekeh]
- do you have a mallet for hammering in the tent pegs? vous auriez un maillet pour enfoncer les sardines ? [vooz ohryay AN ma-yeh poor ONfON-say lay sardeen]

terminal *(in airport)* le terminal [termee-nal]
- where is terminal 1? où se trouve le terminal un ? [oo suh troov luh termee-nal AN]

tetanus le tétanos [tayta-nos]
- I've been vaccinated for tetanus je suis vacciné contre le tétanos [zhuh swee vaksee-nay kONtr luh tayta-nos]

thank remercier [ruhmehr-syay] ◆ **thanks** merci *m* [mersee]
- I can't thank you enough je ne sais comment vous remercier [zhuh nuh seh komON voo ruhmehr-syay]
- thanks for everything (you've done) merci pour tout (ce que vous avez fait) [mersee poor too (skuh vooz avay feh]

thank you! merci ! [mersee]
- thank you very much! merci beaucoup ! [mersee bohkoo]

that *(demonstrative use)* ça [sa]; *(in relative clauses)* que [kuh], qui [kee] ◆ ce [suh], cette [set], ces [say]

▶ who's that? qui est-ce ? [kee es]

▶ that's right c'est ça [seh sa]

▶ the road that goes to Calais la route qui mène à Calais [la root kee men a kaleh]

▶ I'll have that one je vais prendre celui-là [zhuh veh prONdr suhlwee-la]

theater *(for plays)* le théâtre [tay-atr]

▶ where is there a theater? où y a-t-il un théâtre ? [oo ee ateel AN tay-atr]

theft le vol [vol]

▶ I'd like to report a theft je voudrais déclarer un vol [zhuh voodreh daykla-ray AN vol]

then *(at a particular time)* alors [alor], à ce moment-là [a suh momON-la]; *(next)* puis [pwee]; *(in that case)* donc [dONk], alors [alor]

▶ I'll see you then je te verrai à ce moment-là [zhuh tuh veray a suh momON-la]

there là [la]

▶ he's over there il est là-bas [eel eh la-bah]

▶ there is/are... il y a... [eel ya]

▶ there's a problem il y a un problème [eel ya AN problem]

▶ are there any restrooms near here? y a-t-il des toilettes dans les environs ? [ee ateel day twalet dON layz ONvee-rON]

▶ there is/are...! voilà... ! [vwala]

▶ there's the train! voilà le train ! [vwala luh trAN]

▶ there you are *(handing something over)* voilà [vwala]

thermometer le thermomètre [termo-metr]

▶ do you have a thermometer? est-ce que vous avez un thermomètre ? [eskuh vooz avay AN termo-metr]

▶ the thermometer shows 18 degrees (Celsius) le thermomètre indique dix-huit degrés (Celsius) [luh termo-metr ANdeek deez-weet duhgray (selsyUs)]

---

saying thank you

▶ thank you je vous remercie [zhuh voo ruhmehr-see]

▶ thanks, that's very kind of you merci, c'est très gentil à vous [mersee seh treh zhONtee a voo]

▶ I can't thank you enough je ne sais comment vous remercier [zhuh nuh seh komON voo ruhmehr-syay]

▶ thank you for your help je vous remercie de votre aide [zhuh voo ruhmehr-see duh votr ehd]

▶ I wanted to thank you for inviting me je voulais vous remercier de m'avoir invité [zhuh vooleh voo ruhmehr-syay duh mavwar ANvee-tay]

thin *(person)* mince [mANs], maigre [mehgr]; *(slice)* mince [mANs], fin(e) [fAN (feen)]; *(layer)* léger [layzhay], légère [layzhehr]

▸ isn't that jacket too thin for a cold evening like this? cette veste n'est-elle pas trop légère pour une soirée aussi froide ? [set vest neht-el pa troh layzhehr poor Un swaray ohsee frwad]

thing la chose [shohz]; *(object)* l'objet *m* [obzheh] ◆ **things** *(possessions, clothes)* les affaires *f* [afehr]

▸ what's that thing for? à quoi ça sert, ça ? [a kwa sa sehr sa]

▸ I don't know what the best thing to do is je ne sais pas ce qu'il y a de mieux à faire [zhuh nuh seh pa suh keel ya duh myuh a fehr]

▸ could you look after my things for a minute? pouvez-vous surveiller mes affaires un instant ? [poovay-voo sUr-veyay mayz afehr AN ANtstON]

think *(believe)* croire [krwar], trouver [troovay] ◆ *(use mind)* penser [pONsay]

▸ I think (that)... je trouve que... [zhuh troov (kuh)]

▸ I don't think so je crois que non [zhuh krwah kuh nON]

third troisième [trwazyem] ◆ *(fraction)* le tiers [tyer]; *(gear)* la troisième [trwazyem]

▸ this is my third time in France c'est mon troisième séjour en France [seh mON trwazyem sayzhoor ON frONs]

thirsty

▸ to be thirsty avoir soif [avwar swaf]

▸ I'm very thirsty j'ai très soif [zhay treh swaf]

three trois [trwah]

▸ there are three of us nous sommes trois [noo som trwah]

throat la gorge [gorzh]

▸ I have a fish bone stuck in my throat j'ai une arête coincée dans la gorge [zhay Un aret kwANsay dON la gorzh]

throat lozenge la pastille pour la gorge [pasteey poor la gorzh]

▸ I'd like some throat lozenges je voudrais des pastilles pour la gorge [zhuh voodreh day pasteey poor la gorzh]

thunderstorm l'orage *m* [orazh]

▸ will there be a thunderstorm? est-ce qu'il va y avoir de l'orage ? [eskeel va ee avwar duh lorazh]

Thursday jeudi *m* [zhuhdee]

▸ we're arriving/leaving on Thursday nous arrivons/partons jeudi [noo zaree-vON/ partON zhuhdee]

ticket le billet [beeyeh]; *(for a bus, the subway)* le ticket [teekeh]

▸ I'd like a ticket to... je voudrais un billet pour... [zhuh voodreh AN beeyeh poor]

▸ how much is a ticket to...? combien coûte un billet pour... ? [kONbyAN koot AN beeyeh poor]

validating tickets (i)

Before boarding a bus or train you must always make sure that your ticket is validated by getting it punched, date-stamped or electronically read by a *composteur* (ticket machine). If you don't, you run the risk of being fined.

> ▸ a book of tickets, please un carnet de tickets, s'il vous plaît [AN karneh duh teekeh seel voo play]
> ▸ I'd like to book a ticket je voudrais réserver un billet [zhuh voodreh rayzer-vay AN beeyeh]
> ▸ I'd like three tickets for... je voudrais trois places pour... [zhuh voodreh trwah plas poor]

tide la marée [maray]
> ▸ what time does the tide turn? à quelle heure la marée s'inverse-t-elle ? [a kel uhr la maray sANvers-tel]

tight *(piece of clothing)* juste [zhUst], serré(e) [seray]
> ▸ these pants are too tight ce pantalon est trop juste [suh pONta-lON eh troh zhUst]

time le temps [tON]; *(by clock)* l'heure *f* [uhr]; *(occasion)* la fois [fwah], le coup [koo]
> ▸ do we have time to visit the town? avons-nous le temps de visiter la ville ? [avON-noo luh tON duh veezee-tay la veel]
> ▸ what time is it? quelle heure est-il ? [kel uhr eht-eel]
> ▸ what time do you close? à quelle heure fermez-vous ? [a kel uhr fermay-voo]
> ▸ could you tell me if the train from Paris is on time? pourriez-vous me dire si le train en provenance de Paris est à l'heure ? [pooryay-voo muh deer see luh trAN ON pronvnONs duh paree eht a luhr]
> ▸ three times trois fois [trwah fwah]
> ▸ at the same time à la fois [a la fwah]
> ▸ first time du premier coup [dU pruhmyay koo]

timetable l'horaire *m* [orehr]
> ▸ do you have local bus timetables? avez-vous les horaires des bus du quartier ? [avay-voo layz orehr day bUs dU kartyay]

tip *(gratuity)* le pourboire [poorbwar] ◆ *(give a gratuity to)* donner un pourboire [donay AN poorbwar]

tipping (i)

Tipping is not compulsory in France, but people usually leave a tip in cafés or restaurants, even when gratuity is included. Otherwise you risk getting a dirty look from your waiter or waitress. You should also tip taxi drivers, porters, tour guides, hair stylists, beauticians, delivery people, etc.

tobacco stores (i)

A private company called *Altadis* produces or distributes all cigarettes, cigars, tobacco and matches sold in France. At *tabacs* (tobacco stores) you can also buy lottery tickets, stamps, phonecards, *métro* tickets and travel cards, and, in the provinces, newspapers and magazines.

▸ how much should I leave as a tip? combien je dois laisser de pourboire ? [kONbyAN zhuh dwah laysay duh poorbwar]

tire *(for a vehicle)* le pneu [pnuh]

▸ the tire's flat/punctured le pneu est à plat/crevé [luh pnuh eht a plah/kruhvay]

to *(indicating place, direction)* à [a]; *(in telling time)* moins [mwAN]

▸ when is the next train to Brussels? quand part le prochain train pour Bruxelles ? [kON par luh proshAN trAN poor brUsel]

▸ it's twenty to nine il est neuf heures moins vingt [eel eh nuhv uhr mwAN vAN]

tobacco store le bureau de tabac [bUroh duh tabah]

▸ where is the tobacco store? où se trouve le bureau de tabac le plus proche ? [oo suh troov luh bUroh duh tabah luh plU prosh]

today aujourd'hui [ohzhoor-dwee]

▸ what's today's date? on est le combien aujourd'hui ? [ON eh luh kONbyAN ohzhoor-dwee]

toe le doigt de pied [dwah duh pyay], l'orteil *m* [ortey]

▸ I think I've broken my toe je crois que je me suis cassé l'orteil [zhuh krwah kuh zhuh muh swee kasay lortey]

together ensemble [ONsONbl]

▸ let's go together allons-y ensemble [alONz-ee ONsONbl]

toilet les toilettes *f* [twalet]

▸ I need to go to the toilet il faut que j'aille aux toilettes [eel foh kuh zha-yuh oh twalet]

▸ do you have to pay to use the toilets? est-ce qu'il faut payer pour aller aux toilettes ? [eskeel foh peyay poor alay oh twalet]

toilet paper le papier toilette [papyay twalet], le papier hygiénique [papyay eezh-yayneek]

▸ there is no toilet paper il n'y a pas de papier toilette [eel nya pa duh papyay twalet]

toll *(for a road, a bridge)* le péage [pay-azh]

▸ do you have to pay a toll to use the bridge? est-ce que c'est un pont à péage ? [eskuh seht AN pON a pay-azh]

toll-free *(number, call)* non-payant(e) [nON-peyON(-peyONt)]

▸ there's a toll-free number you can call il y a un numéro vert à appeler [eel ya AN nUmay-roh vehr a aplay]

tomato la tomate [tomat]
- a pound of tomatoes une livre de tomates [Un leevr duh tomat]

tomato juice le jus de tomate [zhU duh tomat]
- I'd like a tomato juice j'aimerais un jus de tomate [zhemuh-reh AN zhU duh tomat]

tomorrow demain [duhmAN]
- can you hold my reservation until tomorrow? pouvez-vous me garder la réservation jusqu'à demain? [poovay-voo muh garday la rayzer-vasyON zhUska duhmAN]
- I'm leaving tomorrow morning je pars demain matin [zhuh par duhmAN matAN]
- see you tomorrow à demain [a duhmAN]

tonight ce soir [suh swar]
- do you have any beds available for tonight? vous reste-t-il des lits pour ce soir? [voo rest-teel day lee poor suh swar]

too *(also)* aussi [ohsee]; *(excessively)* trop [troh]
- enjoy your meal! – you too bon appétit! – vous de même [bon apay-tee – voo duh mem]
- she's too tired to... elle est trop fatiguée pour... [el eh troh fatee-gay poor]
- it's too expensive c'est trop cher [seh troh shehr]
- there are too many people il y a trop de monde [eel ya troh duh mONd]

tooth la dent [dON]
- I've broken a tooth je me suis cassé une dent [zhuh muh swee kasay Un dON]

toothache la rage de dents [razh duh dON], le mal de dents [mal duh dON]
- I have a toothache j'ai mal aux dents [zhay mal oh dON]

toothbrush la brosse à dents [bros a dON]
- I've forgotten my toothbrush j'ai oublié ma brosse à dents [zahy ooblee-yay ma bros a dON]

toothpaste le dentifrice [dONtee-frees]
- I'd like to buy some toothpaste je voudrais acheter du dentifrice [zhuh voodreh ashtay dU dONtee-frees]

top le bouchon [booshON]; *(of a pen)* le capuchon [kapU-shON] ♦ *(maximum)* dernier [dernyay], dernière [dernyehr], maximum [maksee-mom]
- the car drove away at top speed la voiture roulait à vitesse maximum [la vwatUr rooleht a veetes maksee-mom]

tour le circuit [seerkwee]
- I'm planning to do a two week tour of the country je compte faire un circuit de deux semaines dans le pays [zhuh kONt fehr AN seerkwee duh duh sumhen dON luh peyee]

tourist touriste [tooreest] ♦ *(season)* touristique [toorees-teek]
- do you get many tourists here? il y a beaucoup de touristes, ici? [eel ya bohkoo duh tooreest eesee]

tourist attraction le site touristique [seet toorees-teek]

▸ what are the main tourist attractions in the area? quels sont les principaux sites touristiques de la région ? [kel sON lay prANsee-poh seet toorees-teek duh la rayzhyON]

tourist class la classe touriste [klas toreest]

▸ in tourist class, please en classe touriste, s'il vous plaît [ON klas tooreest seel voo play]

tourist guide le guide touristique [geed toorees-teek]

▸ we have a good tourist guide with a lot of addresses nous avons un bon guide touristique, avec beaucoup d'adresses [nooz avON AN bON geed toorees-teek avek bohkoo dadres]

tourist office le syndicat d'initiative [sANdee-kah deenee-syateev]

▸ I'm looking for the tourist office je cherche le syndicat d'initiative [zhuh shersh luh sANdee-kah deenee-syateev]

tow remorquer [ruhmor-kay]

▸ could you tow me to a garage? pourriez-vous me remorquer jusqu'à un garage ? [pooryay-voo muh ruhmor-kay zhUska AN garazh]

toward *(in the direction of)* vers [vehr]

▸ we're heading toward Nantes nous allons vers Nantes [nooz alON vehr nONt]

tow away emmener à la fourrière [ONmuh-nay a la fooryehr]

▸ my car's been towed away ma voiture a été emmenée à la fourrière [ma vwatUr a aytay ONmuh-nay a la fooryehr]

towel la serviette (de toilette) [servyet (duh twalet)]

▸ we don't have any towels nous n'avons pas de serviettes de toilette [noo navON pa duh servyet duh twalet]

▸ could we have more towels? pourrions-nous avoir des serviettes supplémentaires ? [pooryON-nooz avwar day servyet sUplay-mOntehr]

getting around town

▸ which bus goes to the airport? quel est le bus qui va à l'aéroport ? [kel eh luh bUs kee va a la-ayro-por]

▸ where does the bus to the station go from? d'où part le bus pour la gare ? [doo par luh bUs poor la gar]

▸ I'd like a one-way (ticket) to... je voudrais un ticket pour... [zhuh voodreh AN teekeh poor]

▸ can I have a book of tickets, please? un carnet (de tickets), s'il vous plaît [AN karneh (duh teekeh) seel voo play]

▸ could you tell me where I have to get off? pourriez-vous m'indiquer quand je dois descendre ? [pooryay-voo mANdee-kay kON zhuh dwah desONdr]

TGV and RER (i)

The *TGV* (*Train à grande vitesse*) is the pride of the *SNCF* (French railroads). It can travel at up to 300 km an hour and is a comfortable, safe, yet surprisingly economical way of getting around France (especially if you book well in advance). You can buy tickets for the *TGV* at any station, or online, for either first or second class. You must make a reservation before traveling. The *TGV* now runs direct from Paris Charles de Gaulle airport to many major cities. The *RER* (*Réseau express régional*) is the rail network linking Paris and its suburbs. There are five lines, named A to E. You take Line A to get to Disneyland Paris and Line B to get to Paris's two airports, Roissy-Charles de Gaulle and Orly.

---

tower *(of a church, a castle)* la tour [toor]
  ▸ can you visit the tower? est-ce qu'on peut visiter la tour ? [eskON puh veezee-tay la toor]

town la ville [veel]
  ▸ to go into town aller en ville [alay ON veel]

town hall la mairie [mehree]
  ▸ where is the town hall? où est la mairie ? [oo eh la mehree]

traffic *(vehicles)* la circulation [seerkU-lasyON]
  ▸ is there a lot of traffic on the freeway? y a-t-il beaucoup de circulation sur l'autoroute ? [ee ateel bohkoo duh seerkU-lasyON sUr lotoh-root]

traffic circle le rond-point [rON-pwAN]
  ▸ you turn right at the traffic circle c'est à droite au rond-point [seht a drwat oh rON-pwAN]

traffic jam l'embouteillage *m* [ONboo-teyazh], le bouchon [booshON]
  ▸ we got stuck in a traffic jam on a été bloqués dans un embouteillage [ON a aytay blokay dONz Un ONboo-teyazh]

traffic lights les feux *m* tricolores/de signalisation [fuh treeko-lor/duh seenya-leeza-syON]
  ▸ turn left at the traffic lights tournez à gauche au feu [toornay a gohsh oh fuh]

trail *(path)* le sentier [sONtyay], la piste [peest]
  ▸ will this trail take us back to the main road? est-ce que cette piste nous ramènera sur la route principale ? [eskuh cet peest noo rameh-nuhra sUr la root prANsee-pal]

train *(on the railroad)* le train [trAN]; *(on the subway)* la rame [ram]
  ▸ when is the next train to Bordeaux? quand part le prochain train pour Bordeaux ? [kON par luh proshAN trAN poor bordoh]
  ▸ I'd like a round-trip ticket for the Paris-to-Berlin train tomorrow, please je

voudrais un aller-retour pour le train Paris-Berlin de demain, s'il vous plaît [zhuh voodreh AN alay-ruhtoor poor luh trAN paree-berlAN duh duhmAN seel voo play]

▶ do you have reduced-price train tickets? y a-t-il des billets de train à tarif réduit ? [ee ateel day beeyeh duh trAN a tareef raydwee]

▶ which platform does the train for Lille leave from? de quel quai part le train pour Lille ? [duh kel keh par luh trAN poor leel]

▶ the train was fifteen minutes late le train a eu quinze minutes de retard [luh trAN a U kANz meenUt duh ruhtar]

tram le tramway [tramweh]

▶ can you buy tickets on the tram? est-ce qu'on peut acheter les billets dans le tramway ? [eskON puht ashtay lay beeyeh dON luh tramweh]

▶ which tram line do we have to take? il faut prendre quelle ligne de tramway ? [eel foh prONdr kel leenyuh duh tramweh]

▶ where is the nearest tram stop? où se trouve l'arrêt de tramway le plus proche ? [oo suh troov lareh duh tramweh luh plU prosh]

transfer *(of money)* le virement [veermON] ◆ *(money)* transférer [trONsfay-ray]

▶ I'd like to transfer some money from my account je voudrais transférer de l'argent de mon compte [zhuh voodreh trONsfay-ray duh larzhON duh mON kONt]

travel le voyage [vwa-yazh] ◆ *(go on a trip)* voyager [vwa-yazhay]

▶ I'd like a window seat facing the direction of travel je voudrais une place côté fenêtre dans le sens de la marche [zhuh voodreh Un plas kotay fuhnetr dON luh sONs duh la marsh]

▶ I'm traveling on my own je voyage seul [zhuh vwa-yazh suhl]

travel agency l'agence *f* de voyages [azhONs duh vwa-yazh]

▶ I'm looking for a travel agency je cherche une agence de voyages [zhuh shersh AN azhONs duh vwa-yazh]

traveler's check le chèque de voyage [shek duh vwa-yazh]

▶ do you take traveler's checks? acceptez-vous les chèques de voyage ? [aksep-tay-voo lay shek duh vwa-yazh]

tree l'arbre *m* [arbr]

▶ what type of tree is that? qu'est-ce que c'est comme arbre ? [keskuh seh kom arbr]

trip *(journey)* le voyage [vwa-yage]

▶ have a good trip! bon voyage ! [bON vwa-yazh]

trouble *(difficulty)* les problèmes *m* [problem], les ennuis *m* [ONnwee]; *(effort)* la difficulté [deefee-kUltay], la peine [pen]

▶ we had trouble finding the hotel nous avons eu du mal a trouver l'hôtel [nooz avONz U dU mal a troovay lotel]

▶ I don't want to be any trouble je ne veux pas créer d'ennuis [zhuh nuh vuh pa kray-ay dONnwee]

▶ it's no trouble cela ne me dérange pas [suhla nuh muh dayrONzh pa]

trunk *(of a car)* le coffre [kofr]; *(piece of luggage)* la malle [mal]
- my things are in the trunk of my car mes affaires sont dans le coffre de la voiture [mayz afehr sON dON luh kofr duh la vwatUr]
- I've got two bags and a trunk j'ai deux valises et une malle [zhay duh valeez ay Un mal]

try *(attempt)* essayer [ay-seyay], tâcher de [tashay duh]; *(sample)* goûter [gootay]
- I'd like to try the local beer j'aimerais goûter la bière locale [zhemuh-reh gootay la byehr lokal]

try on *(dress, shoes)* essayer [ay-seyay]
- I'd like to try on the one in the window je voudrais essayer celui qui est en vitrine [zhuh voodreh ay-seyay suhlwee kee eht ON veetreen]

tub *(of ice cream)* le pot [poh]
- I'd like a tub with three scoops j'aimerais un pot avec trois boules [zhemuh-rehz AN poh avek trwah bool]

Tuesday mardi *m* [mardee]
- we're arriving/leaving on Tuesday nous arrivons/partons mardi [noo zaree-vON/partON mardee]

tunnel le tunnel [tUnel]
- there's a long tunnel just before you arrive at the station il y a un long tunnel juste avant d'arriver à la gare [eel ya AN lON tUnel zhUst avON daree-vay a la gar]

turn *(in a game, order)* le tour [toor]; *(off a road)* le tournant [toornON]
- *(change direction)* tourner [toornay]
- it's your turn c'est à ton tour de jouer [seht a tON toor duh zhway]
- is this the turn for the campground? est-ce ici que je tourne pour aller au terrain de camping ? [es eesee kuh zhuh toorn poor alay oh terAN duh kONpeeng]
- turn left at the lights tournez à gauche au feu rouge [toornay a gohsh oh fuh roozh]
- you have to turn right il faut tourner à droite [eel foh toornay a drwat]

turn down *(radio, volume, gas)* baisser [baysay]; *(bed)* préparer [praypa-ray]
- can we turn the air-conditioning down? est-ce qu'on peut baisser la climatisation ? [eskON puh baysay la kleema-teeza-syON]
- how do you turn the volume down? comment on baisse le volume ? [komONt ON behs luh volUm]

turn off fermer [fermay]; *(light, appliance)* éteindre [aytANdr]
- my cell was turned off mon portable était éteint [mON portabl ayteht aytAN]

turn on *(light, radio)* allumer [alU-may]; *(engine)* mettre en marche [metr ON marsh]; *(faucet)* ouvrir [oovreer]
- where do I turn this light on? où est-ce qu'on allume la lumière ? [oo eskON alUm la lUmyehr]

turn up *(sound, central heating)* monter [mONtay]
- how do you turn up the heating? comment fait-on pour monter le chauffage ? [komON feht-ON poor mONtay luh shohfazh]

TV la télé [taylay]

▸ I don't have a TV je n'ai pas la télé [zhuh nay pa la taylay]

TV lounge la salle de télévision [sal duh taylay-veezyON]

▸ is there a TV lounge? y a-t-il une salle de télévision ? [ee ateel Un sal duh taylay-veezyON]

twelve douze [dooz] ◆ *(noon)* midi [meedee]; *(midnight)* minuit [meenwee]

▸ there are twelve of us nous sommes douze [noo som dooz]

▸ it's twelve o'clock *(noon)* il est midi [eel eh meedee]; *(midnight)* il est minuit [eel eh meenwee]

twice deux fois [duh fwah]

▸ the ferry runs twice a day le ferry passe deux fois par jour [le feree pas duh fwah par zhoor]

twin le jumeau [zhUmoh], la jumelle [zhUmel]

▸ twin brother frère jumeau [frehr zhUmoh]

▸ twin sister sœur jumelle [suhr zhUmel]

twin beds les lits *m* jumeaux [lee zhUmoh]

▸ a room with twin beds une chambre avec des lits jumeaux [Un shONbr avek day lee zhUmoh]

two deux [duh]

▸ there are two of us nous sommes deux [noo som duh]

U

umbrella le parapluie [para-plwee]

▸ could you lend me an umbrella? est-ce que vous pourriez me prêter un parapluie ? [eskuh voo pooryay muh prehtay AN para-plwee]

unacceptable inadmissible [eenad-meeseebl]

▸ it's completely unacceptable! c'est inadmissible ! [seht eenad-meeseebl]

underpass le passage souterrain [pasazh sooteh-rAN]

▸ is the underpass safe at night? le passage souterrain est-il sans danger la nuit ? [luh pasazh sooteh-rAN eht-eel sON dONzhay la nwee]

understand comprendre [kONprONdr]

▸ I can understand French, but I can't really speak it j'arrive à comprendre le français mais je ne le parle pas bien [zhareev a kONprONdr luh frONsay meh zhuh nuh luh parl pa byAN]

▸ I understand a little je comprends un petit peu [zhuh kONprONz AN puhtee puh]

▸ I don't understand a word je ne comprends rien [zhuh nuh kONprON ryAN]

▸ do you understand? est-ce que vous comprenez ? [eskuh voo kONpruh-nay]

United States (of America)

▸ the United States les États-Unis [layz aytaz-Unee]
▸ I'm from the United States je viens des États-Unis [zhuh vyAN days aytaz-Unee]
▸ I live in the United States j'habite aux États-Unis [zhabeet ohz aytaz-Unee]
▸ have you ever been to the United States? êtes-vous déjà allé aux États-Unis ? [et-voo dayzha alay ohz aytaz-Unee]

unleaded *(gas)* (le) sans plomb [sON plON]

▸ does it take unleaded? est-ce qu'elle marche au sans plomb ? [eskel marsh oh sON plON]
▸ 20 euros worth of unleaded, please vingt euros de sans plomb, s'il vous plaît [vANt uhroh duh sON plON seel voo play]

until jusqu'à [zhUska]

▸ I'm staying until Sunday je reste jusqu'à dimanche [zhuh rest zhhUska deemONsh]
▸ until noon jusqu'à midi [zhUska meedee]

up *(to or in a higher position)* en haut [ON oh] ◆ **up to** jusqu'à [zhUska]

▸ is something up? qu'est-ce qui se passe ? [kes kee suh pas]
▸ what's up? *(what's wrong)* qu'est-ce qu'il y a ? [kes keel ya]; *(as greeting)* quoi de neuf ? [kwa duh nuhf]
▸ up to now jusqu'ici [zhUskee-see]

urgent urgent(e) [UrzhON(UrzhONt)]

▸ it's not urgent ce n'est pas urgent [suh neh paz UrzhON]

urgently en urgence [ON UrzhONs]

▸ I have to see a dentist urgently je dois voir un dentiste de toute urgence [zhuh dwah vwar AN dONteest duh toot UrzhONs]

US(A)

▸ the US les États-Unis [layz aytaz-Unee]
▸ I'm from the US je viens des États-Unis [zhuh vyAN dayz aytaz-Unee]
▸ I live in the US j'habite aux États-Unis [zhabeet ohz aytaz-Unee]

---

saying that you have understood/not understood

▸ oh, I see...! ah d'accord... ! [ah dakor]
▸ sorry, but I didn't understand excusez-moi, mais je n'ai pas compris [ekskU-zay-mwa meh zhuh nay pa kONpree]
▸ I'm a little confused... je suis un peu perdu là... [zhuh sweez AN puh perdU la]
▸ I don't understand your question je n'ai pas compris la question [zhuh nay pa kONpree la kestyON]
▸ sorry, but I still don't understand désolé, mais je ne comprends toujours pas [dayzo-lay meh zhuh nuh kONprON toozhoor pa]

▶ have you ever been to the US? êtes-vous déjà allé aux États-Unis ? [et-voo dayzha alay ohz aytaz-Unee]

use utiliser [Utee-leezay], se servir de [suh serveer duh]

▶ could I use your cellphone? pourrais-je me servir de votre téléphone portable ? [poorehzh muh serveer duh votr taylay-fon portabl]

vacancy la disponibilité [deespo-neebee-leetay]

▶ do you have any vacancies for tonight? avez-vous des chambres libres pour cette nuit ? [avay-voo day shONbr leebr poor set nwee]

vacation les vacances f [vakONs]

▶ are you here on vacation? êtes-vous ici en vacances ? [et-vooz eesee ON vakONs]

▶ I'm on vacation je suis en vacances [zhuh sweez ON vakONs]

valid valable [valabl]

▶ is this ticket valid for the exhibit too? le ticket est valable aussi pour l'exposition ? [luh teekeh eh valabl ohsee poor lekspo-zeesyON]

▶ how long is this ticket valid for? combien de temps ce ticket est-il valable ? [kONbyAN duh tON ticket est-il valable ? [kONbyAN duh tON suh teekeh eht-eel valabl]

▶ my passport is still valid mon passeport est en cours de validité [mON paspor eht ON koor duh valee-deetay]

vegetable le légume [laygUm]

▶ does it come with vegetables? est-ce servi avec des légumes ? [es servee avek day laygUm]

vegetarian (le) végétarien [vayzhay-taryAN], (la) végétarienne [vayzhay-taryen]

▶ I'm a vegetarian je suis végétarien [zhuh swee vayzhay-taryAN]

▶ do you have vegetarian dishes? est-ce que vous avez des plats végétariens ? [eskuh vooz avay day plah vayzhay-taryAN]

vending machine le distributeur [deestree-bUtuhr]

▶ the vending machine isn't working le distributeur ne marche pas [luh deestree-bUtuhr nuh marsh pa]

vertigo le vertige [verteezh]

▶ I suffer from vertigo j'ai le vertige [zhay luh verteezh]

very très [treh]

▶ I'm very hungry j'ai très faim [zhay treh fAN]

▶ very much beaucoup [bohkoo]

▶ very near tout près [too preh]

view *(panorama)* la vue [vU]
> I'd prefer a room with an ocean view je préférerais une chambre avec vue sur la mer [zhuh prayfay-ruhreh Un shONbr avek vU sUr la mehr]

villa la villa [veela]
> we'd like to rent a villa for one week nous voudrions louer une villa pour une semaine [noo voodree-ON lway Un veela poor Un suhmen]

virus le virus [veerUs]
> I must have picked up a virus j'ai certainement attrapé un virus [zhay serten-mONt atra-pay AN veerUs]

visa le visa [veeza]
> do you need a visa? est-ce qu'il faut un visa ? [eskeel foht AN veeza]

visit la visite [veezeet] ♦ visiter [veezee-tay]
> is this your first visit to Paris? c'est votre première visite à Paris ? [seh votr pruhmyehr veezeet a paree]
> I'd like to visit the castle je voudrais visiter le château [zhuh voodreh veezee-tay luh shatoh]

voucher le bon [bON]
> I haven't received the voucher je n'ai pas reçu le bon [zhuh nay pa ruhsU luh bON]

waist la taille [ta-yuh]
> it's a little bit tight at the waist c'est un peu serré à la taille [seht AN puh seray a la ta-yuh]

wait attendre [atONdr]
> have you been waiting long? vous attendez depuis longtemps ? [vooz atON-day duhpwee lONtON]

waiter le garçon (de café) [garsON (duh kafay)]
> waiter, could we have the check, please? garçon, l'addition ! [garsON ladee-syON]

wait for attendre [atOndr]
> I'm waiting for them to call back j'attends qu'on me rappelle [zhatON kON muh rapel]
> don't wait for me ne m'attendez pas [nuh matON-day pa]

waiting room la salle d'attente [sal datONt]
> is there a waiting room on the platform? est-ce qu'il y a une salle d'attente sur le quai ? [eskeel ya Un sal datONt sUr luh keh]

waitress la serveuse [servuhz]
> the waitress has already taken our order la serveuse a déjà pris notre commande [la servuhz a dayzha pree notr komONd]

wake (se) réveiller [(suh) ray-veyay]

▶ could you wake me at 6.45? pourriez-vous me réveiller à six heures quarante-cinq ? [pooryay-voo muh ray-veyay a seez uhr karONt-sANk]

▶ I always wake early je me réveille toujours tôt [zhuh muh rayvey toozhoor toh]

wake up (se) réveiller [(suh) ray-veyay]

▶ a noise woke me up in the middle of the night un bruit m'a réveillé au milieu de la nuit [AN brwee ma ray-veyay oh meelyuh duh la nwee]

▶ I have to wake up very early tomorrow to catch the plane je dois me réveiller très tôt demain pour prendre l'avion [zhuh dwah muh ray-veyay treh toh duhmAN poor prONdr lavyON]

walk la promenade [promnad], la marche [marsh] ♦ (go on foot) marcher [marshay] ♦ (person) raccompagner (à pied) [rakON-panyay (a pyay)]; (distance) faire à pied [fehr a pyay]

▶ are there any interesting walks in the area? y a-t-il des promenades intéressantes à faire dans les environs ? [ee ateel day promnad ANtay-resONt a fehr dON layz ONvee-rON]

▶ let's go for a walk allons faire une promenade [alON fehr Un promnad]

walking boots les chaussures f de marche [shohsUr duh marsh]

▶ do you need walking boots? est-ce qu'il faut avoir des chaussures de marche ? [eskeel foht avwar day shohsUr duh marsh]

wallet le portefeuille [portfoy]

▶ I've lost my wallet j'ai perdu mon portefeuille [zhay perdU mON portfoy]

want (wish, desire) vouloir [voolwar], avoir envie de [avwar ONvee duh]

▶ I don't want to go there je n'ai pas envie d'y aller [zhuh nay paz ONvee dee alay]

warm chaud(e) [shoh(shohd)]

▶ it's warm il fait chaud [eel feh shoh]

▶ take some warm clothing with you prenez des affaires chaudes avec vous [pruhnay dayz afehr shohd avek voo]

wash (se) laver [(suh) lavay]

▶ I need to wash this shirt il faut que je lave cette chemise [eel foh kuh zhuh lav set shuhmeez]

▶ where can I wash my hands? où puis-je me laver les mains ? [oo pweezh muh lavay lay mAN]

watch la montre [mONtr] ♦ (look at) regarder [ruhgar-day]; (guard) surveiller [sUr-veyay]

▶ my watch has been stolen on m'a volé ma montre [ON ma volay ma mONtr]

▶ can you watch my bags for a minute? pouvez-vous surveiller mes affaires une minute ? [poovay-voo sUr-veyay mayz afehr Un meenUt]

water l'eau f [oh]

▶ could I have some water, please? pourriez-vous m'apporter de l'eau, s'il vous plaît ? [pooryay-voo mapor-tay duh loh seel voo play]

- there's no hot water il n'y a pas d'eau chaude [eel nya pa doh shohd]
- can you check the water, please? pouvez-vous vérifier le niveau d'eau ? [poovay-voo vayree-fyay luh neevoh doh]

water ski le ski nautique [skee nohteek]

- can I rent water skis here? est-il possible de louer des skis pour faire du ski nautique ici ? [eht-eel poseebl duh lway day skee poor fehr dU skee nohteek eesee]

water skiing le ski nautique [skee nohteek]

- can I go water skiing anywhere around here? on peut faire du ski nautique dans le coin ? [ON puh fehr dU skee nohteek dON luh kwAN]

wave *(of water)* la vague [vag]

- the waves are very big today les vagues sont très hautes aujourd'hui [lay vag sON treh oht ohzhoor-dwee]

way *(means)* le moyen [mwa-yAN]; *(direction)* la direction [deerek-syON]; *(route, path)* le chemin [shuhmAN]

- what's the best way of getting there? quel est le meilleur chemin pour y aller ? [kel eh luh meyuhr shuhmAN poor ee alay]
- which way is it to the station? quelle est la route de la gare ? [kel eh la root duh la gar]
- I went the wrong way je me suis trompé de direction [zhuh muh swee trONpay duh deerek-syON]
- is this the right way to the cathedral? est-ce le bon chemin pour aller à la cathédrale ? [es luh bON shuhmAN poor alay a la katay-dral]
- on the way en chemin [ON shuhmAN]
- all the way *(push)* à fond [a fON]
- to give way *(on the road)* laisser la priorité [laysay la pree-oree-tay]
- no way! pas question ! [pa kestyON]

way out la sortie [sortee]

- where's the way out? où est la sortie ? [oo eh la sortee]

asking the way

- can you show me where we are on the map? pouvez-vous me montrer sur le plan où nous sommes ? [poovay-voo muh mONtray sUr luh plON oo noo som]
- where is the station/the post office? où est la gare/le bureau de poste ? [oo eh la gar/luh bUroh duh post]
- excuse me, how do you get to Boulevard Saint-Germain? excusez-moi, je cherche le boulevard Saint-Germain [ekskU-zay-mwa zhuh shersh luh boolvar sAN-zhermAN]
- is it far? est-ce loin ? [es lwAN]
- is it within walking distance? peut-on y aller à pied ? [puht-ON ee alay a pyay]

weak *(person)* faible [fehbl]; *(drink)* léger [layzhay], légère [layzhehr]
- I feel very weak je me sens très faible [zhuh muh sON treh fehbl]
- could I have a very weak coffee? pourrais-je avoir un café très léger ? [poorehzh avwar AN kafay treh layzhay]

wear *(piece of clothing, glasses)* porter [portay]
- is what I'm wearing all right? est-ce que ça va, ce que je porte ? [eskuh sa va suh kuh zhuh port]

weather le temps [tON]; *(on the TV, the radio)* la météo [maytay-oh]
- what is the weather like today? quel temps fait-il aujourd'hui ? [kel tON feht-eel ohzhoor-dwee]
- is the weather going to change? est-ce que le temps va changer ? [eskuh luh tON va shONzhay]

weather forecast le (bulletin) météo [(bUltAN) maytay-oh]
- what's the weather forecast for tomorrow? quelles sont les prévisions météo pour demain ? [kel sON lay prayvee-zyON maytay-oh poor duhmAN]

website address l'adresse ƒ de site Internet [adres duh seet ANter-net]
- can you give me your website address? pouvez-vous m'indiquer l'adresse de votre site Internet ? [poovay-voo mANdee-kay ladres duh votr seet ANter-net]

Wednesday mercredi *m* [merkruh-dee]
- we're arriving/leaving on Wednesday nous arrivons/partons mercredi [noo zaree-vON/partON merkruh-dee]

week la semaine [suhmen]
- how much is it for a week? combien coûte une semaine ? [kONbyAN koot Un suhmen]
- I'm leaving in a week's time je repars dans une semaine [zhuh ruhpar dONz Un suhmen]
- two weeks une quinzaine [Un kANzen]

weekly de la semaine [duh la suhmen], hebdomadaire [ebdo-madehr]
- is there a weekly rate? est-ce qu'il y a un tarif à la semaine ? [eskeel ya AN tareef a la suhmen]

welcome
- welcome! bienvenu(e) ! [byANvnu]
- you're welcome *(in reply to thanks)* de rien [duh ryAN]
- you're welcome to join us n'hésitez pas à vous joindre à nous [nayzee-tay paz a voo zhwANdr a noo]

well bien [byAN]
- I'm very well, thank you je vais très bien, merci [zhuh veh treh byAN mersee]
- get well soon! remets-toi vite ! [ruhmeh-twa veet]
- well played bien joué ! [byAN zhway]

well done *(steak)* bien cuit(e) [byAN kwee(kweet)]
- well done, please bien cuit, s'il vous plaît [byAN kwee seel voo play]

what quel(le) [kel], quels [kel], quelles [kel] ♦ quoi [kwa]
- what? *(asking for repetition)* quoi ? [kwa], comment ? [komON]
- what is it? *(what's this thing?)* c'est quoi ? [seh kwa]; *(what's the matter?)* qu'est-ce qu'il y a ? [keskeel ya]
- what's up? *(what's wrong)* qu'est-ce qui se passe ? [keskee suh pas]; *(as greeting)* quoi de neuf ? [kwa duh nuhf]
- what's your name? comment tu t'appelles ? [komON tU tapel]
- what's it called? comment on appelle ça ? [komONt ON apel sa]
- what time is it? quelle heure est-il ? [kel uhr eht-eel]
- what day is it? quel jour sommes-nous ? [kel zhoor som-noo]
- what desserts do you have? qu'est-ce que vous avez comme desserts ? [keskuh vooz avay kom dayser]

wheel la roue [roo]
- could you help me change the wheel? vous pouvez m'aider à changer la roue ? [voo poovay mayday a shONzhay la roo]

when quand [kON]
- when was it built? quand est-ce que ça a été construit ? [kONt eskuh sa a aytay kONstrwee]
- when is the next train to Paris? à quelle heure est le prochain train pour Paris ? [a kel uhr eh luh proshAN trAN poor paree]

where où [oo]
- where do you live? où habitez-vous ? [oo abee-tay-voo]
- where are you from? d'où êtes-vous ? [doo et-voo]
- excuse me, where is the nearest bus stop, please? excusez-moi, où est l'arrêt de bus le plus proche, s'il vous plaît ? [ekskU-zay-mwa oo eh lareh duh bUs luh plU prosh seel voo play]

which quel(le) [kel] ♦ *(in questions)* lequel [luhkel], laquelle [lakel]; *(in relative clauses)* qui [kee], que [kuh]
- which hotel would you recommend for us? quel hôtel nous recommandez-vous ? [kel otel noo ruhko-mONday-voo]
- which way should we go? quelle direction devons-nous prendre ? [kel deerek-syON duhvON-noo prONdr]
- which do you prefer? lequel préfères-tu ? [luhkel prayfehr-tU]
- I can't decide which to have je n'arrive pas à décider lequel je prends [zhuh nareev paz a daysee-day luhkel zhuh prON]

while le moment [momON], quelque temps [kelkuh tON]
- I'm only planning to stay for a while je ne compte rester que quelque temps [zhuh nuh kONt restay kuh kelkuh tON]

white *(in color)* blanc [blON], blanche [blONsh]; *(coffee, tea)* au lait [oh leh]
- two white coffees, please deux cafés au lait, s'il vous plaît [duh kafay oh leh seel voo play]

white wine le vin blanc [vAN blON]
- a glass of white wine, please un verre de vin blanc, s'il vous plaît [AN vehr duh vAN blON seel voo play]

who qui [kee]
- who are you? qui êtes-vous ? [kee et-voo]
- who should I speak to? à qui dois-je m'adresser ? [a kee dwazh madreh-say]
- who's calling? c'est de la part de qui ? [seh duh la par duh kee]

whole tout(e) [too(toot)]
- we spent the whole day walking on a marché toute la journée [ON a marshay toot la zhoornay]
- on the whole we had a good time dans l'ensemble on s'est bien amusés [dON lONsONbl ON seh byAN amU-zay]

whole-wheat complet [kONpleh], complète [kONplet]
- I'd like some whole-wheat bread je voudrais du pain complet [zhuh voodreh dU pAN kONpleh]

why pourquoi [poorkwa]
- why not? pourquoi pas ? [poorkwa pa]

wide *(river, road)* large [larzh]
- 2 meters wide deux mètres de large [duh metr duh larzh]

will
- I'll be arriving at six j'arriverai à six heures [zharee-vuhray a seez uhr]

win *(competition, race)* gagner [ganyay] ◆ *(be ahead)* mener [muhnay]
- who's winning? qui est-ce qui gagne ? [kee es kee ganyuh]

wind le vent [vON]
- it's a westerly wind c'est un vent d'ouest [seht AN vON dwest]

window *(of a building)* la fenêtre [fuhnetr]; *(of a car)* la vitre [veetr], la glace [glas]; *(of a plane)* le hublot [Ubloh]; *(of a store)* la vitrine [veetreen]; *(at a station, in a post office)* le guichet [geesheh]
- I can't open the window je ne peux pas ouvrir la fenêtre [zhuh nuh puh pa oovreer la fuhnetr]
- I'd like to see the dress in the window j'aimerais voir la robe qui est en vitrine [zhehmuh-reh vwar la rob kee eht ON veetreen]

window seat la place côté fenêtre [plas kotay fuhnetr]
- I'd like a window seat if possible je voudrais une place côté fenêtre si possible [zhuh voodreh Un plas kotay fuhnetr see poseebl]

windshield le pare-brise [par-breez]
- could you clean the windshield? pourriez-vous nettoyer le pare-brise ? [pooryay-voo netwa-yay luh par-breez]

wishes and regrets

▶ I hope it won't be too busy j'espère qu'il n'y aura pas trop de monde [zhespehr keel nyohra pa troh duh mONd]

▶ it'd be great if you stayed ça serait vraiment bien que tu restes [sa suhreh vrehmON byAN kuh tU rest]

▶ if only we had a car! si seulement nous avions une voiture ! [see suhlmON nooz avyON Un vwatUr]

▶ unfortunately, we couldn't get there in time malheureusement, nous n'avons pas pu arriver à temps [maluh-ruhzmON noo navON pa pU aree-vay a tON]

▶ I'm really sorry you couldn't make it je regrette vraiment que vous n'ayez pas pu venir [zhuh ruhgret vrehmON kuh voo neyay pa pU vuhneer]

---

windsurfing la planche à voile [plONsh a vwal]

▶ is there anywhere round here I can go windsurfing? est-ce que l'on peut faire de la planche à voile par ici ? [eskuh lON puh fehr duh la plONsh a vwal par eesee]

windy *(day, weather)* venté(e) [vONtay]

▶ it's windy il y a du vent [eel ya dU vON]

wine le vin [vAN]

▶ this wine is not chilled enough ce vin n'est pas assez frais [suh vAN neh paz asay freh]

wine list la carte des vins [kart day vAN]

▶ can we see the wine list, please? pouvons-nous voir la carte des vins, s'il vous plaît ! [poovON-noo vwar la kart day vAN seel voo play]

wish le vœu [vuh] ◆ souhaiter [swaytay]

▶ best wishes! meilleurs vœux ! [meyuhr vuh]

▶ we wish you good luck nous vous souhaitons bonne chance [noo voo swaytON bon shONs]

---

wishing someone something

▶ Happy Birthday! joyeux anniversaire ! [zhwayuhz anee-versehr]

▶ Merry Christmas! joyeux Noël ! [zhwayuh no-el]

▶ Happy New Year! bonne année ! [bon anay]

▶ enjoy your vacation! bonnes vacances ! [bon vakONs]

▶ enjoy your meal! bon appétit ! [bon apay-tee]

▶ good night! bonne nuit ! [bon nwee]

▶ congratulations! félicitations ! [faylee-seeta-syON]

with avec [avek]

▸ I'm with my boyfriend je suis avec mon copain [zhuh sweez avek mON kopAN]

withdraw *(money)* retirer [ruhtee-ray]

▸ I'd like to withdraw 100 euros je voudrais retirer cent euros [zhuh voodreh ruhtee-ray sONt uhroh]

without sans [sON]

▸ a chicken sandwich without mayonnaise un sandwich au poulet sans mayonnaise [AN sONdweesh oh pooleh sON ma-yonehz]

woman la femme [fam]

▸ who is the woman he's with? qui est la femme qui est avec lui ? [kee eh la fam kee eht avek lwee]

wonderful formidable [formee-dabl]

▸ that's wonderful! c'est formidable ! [seh formee-dabl]

▸ the weather was wonderful il a fait un temps magnifique [eel a feh AN tON manyee-feek]

word le mot [moh]

▸ I don't know what the word is in French je ne sais pas quel est le mot en français [zhuh nuh seh pa kel eh luh moh ON frONsay]

▸ I don't understand a word je ne comprends rien [zhuh nuh kONprON ryAN]

work *(employment)* le travail [trava-yuh] ◆ *(do a job)* travailler [trava-yay]; *(function)* marcher [marshay]

▸ to be out of work être sans travail [etr sON trava-yuh]

▸ what do you work as? tu travailles dans quoi ? [tU trava-yuh dON kwa]

▸ I work in marketing je travaille dans le marketing [zhuh trava-yuh dON luh markay-teeng]

▸ the heating isn't working le chauffage ne marche pas [luh shohfazh nuh marsh pa]

▸ how does the shower work? comment marche la douche ? [komON marsh la doosh]

workday le jour ouvrable [zhoor oovrabl]

▸ is tomorrow a workday? est-ce que demain est un jour ouvrable ? [eskuh duhmAN eht AN zhoor oovrabl]

world le monde [mONd]

▸ people from all over the world des gens de toutes origines [day zhON duh tootz oree-zheen]

worried inquiet [ANkyeh], inquiète [ANkyet]

▸ I'm worried about his health je suis inquiet pour sa santé [zhuh sweez ANkyeh poor sa sONtay]

worry s'inquiéter [sANkyay-tay]

▸ don't worry! ne t'inquiète pas ! [nuh tANkyet pa]

worth

▸ it's well worth a visit ça mérite bien une visite [sa mayreet byAN Un veezeet]

▸ what's worth seeing in this town? qu'y a-t-il d'intéressant à voir dans cette ville ? [kee ateel dANtay-resON a vwar dON set veel]

wound la plaie [pleh]

▸ the wound needs to be disinfected il faut désinfecter cette plaie [eel foh dayzAN-fektay set pleh]

wrap (up) emballer [ONba-lay]

▸ can you wrap it (up) for me? pouvez-vous me l'emballer ? [poovay-voo muh lONba-lay]

wrist le poignet [pwanyeh]

▸ I've sprained my wrist je me suis foulé le poignet [zhuh muh swee foolay luh pwanyeh]

write écrire [aykreer]

▸ I have some letters to write j'ai quelques lettres à écrire [zhay kelkuh letr a aykreer]

wrong (incorrect) faux [foh], fausse [fohs]

▸ to be wrong (person) se tromper [suh trONpay]

▸ I'm sorry, but I think you're wrong excusez-moi, mais je crois que vous vous trompez [ekskU-zay-mwa meh zhuh krwah kuh voo voo trONpay]

▸ sorry, I dialed the wrong number excusez-moi, j'ai fait un faux numéro [ekskU-zay-mwa zhay feh AN foh nUmay-roh]

▸ you've got the wrong number vous avez fait un faux numéro [vooz avay feht AN foh nUmay-roh]

▸ you've taken the wrong road tu t'es trompé de route [tU teh trONpay duh root]

▸ this is the wrong train c'est le mauvais train [seh luh mohveh trAN]

▸ what's wrong? qu'est-ce qui ne va pas ? [keskee nuh va pa]

▸ there's something wrong with the switch cet interrupteur a quelque chose qui ne va pas [set ANteh-rUptuhr a kelkuh shohz kee nuh va pa]

▸ there's something wrong with my elbow j'ai quelque chose au coude [zhay kelkuh shohz oh kood]

X-ray la radio [radyoh]

▸ do you think I should have an X-ray? croyez-vous que je doive passer une radio ? [krwa-yay-voo kuh zhuh dwav pasay Un radyoh]

year l'année f [anay], l'an m [on]

▸ we came here last year nous sommes venus l'année dernière [noo som vuhnU lanay dernyehr]

▸ I'm 21 years old j'ai vingt-et-un ans [zhay vANt-ay-AN ON]

yellow jaune [zhohn]

▸ the yellow one le jaune [luh zhohn], la jaune [la zhohn]

Yellow Pages®

▸ the Yellow Pages® les Pages jaunes® f [lay pazh zhohn]

yes *(in agreement)* oui [wee]; *(in disagreement)* si [see]

▸ yes, please oui, s'il vous plaît [wee seel voo play]

▸ it doesn't matter – yes it does! ce n'est pas grave – si, c'est grave ! [suh neh pa grav – see seh grav]

yet encore [ONkor]

▸ I've not been there yet je ne suis pas encore allé là-bas [zhuh nuh swee paz ONkor alay la-bah]

yogurt le yaourt [ya-oort]

▸ do you have any natural yogurt? y a-t-il des yaourts nature ? [ee ateel day ya-oort natUr]

young man le garçon [garsON], le jeune homme [zhuhn om]

▸ who is that young man? qui est ce jeune homme ? [kee eh suh zhuhn om]

young person jeune [zhuhn]

▸ are there any discounts for young people? est-ce qu'il y a des réductions pour les jeunes ? [eskeel ya day raydUk-syON poor lay zhuhn]

young woman la jeune fille [zhuhn feey], la jeune femme [zhuhn fam]

▸ who is the young woman he's with? qui est la jeune fille qui est avec lui ? [kee eh la zhuhn feey kee eht avek lwee]

youth hostel l'auberge f de jeunesse [ohberzh duh zhuhnes]

▸ I'd like to book two beds for three nights in a youth hostel j'aimerais réserver deux lits pour trois nuits en auberge de jeunesse [zhemuh-reh rayzer-vay duh lee poor trwah nwee ON ohberzh duh zhuhnes]

▸ do you have to have a youth hostel card? est-ce qu'il faut avoir la carte de membre des auberges de jeunesse ? [eskeel foht avvar la kart duh mONbr dayz ohberzh duh zhuhnes]

zone la zone [zon]

▸ a ticket for zones 1 and 2, please un ticket pour les zones un et deux, s'il vous plaît [AN teekeh poor lay zon AN ay duh seel voo play]

French language
and culture

French around the world: who speaks it and where?

French is spoken as their first or official language by over 200 million people around the world. It is spoken by the 60.5 million inhabitants of the mainland territory of France (*la France métropolitaine*) and in the overseas territories administered by France. These are the *départements d'outre-mer* or *DOM*, consisting of Guadeloupe, Martinique, French Guiana, and Reunion, and the *territoires d'outre-mer* or *TOM*, consisting essentially of New Caledonia, French Polynesia, the Wallis and Futuna Islands – and the St Pierre and Miquelon islands off the coast of Newfoundland.

French is the official language of part of Switzerland, part of Belgium, and of Haiti and Luxembourg. It is also widely spoken, whether as the official language or not, in a number of African countries with which France has historical links through colonialism. Amongst these are Algeria, Tunisia, Morocco, Cameroon, Côte d'Ivoire (Ivory Coast), Mali, Senegal, Congo, Chad, and Burkino Faso.

French in North America

And then of course, much closer to home, French is the joint official language of Canada, with around 5.5 million speakers. In addition, a now antiquated form of French survives among the Cajun communities in parts of Louisiana and, more widely across the south of the US, in the form of *Creole*, which dates back to the time when a large area of the south of the US was colonized by the French. The Cajuns are the descendants of French people who settled in the Canadian province of Nova Scotia, then called Acadia, in the 17th century and who were subsequently deported to Louisiana. Originally called Acadians, the name has, through day-to-day oral use become Cajun over the years. French has survived for these people as part of a rich oral and musical culture as well as a style of cooking renowned thoughout the US. In recent years there has been a growing movement to preserve the language and the teaching of French is now considered a priority in Cajun communities.

Where did the French language come from?

Early beginnings

Like Italian and Spanish, French as it exists today developed essentially out of Latin. This came about through the extraordinary influence that the Romans came to have in the Western world and in particular in Europe as we now know it. The city of Rome was founded by the Etruscans in 753 BC. Over the next 1000 years, in war after war and conquest after conquest, the Romans, effectively the peoples of central Italy, first took under their power almost all of Italy, and the islands of Corsica, Sardinia, and Sicily. Between 200 and 146 BC, in an astonishing series of advances, they conquered Spain and Portugal, much of North Africa, Greece, Macedonia, and Turkey. They then went on to take possession of Syria and Cyprus and then around 60 BC began their advance up through the province they named Gaule – *Gallia* in Latin and roughly speaking equivalent to modern-day France. They also took control of the countries that are now Belgium and Switzerland as well as a fair bit of Germany. In 55 BC, they landed in England and only finally came to a halt just short of what is now Scotland, apparently discouraged in their advance by the weather, the wild landscape, and the ferocity of the inhabitants!

The spread of Latin

By the year 200 AD the Roman Empire stretched from Britain to Egypt and Asia Minor. Such a vast dominion demanded a highly organized administration. In this the Romans proved to be extremely talented and language was a vital tool in their control of their subjects. They did not actually impose Latin on their conquered subjects but rather simply ignored the existence of what they considered to be barbaric tongues. The result was that nobody could advance in the societies of the subjugated territories without speaking Latin. Latin was the language of commerce, of finance, and of the army, into which hundreds of thousands of people were conscripted. In addition, in a clever move, Romans who had served the Empire well were rewarded by being granted vast tracts of land in the conquered provinces, and in this way Latin was taken out into the most rural areas.

In France, the Romans set to building extensive road and waterway systems, making for thriving routes of trade and commerce and by the 5th century, Latin was the language spoken throughout the country. Almost all of the ancient Celtic tongues had disappeared from Europe. Exceptions were made for a few linguistic communities, in exchange for services in defence of the Empire, and this explains the survival to the present day of the Welsh, Breton and Basque languages. The Celtic tongues of Scotland and Ireland had escaped the Roman conquest.

Movements of change

However, the Latin that was spoken in the Roman provinces soon started to move away slowly but very surely from the classical Latin spoken in Rome. Through contact with the various peoples and the influences that individual environments and cultures have on language, a variety of languages loosely resembling Latin began to emerge. The further away from Rome you were, the less your language remained close to Latin. So it was that French and even more so English moved much further away from Latin than did Italian or Spanish for example – and this remains the case to the present day with Italian being much closer to classical Latin than is French. So in Italian the Latin **pater** (*father*), **mater** (*mother*), **panis** (*bread*) and **vinum** (*wine*) become **padre, madre, pane** and **vino** while French moves further but still recognizably to **père, mère, pain** and **vin**.

Romance

As time went on, the Romans began to lose interest in the northern outposts of their empire and increasingly handed over military control to mercenaries from the countries east of France The 4th and 5th centuries saw vast movements of peoples all over Europe and in particular invasion after invasion of tribes from Germany and Eastern Europe, invasions that contributed a great deal to making the Europe we know today. The Angles and the Saxons established themselves in Britain, the former giving their name to England, in French more directly **Angleterre**. The Francs took northern France and Germany, eventually giving **France** its name and the language **français** (*French*), while the Burgundians established the kingdom of Burgundy in east central France. People began to speak a language that was no longer Latin but not yet French or Italian etc. This was the language we call Romance, in French **roman**, and French, Spanish, Portuguese, Italian, Catalan, Occitan, and Romanian are all derived from it. This language had a near infinite number of variants according to region. We still refer to this family of languages as the **Romance languages**.

In the north, the Germanic language of the Francs dominated all others. English is considered to be a Germanic language with basic words like *man* and *house* and *garden* coming straight from Germanic. And although French is a Romance language, many words in French show the influence of Germanic, for example the colors **bleu** (*blue*), modern German *blau*, **gris** (*gray*), German *grau*, and **brun** (*brown*), German *braun*. And **est**, **ouest**, **nord** and **sud** (*east, west, north, and south*) came in from the English Germanic in the 12th century.

The languages of France

Meanwhile in France, Hugues Capet in the 10th century was the first king to speak the Romance vernacular, the language of the common people. But he controlled only a tiny area around Paris. In the rest of the country, any number of local languages or **patois** were spoken. This situation prevailed among rural communities until well into the 19th century. Indeed, it was only with the move to universal education that French became standardized. Today, most **patois** have died out or are in the process of doing so, although in many areas moves are afoot to try to keep them alive. In many cases, this is a difficult task as the **patois** have virtually no existence other than as oral languages passed down from generation to generation.

Gradually, the languages of France began to fall into three broad groups, the **langue d'oïl**, the language spoken in the *Ile de France* – the area around Paris, the **langues d'oc** in the southwest and the **langues franco-provençales** – in the southeast. The first of these incorporated a good deal of Germanic influence, while the others remained much closer to Latin.

The spread of French

It was not until the reign of Louis IX in the 13th century that **le français** (*French*) replaced the other **langues d'oïl** and, as Louis became the most powerful monarch in Europe, replaced most of the other languages as well. Nonetheless, because of the immense power of the Roman Catholic Church, Latin remained the international language of communication in Europe, though after the invasion of England by the Norman William the Conqueror in 1066, communication between England and France was conducted in French. French remained the language of the English parliament in London until 1363. Indeed it has been suggested that if the English had not finally lost the Hundred Years' War and become very patriotic as a result, French might well have remained the principal language of England and the language the English took to the future United States of America and elsewhere!

It was the prestige of Latin among the tiny minority of learned people and grammarians that caused the spoken and written languages to move away from each other and led to **Richelieu** setting up the **Académie française** in 1635, effectively as a language watchdog, a role it continues to play to this day. In some respects it has traditionally put a brake on the spontaneous growth and development that has been – and continues to be – such a notable feature of the English language. But it has not always been as successful in this as it would have liked to be! And it was inevitable that the 18th century, the Age of the Enlightenment, the flowering of science and reason, brought to French, as it did to the other major European languages a veritable explosion of terms from Greek and Latin, from **technologie** and **biographie** to **nationalisme**.

French and patois

French slowly became the language of official publications throughout France but right through to the 19th century, was the language of only a tiny minority of the people. In towns and villages all over the land, the local **patois** was the language of church and school. In the 17th century, an expert in rural languages listed 636 **patois** in France. Astonishingly, French was more widely spoken in North America, England, Holland and Moscow than it was in France itself!

With the Revolution in 1789, things changed dramatically. French was imposed everywhere in a series of decrees and the war on **patois** began. However, for lack of educational resources, the many regional languages survived nonetheless and indeed under Napoleon flourished once more. France also became discredited in the wider world due to Napoleon's imperialism. And the influence of French in the US waned greatly after Napoleon sold Louisiana to the United States for $15 million in 1803. At the time Louisiana was an immense territory that included present-day Louisiana, Arkansas, Missouri, Iowa, North Dakota, Texas, South Dakota, New Mexico, Nebraska, Kansas, Wyoming, Minnesota, Oklahoma, Colorado and Montana.

By the middle of the 19th century most people in France spoke French, even if a great many continued to speak **patois** in the family. In 1882, the great social reformer **Jules Ferry** made primary education (in French) free and obligatory for all and French was thus imposed nation-wide.

Nowadays, the various **patois** are dying out, though there are increasing efforts to keep them alive. However, the more widely spoken and distinctive languages such as Basque, Breton, Catalan, and Occitan are on the whole flourishing. It seems that the minority tongues of France have finally succeeded in casting off the stigma so long attached to them.

The influence of French on English

The prestige of French

French was officially the language of international diplomacy from 1714 until the First World War (1914 – 1918) and it is perhaps, to some extent at least, because of this that it has gone through phases of being very fashionable among certain classes of English speaker. It is as if it has retained into the present day the gloss of glamor and sophistication it acquired as the language of the elite of Europe for centuries. In the 20th century, particularly the first half, it was considered sophisticated among a certain class of people, in both Britain and the US to drop French words and phrases into one's conversation and many of these are now virtually clichés and often have no exact equivalent in English: **double-entendre** (*inuendo*), **tête-à-tête**, (*private conversation between two people*), **rendez-vous** (*date, arrangement to meet*), **femme fatale**…! Which just goes to show that the reputation of French as the language of seduction **par excellence** may not be entirely undeserved – *seduction* itself of course being a French import – in word if not in deed!

Diplomacy and the arts

French has retained its prestige in diplomacy and international politics, giving us **coup d'état**, **agent provocateur**, **attaché**, **chargé d'affaires** but there is little doubt that the areas it has contributed most to are the arts, fashion – and above all, food and cooking or, as we say, **cuisine**. In the arts we have the 1930s fashion **art déco**, while oddly **art nouveau** is a purely Anglo-Saxon coinage – and a good example of it being more **chic** to give something a French name (the French call *art nouveau modern style* – in English). Then there are **genre** and **film noir** and **matinée** and a good many more.

Fashion

In the field of **haute couture** (*high fashion*: though *couture* really just means *sewing* or *dressmaking*) we have **décolleté** (*a low neckline*), **démodé** (*out of fashion*), **eau de toilette**, **blouson** and amusingly enough, although the French ages ago stole **le blue jean** from American, they gave the US *denim*, which goes back to the early French settlers in the US in the 17th century. These settlers took with them the stout fabric made in the southern French manufacturing town of Nîmes called **serge de Nîmes**, subsequently (**serge**) **denim**.

Note that **un jean** is a singular in French. In the same way, we say *pants* and *pyjamas* in the plural while the French say **un pantalon** and **un pyjama**.

Food

When it comes to food, the list of French terms used in English is just about endless – from the **maître d('hôtel)**, to **apéritif** and **hors d'oeuvres.** However, the Anglo-Saxons have oddly taken in **entrée**, the French for starter, to mean main dish. You may decide to eat **à la carte**, *carte* being French for the menu itself and **menu** being a semi-false friend, meaning in fact a fixed-price menu. The French reputation for gastronomy has influenced at least every country in the Western Hemisphere and a good many others farther afield. We have **purée**, **gratin**, **béchamel**, **crème**, **pâté**, **terrine**, **crêpe**, **croissant**, **brioche**, **baguette** and so more or less *ad infinitum*.

English borrowings in French

If it seems that Anglo-Saxon cultures have taken a great deal from French, the trade in the other direction has also flourished, especially in recent times. The major linguistic influences have come through the Anglo-Saxon film industry, popular music – and of course in recent times, the huge impact of computer technology and the internet.

The **Académie française** is a learned body made up of 40 life members. It is considered a very great honor to be elected as one of its members. It is nowadays best known for its role in attempting to control the French language and particularly what is seen as the pernicious invasion of anglicisms. The **Académie** makes rulings on what it considers to be correct and accepted usage but these rulings are not always taken terribly seriously. State supported radio and television channels are theoretically supposed to observe 'correct' usage but even there this is far from strictly observed.

Everyday English

In many contexts the use of anglicisms is thought to give a trendy, up-beat turn to current discourse. In the world of work, **meeting**, **manager**, **management**, **feedback**, **marketing**, **telemarketing**, **business**, **brainstorming**, **leadership**, **timing** are in everyday use, while sports enthusiasts – and commentators – will happily use **fan**, **supporter**, **match** and **hooligan**. Then when it comes to anything to do with computers, just about anything goes, for example **chat**, also written **tchat** and even **tchatche**, giving the verb **tchatcher**! Then there are **blog** and **cookie** and **on-line**, **off-line**, **login** all the way to **bug** (or **bogue** in its frenchified form, giving the verb **déboguer**).

More generally, other frequently used borrowings are **week-end** (with a hyphen), **shuttle**, **barman**, **cowboy**, **gangster**, **dealer**, **gay**, **zoom**, **flash-back**. When it comes to food, you can have **un hot-dog**, **un hamburger**, **un sandwich**, or **un steak**, with or without **le ketchup** – and washed down, if you like, with **un Coca**.

Some odd borrowings!

But perhaps the most interesting thing about English borrowings or anglicisms is that they very often don't quite arrive in French in exactly the same way as they left English. So in French **le jogging** is not an activity but a *tracksuit*, the activity being **le footing**. Then **un smoking** is a *tuxedo*, and though a **T-shirt** will be instantly recognizable wherever you find it, you might have trouble with **le**

sweat, especially in spoken French, as it's pronounced *sweet* but is used to mean *sweatshirt*. Then again there is the vexed question of **le slip**, not at all a slinky petticoat but just plain *underpants* or *panties*. And just why *foosball* should be called **baby-foot** in French is anybody's guess.

You'll have no problem with knowing what **fast food** is but you might be surprised if somebody invites you to meet them in one: it's also used to mean a *fast food restaurant*. People use **look** a lot – but only in the sense of the way you look, so **elle a un look très sexy** or the way somebody's apartment looks: **un look plutôt design**. Thus, **design** is used as an adjective in more or less the same way as we might use *designer*. Then you might go to a **concert en live** and find it really **cool**. You can use **cool** in just about the same way as in English. In fact, **c'est un must**!

The French seem to have the feeling that using words ending in **-ing** is particularly Anglo-American, so lots of imports end up like this even though they're not used in that way in English: a **parking** is a *parking lot*, a **camping** is a *campground* (and a **camping-car** is a *camper*), a **mailing** is a *mail shot*, a **peeling** is a *chemical peel* – and, believe it or not, a **brushing** is a *blowdry*. Talking about feeling, if you do something **au feeling** you do it the way your intuitions tell you: **c'est une question de feeling**! Paradoxically, however, the French have adopted **happy end** rather than *happy ending*!

As far as music goes, just about anything goes: **le jazz**, **le rock**, **le rap**, **un rappeur**. In sport **le foot** is *football* but this is always taken to mean *soccer*, so for American football you need to specify **le football américain**. Finally, the world of stars and celebrities is **le people**, a celebrity scandal magazine is **un magazine people** and you can even hear it said that somebody is **un people**. But possibly the oddest anglicism around is **speakerine** for a female TV presenter!

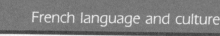

False friends and true friends

Although French is a Romance language and English essentially a Germanic one, there is nonetheless a good deal of common stock, due mainly to both languages having derived words from Latin or Greek or else from one having taken a word from the other. However, it quite frequently happens that a word's meaning develops differently in the two languages – or even that a different meaning has been adopted from French. So two words that look the same or similar may not mean the same at all. Linguists call these pairs *false cognates* but they are more commonly known as *false friends*. These need to be watched: it's just as well to know that **gasoil** is *diesel fuel* and not *gasoline*, that a person who is **sensible** is *sensitive* rather than *sensible* and that one who is **sympathique** is *nice* but not necessarily *sympathetic*! Then again, if you lose your **agenda** you've only lost your *diary*, not your grip on life. Here is a list of some of the most common false friends followed by what they in fact mean in French:

actuel	*present, current*
assister	*to attend, to be present*
attendre	*to wait*
avertissement	*warning*
blesser	*to wound*
car	*coach*
chair	*flesh*
coin	*corner*
complet	*full*
demander	*to ask (for)*
eventuellement	*if need be*
formidable	*great, terrific*
librairie	*bookstore*
quitter	*to leave*
raisin	*grapes*
rester	*to stay*
robe	*dress*
veste	*jacket*

It is however, fortunate for English speakers learning French that friends are more often true than false. Here are just a very few of the many 'true' friends that do mean what you'd think they mean:

absence, absent, accident, accusation, biscuit, budget, cause, certificat, client, couleur, international, machine, miracle, musique, national, piano, public, secret, signature, village, violon, visite.

Influences of French culture in the US

C'est si chic!

The French are extremely proud of their culture, some might even think positively arrogant on occasion! However, there is no doubt about the fact that we owe a good deal to them. Again, there is an undeniable notion of French style – in a variety of areas. The idea of high fashion, **haute couture**, originated in France and still carries tremendous prestige. It was, however, an Englishman who started it all. Charles Worth moved from London to Paris and in 1857 set up a fashion house in a neighborhood then not at all fashionable but that has now become the center of the fashion industry. He was the first **couturier** to show his seasonal collections on live models, thus setting off the cat-walk craze known all over the world today. Names like Paul Poiret, Coco Chanel, Christian Dior, and Yves Saint Laurent have taken on legendary status in the world of high fashion.

French taste has also been highly influential in architecture and interior design as can be seen from just about any glossy lifestyle magazine. It goes from the intricate carving and elegant, graceful forms of antique and reproduction French style chairs, sofas and mirrors to the much more rustic 'provençal' styles of furniture, artifacts, fabrics and cooking utensils that are so popular everywhere today.

The art world

Then again there is the world of art, where French influence has been immeasurable. Although France has a noble history in all the arts, it is perhaps the painting and sculpture of the late 19th century and the 20th century that is familiar to just about everybody in the Western world. The Impressionist, Post-Impressionist, and Fauvist movements are associated with such painters as Monet, Manet, Renoir, Degas, van Gogh, Cézanne, and Matisse, all of them household names today and familiar from the reproductions to be found everywhere, as well as from exhibits throughout the world of course. Pablo Picasso, probably the most famous artist of the 20th century, though Spanish by birth, spent most of his long and intensely productive life in France.

Music

France has also given birth to a number of great composers and musicians from Rameau and Lully to Bizet, Berlioz and Debussy, though it would perhaps be true to say that its heritage in this respect is less illustrious than that of say Germany or Italy. The later years of the 19th century and the early years of the 20th, the era known as *La Belle Epoque* was the grand age of vaudeville and the tremendously popular operettas of Offenbach. Out of this a tradition of popular music has continued, with legendary performers such as Edith Piaf, Georges Brassens, Jacques Brel (who was Belgian), Juliette Gréco and Serge Gainsbourg, to mention but a tiny handful, achieving international acclaim.

Cuisine

The French take great pride in their **cuisine** and in turn it has been prized above any other all over the Western world. A great many of the Western world's grandest and most prestigious restaurants boast French cuisine, and French cooking schools and courses are everywhere to be found. Then of course there is wine. Many of the varieties of grape grown in the US came originally from France, where wine has been made from earliest times. However, the trade has not always been only one way: when the French vine stock was devastated in the late 19th century by the disease phylloxera, which originated in the US, the situation was saved by grafting onto vines imported from the US, as these were naturally resistant to the disease.

Life and language in France today

The French continue to be justifiably proud of their culture and lifestyle and to play an active part in these. Cinema is very popular and of course huge numbers of American movies are screened, very often dubbed into French, though in 'art cinemas' you can often see them in the original language (**en version original** or **VO**). However, France has its own very thriving film industry and of course hosts the celebrated Cannes Film Festival every year.

Outdoor pursuits

France is a very beautiful country with plenty of stunning countryside. People tend to take advantage of this and walking, cycling, and skiing are particularly popular outdoor activities. One of the great national events of the year is the **Tour de France**, a three-week cycle race that covers around 3,000 miles and is renowned for its very tough mountain stages. The national pastime is undoubtedly **boules**, also known as **pétanque**. This is a game played between two teams with metal balls or **boules** and the idea is to get your ball as close as possible to the jack – **le cochonet**. The game is played by all ages, especially after large family lunches on Sundays. However, you can also generally see groups of elderly men playing almost any summer afternoon in just about every town and village in France. Soccer is extremely popular and enthusiastically supported, as is rugby in some areas. American football and baseball are, however, pretty much unknown.

Politics

French people tend to be more actively politically engaged than Americans. Trade unions are very active and strikes are common, especially those involving public transportation. There is a strong tradition of public protest that has its roots in the Revolution and in the near legendary status that the **Commune** of 1871 has in people's minds. This was a popular insurrection in Paris that was brutally put down. It was to some extent re-enacted in the student demonstrations and riots of May 1968 as a protest against the government of the day and the colonial war in Algeria. It is still very common for people to take to the streets to protest against proposed legislation and for even high school students to go on strike or stage sit-ins. Government tends to take more note of popular protest than is the case in many other countries.

Gastronomy

Food and wine of course play a big part in national life. Big family meals on Sundays are still a thriving tradition and celebrations of special occasions can involve meals that stretch on through the day with much conviviality. Generally speaking the French love parties – and eating and drinking. Agriculture remains a central part of the economy and each region has dozens of local food specialities. General de Gaulle, president of France in the 1960s famously mused aloud about how it could be possible to govern a country that boasted 258 varieties of cheese! And then of course the wine is renowned and appreciated throughout the world. Markets are a great feature of everyday life and there are few things more appetizing and colorful than a bustling street market full of stalls stacked with local produce.

Social life

Young people tend to grow up more closely involved with their families than is perhaps generally the case in the US. But there is nonetheless a strong youth culture surrounding sports activities, computer games, the Internet – and of course going out on weekends. Bars and cafés are to be found at every turn and some tend to be patronized particularly by young people. Groups of young people will often meet up on weekends for a meal or a few drinks and then go on to a club or disco (**sortir en boîte**). Much as in the US, most people tend to socialize through school, college, sports activities or work. Dress is informal and jeans (**le jean**) just about universal. Restaurants and clubs do not tend to have strict dress codes and even in really sophisticated places, you will see people dressed casually in jeans and a sweater. One thing is common to young and old alike and wherever you go in France. If you meet someone you know only distantly, you will always shake hands and when you meet (or leave) someone you know well, there will be the ritual of kissing on the cheek. The number of times varies according to region but once on each cheek is the minimum and the count can go up to four times! Children are taught this ritual from the youngest age and the parental instruction **dis bonjour!** is to remind the child that kissing is called for.

Informal French

The Internet has greatly influenced informal chat among young people and conversation is often full of English computer terms. It is also trendy (**branché**) to use abbreviated forms of words and these appear all the time: **ordi** for **ordinateur** (*computer*), **perso** for **personnel**: **mon adresse perso** (*my personal email address*), **pub** for **publicité** (*advertisement*), **appart** for **appartement**, **sympa** for **sympathique** (*nice*) and **les infos** for **les informations** (*news*). Another current trend is to transform words into a form ending in **-os**: **matos** for **matériel** (*equipment, gear*), **coolos** for **cool** and **débilos** for **débile** (*stupid*). Equally popular is **-oche** as in **cinoche** for **cinéma** and **cantoche** for **cantine**. And there are plenty of other slang words that are in everyday use: **flic** instead of **policier** for *policeman*, **bagnole** instead of **voiture** for *automobile*, **fringues** or **fripes** instead of **vêtements** for *clothes* and **frangin** and **frangine** for your *brother* and *sister* rather than the standard **frère** and **soeur**.

But perhaps the most fascinating form of French slang is one that has been around for decades and is tremendously popular with young people. This is **verlan** which is, in terms of the spoken syllables, **l'envers** backwards and *backwards* is exactly this is what **l'envers** means. Examples of this endlessly inventive phomenon are **zarbi** for **bizarre**, **tromé** for **métro** (*subway*), **auche** for **chaud** (*hot*), **laisse béton** for **laisse tomber** (*drop it*) and of course... **céfran** for **français**!

Finally the informal way of saying both *hi!* and *goodbye!* is **salut!** but people increasingly use the Italian **ciao** for goodbye, as well as **à plus**, short for **à plus tard** and **à toute**, short for **à tout à l'heure**, both meaning *see you later*. Knowing a few informal words can go a long way towards making you feel at ease in social situations.

French–English dictionary

a

à [a] *prep* ▸ aller à Paris to go to Paris ▸ être à Paris to be in Paris ▸ aller à la gare to go to the station ▸ à deux km 2 km away ▸ je vais à Paris/à la gare I'm going to Paris/to the station ▸ à trois heures at 3 o'clock

abbaye [abeh-yee] *f* abbey

abeille [abey] *f* bee

abîmé, e [abee-may] *adj* damaged

abonnement [abon-mON] *m* subscription; season ticket

abord [abor] ▸ d'abord first (of all)

abordable [abor-dabl] *adj* affordable

absent, e [absON(absONt)] *adj (person)* absent; *(thing)* missing

absolument [abso-lUmON] *adv* absolutely ▸ absolument pas absolutely not ▸ absolument rien absolutely nothing

abus [abU] *m* misuse ▸ 'en cas de danger, tirer la sonnette. Tout abus sera puni' 'in case of emergency, pull cord. Any misuse will be prosecuted'

accepter [aksep-tay] *v* to accept

accès [akseh] *m* access ▸ 'accès réservé aux voyageurs munis de billets' 'ticket-holders only'

accessible [akseh-seebl] *adj* accessible

accident [aksee-dON] *m* accident

accompagner [akON-panyay] *v* to go with; to come with ▸ accompagner quelqu'un en voiture to take somebody by car

accord [akor] *m* ▸ d'accord OK ▸ je suis d'accord I agree

accueil [akoy] *m* welcome, reception desk

accueillant, e [akoy-ON(-ONt)] *adj* welcoming

accusé [akU-zay] *m* ▸ accusé de réception acknowledgement of receipt

acheter [ashtay] *v* to buy

adaptateur [adap-tatuhr] *m* adaptor

addition [adee-syON] *f* check; addition

admis, e [admee(z)] *adj* admitted ▸ 'les chiens ne sont pas admis' 'no dogs allowed'

admission [admee-syON] *f* admission ▸ 'admissions' *(hospital)* 'admissions'

adolescent, e [adoleh-sON(-sONt)] *m,f* teenager

adorer [ado-ray] *v* to love

adresse [adres] *f* address ▸ adresse e-mail e-mail address

adulte [adUlt] *mf & adj* adult

aéroport [a-ayro-por] *m* airport

affaires [afehr] *fpl (commerce)* business; *(personal)* things ▸ affaires de toilette toiletries

affiche [afeesh] *f* poster

âge [azh] *m* age ▸ quel âge as-tu ? how old are you?

agence [azhONs] *f* agency; *(of bank, company)* branch ▸ agence de voyages travel agency

aggraver [agra-vay] ◆ **s'aggraver** *v* to get worse

agréable [agray-abl] *adj* nice

agresser [agreh-say] *v* to attack

aide [ed] *f* help

aider [ayday] *v* to help

ailleurs [a-yuhr] *adv* somewhere else ▸ d'ailleurs by the way

aimer [aymay] *v* to like; to love ▸ j'aimerais I'd like

air [ehr] *m* air ▸ en plein air outside ▸ avoir l'air... to look...

alcool [alkol] *m* alcohol ▸ alcool à 90 rubbing alcohol

algues [alg] *fpl* seaweed

alimentation [alee-mONta-syON] *f* food; grocery store

aller [alay] *v* to go ◆ *m* outward journey ◆ **s'en aller** *v* to go (away) ▸ comment allez-vous ? how are you? ▸ je vais bien I'm very well ▸ ça va ? how are you? ▸ ça va I'm fine ▸ ça vous va ? does that suit you? ▸ ça vous va bien it really suits you ▸ un aller (simple) a one-way (ticket)

allergique [aler-zheek] *adj* allergic

aller-retour [alay-ruhtoor] *m* round-trip (ticket)

allô [aloh] *excl (on phone)* hello

allumer [alU-may] *v (fire, cigarette)* to light; *(light)* to switch on

allumette [alU-met] *f* match ▸ une boîte d'allumettes a box of matches

alors [alor] *adv* so; then

ambassade [ONba-sad] *f* embassy

ambiance [ONbyONs] *f* atmosphere

ambulance [ON-bUIONs] *f* ambulance

amende [amONd] *f* fine

amener [amnay] *v* to bring

américain, e [amay-reekAN(-reeken)] *adj* American ◆ **américain** *m (language)* American English

Américain, e [amay-reekAN(-reeken)] *m,f* American

ami, e [amee] *m,f* friend

amour [amoor] *m* love

ampoule [ONpool] *f (electric)* (light) bulb; *(on skin)* blister

amusant, e [amU-zON(-zONt)] *adj* funny

amuser [amU-zay] ◆ **s'amuser** *v* to enjoy oneself

an [ON] *m* year ▸ j'ai vingt-deux ans I'm 22 (years old)

analgésique [anal-zhayzeek] *m* painkiller

ancien, enne [ONsyAN(ONsyen)] *adj* old; former

anesthésie [anes-tayzee] *f* anesthetic

angine [ONzheen] *f* sore throat

anglais, e [ONglay(ONglez)] *adj* English

apéritif

The French take their time over the *apéro*, whether in a bar with friends or with guests at home. As well as wine and beer, popular *apéritifs* are *Ricard* or *Pastis* (aniseed-flavored liqueur) and *kir* (white wine with blackcurrant liqueur). If you'd prefer something a little more up-market, opt for a *kir royal* which is made with champagne. The accompanying snacks, *amuse-bouches* or *amuse-gueules* range from olives, chips and peanuts to more gastronomic delights.

◆ **anglais** *m (language)* English

Anglais, e [ONglay(ONglez)] *m,f* English person

Angleterre [ONgluh-tehr] *f* England

animal [anee-mal] *m* animal

animé, e [anee-may] *adj (place)* lively

année [anay] *f* year ▸ bonne année ! Happy New Year!

anniversaire [anee-versehr] *m* birthday; anniversary ▸ bon anniversaire ! happy birthday! ▸ anniversaire de mariage wedding anniversary

annonce [anONs] *f* announcement

annuaire [anU-ehr] *m* directory ▸ annuaire (téléphonique) telephone directory

annuler [anU-lay] *v* to cancel

antibiotique [ONtee-byoteek] *m* antibiotic

antiquités [ONtee-keetay] *fpl* antiques

août [oot] *m* August

apéritif [apay-reeteef] *m* aperitif ▸ prendre l'apéritif to have a drink before lunch/dinner

appareil [apa-rey] *m* ▸ qui est à l'appareil ? who's calling? ▸ appareil photo camera

appartement [apar-tuhmON] *m* apartment

appartenir [apar-tuhneer] *v* ▸ appartenir à to belong to

appel [apel] *m* (telephone) call

appeler [aplay] *v* to call ◆ **s'appeler** *v* to be called ▸ je m'appelle... my name is...

appendicite [apON-deeseet] *f* appendicitis

appétit [apay-tee] *m* ▸ bon appétit ! enjoy your meal!

appoint [apwAN] *m* change ▸ 'veuillez faire l'appoint' 'exact change only'

apporter [apor-tay] *v* to bring

apprendre [aprONdr] *v* to learn; *(news)* to hear

appuyer [apwee-yay] *v* to press ▸ appuyer sur quelque chose to press (on) something

après [apreh] *prep* after

après-demain [apreh-duhmAN] *adv* the day after tomorrow

après-midi [apreh-meedee] *m* afternoon

araignée [aren-yay] *f* spider

arbre [arbr] *m* tree

argent [arzhON] *m* money

arnaque [arnak] *f* rip-off

arrêt [areh] *m* stop ▸ sans arrêt continuously ▸ train sans arrêt non-stop train ▸ arrêt de bus bus stop ▸ 'arrêt demandé' 'stop requested' ▸ 'ce train ne marque pas l'arrêt à la station...' 'this train will not stop at...'

arrêter [areh-tay] *v* to stop ◆ **s'arrêter** *v* to stop

arrhes [ar] *fpl* deposit

arrière [ayrehr] *m & adj* back

arrivée [aree-vay] *f* arrival

arriver [aree-vay] *v* to arrive; to happen; to reach ▸ arriver à to manage to

art [ar] *m* art

article [arteekl] *m* item

artisanal [artee-zanal] *adj (item)* traditionally made

artiste [arteest] *mf* artist

ascenseur [asON-suhr] *m* elevator

aspirine [aspee-reen] *f* aspirin

asseoir [aswar] ◆ **s'asseoir** *v* to sit down

assez [asay] *adv* enough; quite ▸ assez de enough

assiette [asyet] *f* plate

assurance [asU-rONs] *f* insurance ▸ assurance tous risques comprehensive insurance

assurer [asU-ray] *v (vehicle)* to insure

asthme [asm] *m* asthma

attendre [atONdr] *v* to wait ▸ at-

tendre quelqu'un/quelque chose to wait for someone/something ▸ 'veuillez attendre derrière cette ligne' 'please wait behind this line' ▸ 'le petit Thomas attend ses parents à la caisse centrale' 'a little boy by the name of Thomas is waiting for his parents at the customer service desk'

attention [atON-syON] *f* ▸ faire attention to be careful ▸ attention ! watch out! ▸ 'attention à la fermeture (automatique) des portes' 'stand clear of the doors'

atterrir [ateh-reer] *v (airplane)* to land

atterrissage [ateh-reesazh] *m (of flight)* landing

attrape-touristes [atrap-tooreest] *m* tourist trap

au [oh] *art* = à + le

auberge [ohberzh] *f* inn ▸ auberge de jeunesse youth hostel

aucun, e [ohkAN(ohkUn)] *adj* no, not any ◆ *pron* none ▸ aucune idée no idea

aujourd'hui [ohzhoor-dwee] *adv* today

aussi [ohsee] *adv* too, also ▸ moi aussi me too ▸ tu le sais aussi bien que moi you know as well as I do

auteur [ohtuhr] *m* author

autobus [ohtoh-bUs] *m* bus

automatique [ohtoh-mateek] *adj* automatic

automne [ohton] *m* fall

autoroute [ohtoh-root] *f* freeway

auto-stop [ohtoh-stop] *m* hitchhiking

autour [ohtoor] *adv* around

autre [ohtr] *adj* other ▸ un(e) autre

another ‣ d'autres others ‣ les autres the others ‣ autre chose something else

aux [oh] *art* = à + les

avance [avONs] *f* ‣ à l'avance in advance ‣ en avance early

avancer [avON-say] *v (object)* to move forward; *(date, event)* to bring forward

avant [avON] *prep* before ‣ avant de faire before doing

avant-hier [avON-yer] *adv* the day before yesterday

avec [avek] *prep* with ‣ et avec ceci ?

(in grocery store) (would you like) anything else?

avenue [avnU] *f* avenue

aveugle [avuhgl] *adj* blind

avion [avyON] *m* airplane ‣ par avion airmail

avis [avee] *m* ‣ changer d'avis to change one's mind

avocat, e [avoh-kah(-kat)] *m,f* lawyer
• **avocat** *m (fruit)* avocado

avoir [avwar] *v* to have

avril [avreel] *m* April

b

baby-sitter [babee-seetuhr] *mf* baby-sitter

bagages [bagazh] *mpl* luggage, baggage ‣ bagages à main carry-on baggage

baguette [baget] *f* baguette ‣ baguette moulée *baguette baked in a shaped pan* ‣ baguette de campagne *country baguette* ‣ baguette viennoise *type of sweet baguette*

baigner [benyay] • **se baigner** *v* to go for a swim

baignoire [ben-ywar] *f* bathtub

bain [bAN] *m* bath ‣ prendre un bain to take a bath

balader [bala-day] • **se balader** *v* to go for a walk; to go for a drive

balcon [balkON] *m* balcony ‣ premier balcon first balcony ‣ deuxième balcon second balcony ‣ dernier balcon top balcony

balle [bal] *f* ball; bullet

ballon [balON] *m* ball ‣ ballon de football football

banane [banan] *f* banana

bandage [bONdazh] *m* bandage

bande [bONd] *f* bandage; band ‣ bande d'arrêt d'urgence *(on road)* shoulder ‣ bande blanche *(on road)* white line ‣ bande dessinée comic strip

banlieue [bON-lyuh] *f* suburb

banque [bONk] *f* bank

Beaubourg

This is the name given to the *Centre Pompidou* and the neighborhood around it in Paris. With its striking architectural design, the Center is a popular tourist attraction. It contains the National Museum of Modern Art and a large public library, as well as movie theaters, a café, and restaurant.

bar [bar] *m* bar

barbe [barb] *f* beard ▸ barbe à papa cotton candy

barbecue [barbuh-kyoo] *m* barbecue

bas [bah] *m (lower part)* bottom; downstairs ◆ *adj* low ▸ en bas at the bottom

basilique [bazee-leek] *f* basilica

bassin [basAN] *m* pond; pelvis ▸ grand bassin main pool ▸ petit bassin children's pool

bateau [batoh] *m* boat

bâtiment [batee-mON] *m* building

bâton [batON] *m* stick ▸ bâton de ski ski pole

batterie [batree] *f* battery; *(musical instrument)* drums

beau, belle [boh(bel)] *adj (woman)* beautiful; *(man)* handsome

Beaubourg [bohboor] *n* name used to refer to the neighborhood around the Pompidou Center in Paris

beaucoup [bohkoo] *adv* a lot, much ▸ beaucoup de a lot of, many ▸ beaucoup plus a lot more, much more

bébé [baybay] *m* baby

belge [belzh] *adj* Belgian

Belge [belzh] *mf* Belgian

Belgique [belzheek] *f* ▸ la Belgique Belgium

besoin [buh-zwAN] *m* ▸ avoir besoin de to need

bête [bet] *f* animal ◆ *adj* stupid

beurre [buhr] *m* butter

biberon [beebrON] *m* baby bottle

bicyclette [beesee-klet] *f* bicycle

bidon [beedON] *m* can

bien [byAN] *adv* well ◆ *adj* good ▸ j'aimerais bien... I'd like... ▸ bien sûr of course

bientôt [byANtoh] *adv* soon ▸ à bientôt ! see you soon!

bienvenue [byANvuh-nU] *f* welcome ▸ bienvenue ! welcome!

bière [byehr] *f* beer

bijouterie [beezhoo-tree] *f* jewelry store

bijoux [beezhoo] *mpl* jewelry

billet [beeyay] *m (for traveling)* ticket; *(money)* bill

billetterie [beeyeh-tree] *f* ticket office

bio [byoh] *adj* organic, natural

biscuit [beeskwee] *m* cookie; cracker

bise [beez] *f* kiss ▸ faire la bise à quelqu'un to kiss someone on both cheeks

bonne fête

In the Gregorian Calendar established by Pope Gregory XIII in 1582, each day of the year is associated with a particular saint or saints. The French traditionally wish someone with the same first name as a saint *Bonne Fête !* on that saint's day.

bizarre [beezar] *adj* strange, odd

blanc, blanche [blON(blONsh)] *m & adj* white

blanchisserie [blON-sheesree] *f* laundry

blessé, e [blesay] *adj* injured

bleu, e [bluh] *adj (color)* blue; *(steak)* rare ♦ **bleu** *m (color)* blue; *(on skin)* bruise

blond, e [blON(blONd)] *adj* blond

bloqué, e [blokay] *adj* stuck

blouson [bloozON] *m* jacket

bœuf [buhf] *m (meat)* beef; *(animal)* ox

boire [bwar] *v* to drink

bois [bwah] *m* wood

boisson [bwasON] *f* drink

boîte [bwat] *f* box ♦ **boîte aux lettres** *(personal)* letterbox; *(public)* mailbox ♦ **boîte de conserve** can ♦ **boîte de nuit** night club ♦ **boîte de vitesses** gearbox

bol [bol] *m* bowl

bon, bonne [bON(bon)] *adj* good; *(correct)* right ♦ **bon marché** cheap

bondé, e [bONday] *adj* packed

bonjour [bON-zhoor] *excl* hello, good morning; hello, good afternoon

bonnet [boneh] *m* hat

bonsoir [bONswar] *excl* hello!, good evening!

bord [bor] *m* ♦ **au bord de la mer** at the seaside

bosse [bos] *f* bump

bottes [bot] *fpl* boots

bouche [boosh] *f* mouth

boucher [booshay] *v (bottle)* to cork; *(ears, road)* to block

boucherie [booshree] *f* butcher shop

bouchon [booshON] *m* cork; traffic jam

boucle [bookl] *f* ♦ **boucles d'oreilles** earrings

bouée [bway] *f* buoy; *(for floating)* rubber ring ♦ **bouée de sauvetage** lifebelt

bougie [boozhee] *f* candle; spark plug

bouilloire [booy-war] *f* kettle

boulangerie [boolON-zhree] *f* bakery

boule [bool] *f* ♦ **une boule/deux boules** *(of ice cream)* one scoop/ two scoops

boules Quiès® [bool kee-ess] *fpl* ear-plugs

bout [boo] *m* ♦ **au bout de...** *(time)* after...; *(space)* at the end of... ♦ **un**

bout de... a bit of... ▸ jusqu'au bout to the end

bouteille [bootey] *f* bottle ▸ bouteille de gaz gas cylinder

boutique [booteek] *f* store

bouton [bootON] *m (on skin)* pimple; *(on clothes, machine)* button

bracelet [brasleh] *m* bracelet

brancher [brONshay] *v* to plug in

bras [brah] *m (of body)* arm

bravo [bravoh] *excl* bravo!, well done!

briquet [breekeh] *m* lighter

brochure [broshUr] *f* brochure

bronchite [brONsheet] *f* bronchitis

bronzé, e [brONzay] *adj* tanned

bronzer [brONzay] *v* to tan; to sunbathe

brosse [bros] *f* brush ▸ brosse à dents

toothbrush ▸ brosse à cheveux hairbrush

brouillard [broo-yar] *m* fog

bruit [brwee] *m* noise ▸ faire du bruit to make (a) noise

brûler [brUlay] *v* to burn ◆ se brûler *v* to burn oneself

brûlure [brUlUr] *f* burn

brun, e [brAN(brUn)] *m & adj* brown

bruyant, e [brwee-yON(-yONt)] *adj* noisy

bureau [bUroh] *m* office; *(furniture)* desk ▸ bureau de change *(place of business)* currency exchange ▸ bureau de poste post office ▸ bureau de tabac tobacconist

bus [bUs] *m* bus

C

ça [sa] *pron* that; *(nearer)* this; *(indefinite pronoun)* that, it ▸ (comment) ça va ? how are you? ▸ ça va I'm fine

cabine [kabeen] *f* cabin; *(on the beach)* hut ▸ cabine de douche shower stall ▸ cabine d'essayage fitting room ▸ cabine (téléphonique) phone booth ▸ cabine (téléphonique) à carte phone booth that takes cards

cabinet [kabee-neh] *m* office ▸ cabinet médical doctor's office

câble [kabl] *m* cable

Caddie® [kadee] *m (for groceries)* cart

cadeau [kadoh] *m* present

cafard [kafar] *m* cockroach ▸ avoir le cafard *(familiar)* to feel low/down

café [kafay] *m (drink)* coffee; *(place)* café ▸ café au lait coffee with milk ▸ café crème latte ▸ café serré extra-strong espresso ▸ café allongé espresso diluted with hot water ▸ café Internet Internet café

cahier [ka-yay] *m* notebook

caisse [kes] *f* box; *(in a store)* checkout ▸ 'caisse moins de dix articles' 'nine items or fewer' ▸ 'caisse prioritaire femmes enceintes' *priority checkout for pregnant women*

caleçon [kalsON] *m* boxer shorts ▸ caleçon de bain swimming trunks

calme [kalm] *adj* quiet

caméra [kamay-ra] *f* movie camera

camion [kamyON] *m* truck

campagne [kONpan-yuh] *f* country (side) ▸ aller à la campagne to go to the countryside ▸ maison de campagne house in the country

camping [kONpeeng] *m (activity)* camping; *(venue)* campsite ▸ faire du camping to go camping

camping-car [kONpeeng-kar] *m* camper

Camping-Gaz® [kONpeeng-gaz] *m* camping stove

canette [canet] *f* can ▸ une canette de Coca® a can of Coke®

capot [kapoh] *m (of car)* hood

car [kar] *m* bus

carafe [karaf] *f* carafe

caravane [kara-van] *f* caravan

cardiaque [kardyak] *adj* cardiac ▸ avoir une crise cardiaque to have a coronary ▸ être cardiaque to have a heart condition

carie [karee] *f* ▸ avoir une carie to have a cavity

carnet [karneh] *m* notebook; *(of tickets, stamps)* book ▸ carnet d'adresses address book ▸ carnet de chèques checkbook ▸ carnet de tickets book of tickets

carotte [karot] *f* carrot

carrefour [karfoor] *m* crossroads

carte [kart] *f* menu; map; (playing) card; (identification) card ▸ Carte Bleue® debit card ▸ carte de crédit credit card ▸ carte d'identité identity card ▸ carte postale postcard ▸ carte de téléphone phonecard ▸ carte de visite business card

cartouche [kartoosh] *f* cartridge; *(of cigarettes)* carton

cas [kah] *m* ▸ au cas où just in case ▸ en cas de... in case of...

casque [kask] *m* helmet

casquette [kasket] *f* cap

cassé, e [kasay] *adj* broken

casse-croûte [kas-kroot] *m* snack

casser [kasay] *v* to break; *(couple)* to break up ▸ se casser la jambe to break one's leg

casserole [kasrol] *f* saucepan ▸ à la casserole braised

cathédrale [katay-dral] *f* cathedral

catholique [kato-leek] *adj* Catholic

cause [kohz] *f* ▸ à cause de because of

caution [koh-syON] *f* deposit

CD [sayday] *m* CD

ce, cette [suh(set)] *adj & pron* this; *(further away)* that ▸ ce qui/ce que what ▸ c'est it is ▸ ce sont they are, these are

Césars

Césars are the French equivalent of Hollywood Oscars. The awards ceremony takes place in late February or early March and is intended to promote French cinema and recognize the achievements of French actors and film-makers. Awards tend to go to box office successes rather than critics' choices.

ceinture [sANtUr] *f* belt ▸ ceinture de sécurité safety belt

cela [suhla] *pron* that

célibataire [saylee-batehr] *adj* single ◆ *m,f* single person, single man, single woman

celui, celle [suhlwee(sel)] *pron* the one ▸ celui-ci/celle-ci this one ▸ celui-là/celle-là that one

cendrier [sONdree-yay] *m* ashtray

cent [sON] *num* a hundred ▸ pour cent percent

centaine [sONten] *f* hundred ▸ une centaine de... about a hundred...

centime [sONteem] *m* cent

centimètre [sONtee-metr] *m* centimeter

centre [sONtr] *m* center ▸ centre commercial shopping mall

centre-ville [sONtr-veel] *m* downtown

céréales [sayray-al] *fpl* cereal

certain, e [sertAN(-ten)] *adj* certain

ces [say] *adj* these; *(further away)* those

César [sayzar] *n* ▸ les Césars *French cinema awards*

c'est [seh] *pron* it's ▸ c'est très bon it's very good ▸ c'est annulé it's been canceled ▸ c'est-à-dire that is, in other words

cette [set] *adj* this; *(further away)* that

ceux-ci [suh-see] *pron* these ones

ceux-là [suh-la] *pron* those ones

chacun, e [shakAN(shakUn)] *pron* each one

chaîne [shen] *f* chain; hi-fi; (television) channel

le champagne

Real champagne, the sparkling wine without which no celebration is complete, is produced only in the Champagne region of France. It is made by the 'champagne method' (*méthode champenoise*) developed there over the centuries. A special mixture of liqueur and yeasts added to the wine produces its famous bubbles.

chaise [shez] *f* chair

chaleur [shaluhr] *f* heat

chambre [shONbr] *f* room ▸ chambre à air inner tube ▸ chambre d'hôte guest house

champagne [shONpan-yuh] *m* champagne

chance [shONs] *f* luck ▸ bonne chance ! good luck! ▸ avoir de la chance to be lucky

change [shONzh] *m* exchange rate

changement [shONzh-mON] *m* change

changer [shONzhay] *v* to change ◆ se changer *v* to get changed, to change

chanson [shONsON] *f* song

chanter [shONtay] *v* to sing

chapeau [shapoh] *m* hat

chapelle [shapel] *f* chapel

chaque [shak] *adj* each, every

charcuterie [sharkU-tree] *f* butcher shop; cooked meats

chariot [sharyoh] *m* cart ▸ 'chariots pour bagages' 'luggage carts'

chasse [shas] *f* hunting ▸ chasse d'eau *(of toilet)* flusher

chat, chatte [shah(shat)] *m,f* cat

château [shatoh] *m* castle

chaud, e [shoh(shohd)] *adj* hot ▸ il fait chaud it's hot

chauffage [shohfazh] *m* heating

chauffe-eau [shohf-oh] *m* hot-water heater

chauffeur [shohfuhr] *m* driver ▸ chauf-

feur de taxi taxi driver

chaussettes [shohset] *fpl* socks

chaussure [shohsUr] *f* shoe ▸ chaussures de marche walking boots ▸ chaussures plates flats ▸ chaussures de ski ski boots ▸ chaussures à talons high-heeled shoes

chef [shef] *m* boss; chef

chemin [shuhmAN] *m* path; *(direction)* way ▸ en chemin on the way ▸ chemin de grande randonnée way-marked walking route

cheminée [shuh-meenay] *f* fireplace; chimney

chemise [shuhmeez] *f* shirt; *(for paper documents)* folder ▸ chemise de nuit nightgown

chèque [shek] *m* check ▸ chèque de voyage traveler's check

cher, chère [shehr] *adj* expensive; *(in a letter)* dear

chercher [shehr-shay] *v* to look for ▸ aller chercher quelqu'un/quelque chose to go and get someone/something

cheval [shuhval] *m* horse

cheveux [shuhvuh] *mpl* hair

cheville [shuhveey] *f* ankle

chez [shay] *prep* ▸ chez soi at home ▸ je rentre chez moi I'm going home ▸ je suis allé chez lui I went to his place ▸ je vais chez ma sœur I'm going to my sister's (place)

chien, chienne [shyAN] *m,f* dog ▸ chien d'aveugle guide dog ▸ chien policier police dog

choc [shok] *m* shock

chocolat [shoko-lah] *m* chocolate ▸ chocolat en poudre drinking chocolate

choisir [shwazeer] *v* to choose

choix [shwah] *m* choice

choquant, e [shokON(shokONt)] *adj* shocking

chose [shohz] *f* thing ▸ autre chose something else

ciel [syel] *m* sky

cigare [seegar] *m* cigar

cigarette [seega-ret] *f* cigarette

cimetière [seem-tyehr] *m* cemetery

cinéma [seenay-ma] *m* movies; *(venue)* movie theater

cinq [sANk] *num* five

cinquante [sANkONt] *num* fifty

cinquième [sANkyem] *adj* fifth

cintre [sANtr] *m* coathanger

circulation [seerkU-lasyON] *f* traffic; *(of blood)* circulation

cirque [seerk] *m* circus

ciseaux [seezoh] *mpl* scissors

citron [seetron] *m* lemon ▸ citron pressé freshly-squeezed lemon juice

clair, e [klehr] *adj* clear ▸ bleu clair light blue

classe [klas] *f* class ▸ première/deuxième classe first/second class ▸ classe affaires/économique business/economy class

classique [klaseek] *adj* classic; *(music)* classical

clé [klay] *f* key

cliché [kleeshay] *m* cliché; *(photo)* negative

clignotant [kleen-yotON] *m* flasher

climat [kleemah] *m* climate

climatisation [kleema-teeza-syON] *f* air conditioning

club [kluhb] *m* club

cochon [koshON] *m* pig

code [kod] *m* code ▸ code confidentiel PIN (number) ▸ code d'entrée *(for apartment building)* door code ▸ code postal postal code

cœur [kuhr] *m* heart

coffre [kofr] *m* *(of a car)* trunk

cognac [konyak] *m* cognac

coiffeur, euse [kwafuhr(kwafuhz)] *m,f* hairdresser

coin [kwAN] *m* corner ▸ un coin magnifique a beautiful spot ▸ dans le coin around here

coincé, e [kwANsay] *adj* stuck

colère [kolehr] *f* ▸ être en colère to be angry

colis [kolee] *m* parcel

collants [kolON] *mpl* pantyhose

colle [kol] *f* glue

colline [koleen] *f* hill

colonie [kolo-nee] *f* ▸ colonie de vacances summer camp

combien [kONbyAN] *conj* how many?; how much? ▸ combien ça coûte ? how much does it cost? ▸ combien de temps... ? how long...? ▸ depuis combien de temps... ? for how long...? ▸ combien êtes-vous ? how many of you are there? ▸ on est le combien ? what's today's date?

combinaison [kONbee-nezON] *f* ▸ combinaison de plongée wetsuit ▸ combinaison de ski ski suit

commander [komON-day] *v (food)* to order

comme [kom] *conj (in comparisons)* like, as; *(because)* as, since ▸ comme si as if

commencer [komON-say] *v* to start, to begin

comment [komON] *adv* how ▸ comment ? *(pardon?)* excuse me? ▸ comment allez-vous ? how are you? ▸ comment ça va ? how are you?

commerces [komehrs] *mpl* stores

commissariat [komee-saryah] *m* police station

commission [komee-syON] *f* commission

commun, e [komAN(komUn)] *adj* common; *(bathroom, kitchen)* shared

communication [komU-neeka-syON] *f* communication

compagnie [kONpan-yee] *f* company ▸ compagnie aérienne airline

compartiment [kONpar-teemON] *m* compartment

complet, ète [kONpleh(kONplet)] *adj* full; complete

complètement [kONplet-mON] *adv* completely

composer [kONpo-zay] *v* to dial ▸ composer un numéro to dial a number

composter [kONpos-tay] *v* to date-stamp

comprendre [kONprONdr] *v* to understand

comprimé [kONpree-may] *m* tablet

compris, e [kONpree(kONpreez)] *adj (service, insurance)* included ▸ tout compris all inclusive

comptant, e [kONtON(kONtONt)] *adj* ▸ payer comptant to pay cash

compte [kONt] *m* account ▸ compte bancaire bank account

compter [kONtay] *v* to count ▸ compter sur to count on

compteur [kONtuhr] *m* meter ▸ compteur électrique electricity meter

concert [kONsehr] *m* concert

conducteur, trice [kONdUk-tuhr (-trees)] *m* driver

conduire [kONdweer] *v* to drive; *(somebody)* to take

confirmer [kONfeer-may] *v* to confirm

confiture [kONfee-tUr] *f* jam

confortable [kONfor-tabl] *adj* comfortable

congé [kONzhay] *m* leave; vacation ▸ en congé on vacation ▸ jour de congé day off ▸ congé (de) maladie sick leave ▸ congé (de) maternité maternity leave

congélateur [kONzhay-latuhr] *m* freezer

connaissance [koneh-sONs] *f* knowledge; acquaintance ▸ enchanté de faire votre connaissance ! pleased to meet you!

connaître [konetr] v to know

connecter [konek-tay] v to connect
• **se connecter** v to log on • se connecter sur Internet to log onto the Internet

connu, e [konU] adj famous

conseil [kONsey] m • un conseil a piece of advice • des conseils advice • demander conseil à quelqu'un to ask someone's advice

conseiller [kON-seyay] v to advise, to recommend

consigne [kONseen-yuh] f checkroom

consommation [kONso-masyON] f drink

consommer [kONso-may] v to drink

constipé, e [kONstee-pay] adj constipated

construit, e [kONstrwee(kONstrweet)] adj built • construit en... built in...

consulat [kONsU-lah] m consulate

consultation [kONsUl-tasyON] f consultation • 'service des consultations externes' 'outpatient department'

contact [kONtakt] m contact • rester en contact to stay in touch • il y a un mauvais contact (electrical) there's a loose connection

contacter [kONtak-tay] v to contact

contagieux, euse [kONtazh-yuh (-yuhz)] adj contagious

contemporain, e [kONtON-porAN (-poren)] m,f & adj contemporary

content, e [kONtON(kONtONt)] adj pleased, happy • content de faire quelque chose pleased to do something

continuation [kONtee-nUasyON] f • bonne continuation ! all the best!

continuer [kONtee-nUay] v to continue, to go on • continuer à faire quelque chose to carry on doing something

contraceptif [kONtra-septeef] m contraceptive

contraire [kONtrehr] m & adj opposite • le contraire the opposite • au contraire on the contrary

contrat [kONtrah] m contract

contre [kONtr] prep against

contrôle [kONtrol] m (of tickets, documents) inspection • contrôle de passeports passport control

coordonnées [ko-ordo-nay] fpl address and telephone number

copain [kopAN] m friend

copine [kopeen] f friend

corps [kor] m body

correspondance [kores-pONdONs] f correspondence; (of flight, train) connection • 'la station Champs-Elysées Clémenceau est fermée au public, veuillez emprunter les correspondances' 'Champs-Elysées Clémenceau station is closed: please use alternative routes' • 'correspondance avec la ligne PC1' 'connecting service with Line PC1'

corriger [koree-zhay] v to correct

côte [koht] f coast; rib • avoir une côte fêlée (person) to have a crazy side (to one's character) ▸ côte-à-côte side by side

côté [kohtay] *m* side ▸ à côté de beside

coton [kotON] *m* absorbent cotton; *(textile)* cotton

Coton-Tige® [kotON-teezh] *m* Q-tip®

cou [koo] *m* neck

couche [koosh] *f* diaper

coucher [kooshay] *v* ▸ coucher avec quelqu'un to sleep with someone ▸ coucher du soleil sunset ♦ **se coucher** *v* to go to bed, to lie down

couchette [kooshet] *f* (on a train) couchette; (on a boat) berth

couleur [kooluhr] *f* color

couloir [koolwar] *m* corridor; (of bus) lane

coup [koo] *m* ▸ ça vaut le coup it's worth it ▸ aller boire un coup to go for a drink ▸ prendre un coup de soleil to get sunburnt ▸ passer un coup de téléphone to make a telephone call ▸ tout à coup suddenly ▸ du coup as a result

coupe-ongles [koop-ONgl] *m* nail clippers

couper [koopay] *v* to cut ♦ **se couper** *v* to cut oneself ▸ on a été coupés *(on the telephone)* we got cut off ▸ coupé en tranches sliced

couple [koopl] *m* couple

cour [koor] *f* court

courage [koorazh] *m* courage ▸ bon courage ! good luck!

courant, e [koorON(koorONt)] *adj* everyday ▸ être au courant (de) to know (about)

courir [kooreer] *v* to run

courrier [koor-yay] *m* mail

cours [koor] *m* (in school, university) class, course

courses [koors] *fpl* shopping ▸ faire des/les courses to do some/the shopping

court, e [koor(koort)] *adj* short

cousin, e [koozAN(koozeen)] *m,f* cousin

couteau [kootoh] *m* knife

coûter [kootay] *v* to cost ▸ combien ça coûte ? how much is it?, how much does it cost?

couvert, e [koovehr(koovert)] *adj* covered ♦ **couverts** *mpl* cutlery

couverture [koover-tUr] *f* blanket; (of book) cover

couvrir [koovreer] *v* to cover

cravate [kravat] *f* tie

crayon [kreyON] *m* pencil ▸ crayon de couleur crayon

crédit [kraydee] *m* credit ▸ 'crédit épuisé' 'no credit remaining'

crème [krem] *f* cream ▸ crème fraîche crème fraîche ▸ crème hydratante moisturizer ▸ crème à raser shaving cream ▸ crème solaire sunscreen

crêpe [krep] *f* pancake

crever [kruhvay] *v* (tire) to burst

crise [kreez] *f* (economic) crisis; (of laughter) fit ▸ crise d'appendicite appendicitis ▸ crise cardiaque heart attack

croire [krwar] *v* to believe; to think ▸ je crois que... I think (that)... ▸ croire en Dieu to believe in God

croisière [krwaz-yehr] *f* cruise

croissant [krwasON] *m* croissant ▸ croissant nature plain croissant ▸ croissant au beurre butter croissant ▸ croissant aux amandes almond croissant

cru, e [krU] *adj* raw

cuillère [kwee-yehr] *f* spoon ▸ cuillère à café teaspoon ▸ cuillère à soupe tablespoon

cuire [kweer] *v* to cook; (cakes, bread) to bake

cuisine [kweezeen] *f* cooking; kitchen ▸ faire la cuisine to do the cooking, to cook

cuisse [kwees] *f* thigh ▸ cuisse de poulet chicken thigh

cuit, e [kwee(kweet)] *adj* cooked ▸ bien cuit well done ▸ trop cuit overdone

culotte [kUlot] *f (of woman)* panties; *(of child)* pants

cybercafé [seeber-kafay] *m* Internet café

d

danger [dONzhay] *m* danger ▸ 'en cas de danger, brisez la vitre' 'in case of emergency, break glass'

dangereux, euse [dONzhuh-ruh (-ruhz)] *adj* dangerous

dans [dON] *prep* in ▸ dans une heure in an hour ▸ dans la soirée in the evening

danse [dONs] *f* dance

danser [dONsay] *v* to dance

date [dat] *f* date ▸ date d'expiration expiration date ▸ date limite deadline ▸ date de naissance date of birth

dater [datay] *v (journal entry, form)* to date ▸ dater de date from

de [duh] *art & prep* ▸ le vélo de David

David's bike ▸ de... à... from... to... ▸ du pain (some) bread ▸ des œufs (some) eggs

dé [day] *m (for games)* die, dice

début [daybU] *m* beginning, start ▸ au début at the beginning ▸ en début de at the beginning of

débutant, e [daybU-tON(-tONt)] *m,f* beginner

décaféiné, e [day-kafay-eenay] *adj* decaffeinated

décalage [dayka-lazh] *m* ▸ décalage horaire time difference; jet lag

décapsuleur [daykap-sUluhr] *m* bottle opener

décembre [daysONbr] *m* December

décider [daysee-day] *v* to decide

déclaration [daykla-rasyON] *f* statement ▸ faire une déclaration to make a statement ▸ faire une déclaration de perte de quelque chose to report the loss of something

déclarer [daykla-ray] *v (at customs)* to declare

décoller [dayko-lay] *v (airplane)* to take off

décrocher [daykro-shay] *v* to pick up ▸ 'décrochez (le combiné)' 'pick up (the receiver)'

déçu, e [daysU] *adj* disappointed

dedans [duhdON] *adv* inside ▸ de dedans from inside

défaut [dayfoh] *m* flaw, fault

dégonflé, e [daygON-flay] *adj (tire)* flat

degré [duhgray] *m (temperature)* degree

dehors [duhor] *m & adv* outside ▸ en dehors de cela apart from this

déjà [dayzha] *adv* already

déjeuner [dayzhuh-nay] *v* to have lunch ◆ *m* lunch

demain [duhmAN] *adv* tomorrow ▸ à demain ! see you tomorrow! ▸ demain matin/soir tomorrow morning/evening

demander [duhmON-day] *v* to ask

démanger [daymON-zhay] *v* ▸ ça me démange it's itchy

demi, e [duhmee] *adj* half ▸ un demi-litre/-kilo half a liter/kilo ▸ une demi-heure half an hour ▸ une heure et demie an hour and a half ▸ un demi a

beer ▸ faire demi-tour to turn back

demi-pension [duhmee-pONsyON] *f hotel room with breakfast and one main meal included*

demi-tour [duhmee-toor] *m* U-turn

dent [dON] *m* tooth ▸ les dents teeth

dentifrice [dONtee-frees] *m* toothpaste

dentiste [dONteest] *mf* dentist

déodorant [day-odorON] *m* deodorant

dépannage [daypa-nazh] *m* ▸ service de dépannage breakdown service

départ [daypar] *m* departure

dépêcher [daypay-shay] ◆ **se dépêcher** *v* to hurry (up)

dépendre [daypONdr] *v* ▸ ça dépend (de) that depends (on)

dépenser [daypON-say] *v* to spend

dépliant [dayplee-yON] *m* leaflet

déposer [daypoh-zay] *v* ▸ déposer quelqu'un *(in a car)* to drop someone off

depuis [duhpwee] *prep & adv* since ▸ depuis que since ▸ depuis quand êtes-vous ici ? how long have you been here?

déranger [dayrON-zhay] *v* to disturb ▸ 'ne pas déranger' 'do not disturb'

dernier, e [dern-yay(-yehr)] *adj* last ▸ au dernier moment at the last minute ▸ l'année dernière last year

derrière [deryehr] *adv & prep* behind ◆ *m* back

des [day] *art* = de + les

dès [deh] *prep* from ▸ dès que as soon as

désagréable [dayza-grayabl] *adj* unpleasant

descendre [desOndr] *v (passenger)* to get off

désert [dayzehr] *m* desert

désinfecter [dayzAN-fektay] *v* to disinfect

désolé, e [dayzo-lay] *adj* sorry ▶ je suis désolé I'm sorry

dessert [daysehr] *m* dessert

dessous [duhsoo] *adv & prep* underneath ▶ en dessous (de) below

dessus [duhsU] *adv* above ▶ au-dessus (de) above

destinataire [destee-natehr] *mf* addressee

détendre [daytONdr] ◆ **se détendre** *v* to relax

détester [daytes-tay] *v* to hate

deux [duh] *num & m* two ▶ les deux both

deuxième [duhzyem] *mf & adj* second

devant [duhvON] *adv* in front ◆ *prep* in front of ▶ la porte de devant the front door

développer [dayv-lopay] *v* ▶ faire développer une pellicule to get film developed

devenir [duhvneer] *v* to become

déviation [dayv-yasyON] *f* detour

devise [duhveez] *f* currency

devoir [duhvwar] *v (expressing obligation)* to have to; *(money)* to owe ◆ *m* duty; homework ▶ je dois y aller I have to go, I must go ▶ il doit être cinq heures it must be 5 o'clock ▶ vous devriez... you should... ▶ faire ses devoirs to do one's homework

diabète [dyabet] *m* diabetes ▶ avoir du diabète to suffer from diabetes

diabétique [dyabay-teek] *mf & adj* diabetic

diabolo [dyabo-loh] *m* ▶ diabolo menthe mint syrup and soda ▶ diabolo grenadine grenadine and soda

diapositive [dyapo-zeeteef] *f* diapo

diarrhée [dyaray] *f* ▶ avoir la diarrhée to have diarrhea

diesel [dyayzel] *m* diesel

différent, e [deefay-rON(-rONt)] *adj* different ▶ différent de different from

difficile [deefee-seel] *adj* difficult

dimanche [deemONsh] *m* Sunday

diminuer [deemee-nUay] *v* to reduce

dîner [deenay] *v* to have dinner ◆ *m* dinner

dire [deer] *v* to say ▶ vouloir dire to mean ▶ comment dit-on... ? how do you say... ? ▶ ça te dit ? does that sound OK to you?

direct, e [deerekt] *adj* direct

directement [deerekt-mON] *adv* directly

direction [deerek-syON] *f (way)* direction; *(of business)* management ▶ le train en direction de Paris the train to Paris ▶ 'toutes directions' 'all routes'

discothèque [deesko-tek] *f* disco

disponible [deespo-neebl] *adj* available

disque [deesk] *m* record

distance [deestONs] *f* distance

distributeur [deestree-bUtuhr] *m (of train tickets)* ticket machine; *(of drinks)* vending machine selling drinks ▸ distributeur automatique/ de billets ATM

dix [dees] *num* ten

dix-huit [deez-weet] *num* eighteen

dix-huitième [deez-weetyem] *adj* eighteenth

dixième [deezyem] *adj* tenth

dix-neuf [deez-nuhf] *num* nineteen

dix-neuvième [deez-nuhvyem] *adj* nineteenth

dix-sept [dees-set] *num* seventeen

dix-septième [dees-setyem] *adj* seventeeth

docteur [doktuhr] *m* doctor

documentation [dokU-mONta-syON] *f (information)* literature

doigt [dwah] *m* finger

dommage [domazh] *m* ▸ c'est dommage it's a pity ▸ quel dommage ! what a pity!

donc [dONk] *conj* so, therefore

donner [donay] *v* to give

dont [dON] *pron* whose ▸ l'hôtel dont il me parlait the hotel he told me about

dormir [dormeer] *v* to sleep ▸ dormir à la belle étoile to sleep out in the open

dos [doh] *m* back

douane [dwan] *f* customs ▸ passer la douane to go through customs

double [doobl] *m* copy ◆ *adj & adv* double

doublé, e [dooblay] *adj (film)* dubbed

doubler *v (car)* to pass

doucement [doosmON] *adv* gently; softly, quietly; slowly

douche [doosh] *f* shower ▸ prendre une douche to take a shower

douleur [dooluhr] *f* pain; sorrow

douze [dooz] *num* twelve

douzième [doozyem] *adj* twelfth

drap [drah] *m* sheet

drogue [drog] *f* drug

droit, e [drwah(drwat)] *adj* right ◆ *adv* straight ◆ **droit** *m* law ◆ **droite** *f* right ▸ tout droit straight ahead ▸ le côté droit the right-hand side ▸ avoir le droit de... to have the right to... ▸ à droite (de) to the right (of)

drôle [drohl] *adj* funny

du [dU] *art* = de + le ▸ du vin/lait/pain some wine/milk/bread

dur, e [dUr] *adj* hard

durer [dUray] *v* to last

duvet [dUvay] *m* sleeping bag

e

eau [oh] *f* water ▸ **eau gazeuse** sparkling water ▸ **eau minérale** mineral water ▸ **eau plate** noncarbonated water ▸ **eau potable** drinking water

échanger [ayshON-zhay] *v* to exchange

écharpe [aysharp] *f* scarf

éclair [ayklehr] *m* éclair ▸ **un éclair au chocolat** a chocolate éclair

école [aykol] *f* school

économique [ayko-nomeek] *adj* economical; economic

écouter [aykoo-tay] *v* to listen ▸ **écouter quelqu'un/quelque chose** to listen to someone/something

écrire [aykreer] *v* to write

effort [efor] *m* effort ▸ **faire un effort** to make an effort

égal, e [aygal] *adj* ▸ **ça m'est égal** I don't mind

église [aygleez] *f* church

électricité [aylek-treesee-tay] *f* electricity

électrique [aylek-treek] *adj* electric

elle [el] *pron* she ▸ **elles** they

éloigner [aylwan-yay] *v* to move away ▸ **'veuillez vous éloigner de la bordure du quai'** 'stand clear of the platform edge'

e-mail [eemel] *m* e-mail

embarquement [ONbark-mON] *m* boarding

embarquer [ONbar-kay] *v* to board

embouteillage [ONboo-teyazh] *m* traffic jam

embrasser [ONbra-say] *v* to kiss ▸ **je t'embrasse** lots of love

embrayage [ONbre-yazh] *m* clutch

emmener [ONmuhnay] *v (in car - people)* to take

emplacement [ONplas-mON] *m (in campsite)* spot

emporter [ONpor-tay] *v* to take ▸ **à emporter** takeout

emprunter [ONprAN-tay] *v* to borrow

en [ON] *prep* in ▸ **en France/2006/anglais** in France/2006/English ▸ **je vais en France** I'm going to France ▸ **en voiture** by car

enceinte [ONsANt] *adj* pregnant

enchanté, e [ONshON-tay] *adj* pleased to meet you!

encore [ONkor] *adv* still; more; again ▸ **pas encore** not yet ▸ **encore plus** even more

endormir [ONdor-meer] ◆ **s'endormir** *v* to fall asleep

endroit [ONdrwah] *m* place ▸ **à quel endroit ?** where?

enfant [ONfON] *mf* child ▸ des enfants children

enflé, e [ONflay] *adj* swollen

enlever [ONluh-vay] *v* to remove

ennuyer [ONnwee-yay] ✦ **s'ennuyer** *v* to be bored

enregistrement [ONruh-zheestrhuh-mON] *m* (of baggage) check-in

enregistrer [ONruh-zheestray] *v* (music, CD) to record; (baggage) to check in

enrhumé, e [ONrU-may] *adj* ▸ être enrhumé to have a cold

ensemble [ONsONbl] *adv* together

ensuite [ONsweet] *adv* then, next

entendre [ONtONdr] *v* to hear ▸ bien s'entendre (avec quelqu'un) to get along well (with someone) ▸ mal s'entendre (avec quelqu'un) not to get along (with someone)

entier, ère [ONtyay(ONtyehr)] *adj* whole ▸ le gâteau (en) entier the whole cake

entracte [ONtrakt] *m* interval, intermission

entre [ONtr] *prep* between ▸ entre midi et deux between noon and two pm ▸ entre trois et cinq jours between 3 and 5 days ▸ entre autres among other things

entrée [ONtray] *f* entrance, way in; (in meal) appetizer; admission fee

entreprise [ONtruh-preez] *f* company

entrer [ONtray] *v* to go in; to come in

enveloppe [ONvlop] *f* envelope

envie [ONvee] *f* ▸ avoir envie de to want (to)

environ [ONvee-rON] *adv* about, around ▸ dans les environs in the vicinity

envoyer [ONvwa-yay] *v* to send

épaule [aypohl] *f* shoulder

épeler [ayplay] *v* to spell

épicé, e [aypee-say] *adj* spicy, hot

épicerie [aypee-sree] *f* grocery store

épileptique [aypee-lepteek] *mf & adj* epileptic

éponge [aypONzh] *f* sponge

épuisé, e [aypwee-zay] *adj* exhausted; out of stock, sold out

équipe [aykeep] *f* team

erreur [eruhr] *f* mistake ▸ par erreur by mistake ▸ faire erreur to make a mistake

escalade [eska-lad] *f* climbing

escalier [eskal-yay] *m* stairs

espèces [espes] *fpl* cash

espérer [espay-ray] *v* to hope ▸ j'espère que... I hope that...

essayer [esay-yay] *v* to try; (clothes) to try on ▸ essayer de faire quelque chose to try to do something

essence [esONs] *f* gas

essuyer [eswee-yay] *v* to dry

est [est] *m* east ▸ à l'est in the east ▸ à l'est de... east of...

est-ce que [eskuh] *adv* ▸ est-ce qu'il fait beau ? is the weather good? ▸ est-ce que vous aimez le thé ? do you like tea? ▸ est-ce que tu seras là ? will you be there?

estomac [esto-mah] *m* stomach

et [ay] *conj* and

étage [aytazh] *m* (level) floor

état [aytah] *m* state ▸ l'État the State

États-Unis [aytaz-Unee] *m* ▸ les États-Unis the United States

été [aytay] *m* summer

éteindre [aytANdr] *v* (cigarette) to put out; (machine, light) to switch off

étonner [ayto-nay] *v* to surprise

étranger, ère [aytrON-zhay(-zhehr)] *adj* foreign ◆ *m,f* foreigner ▸ à l'étranger abroad

être [etr] *v* to be ▸ je suis français I'm French ▸ est-ce que tu es content ? are you happy? ▸ c'est beau it's beautiful

études [aytUd] *fpl* studies ▸ faire des études de biologie to study biology

étudiant, e [aytUd-yON(-yONt)] *m,f* student

euro [uhroh] *m* euro

Europe [uhrop] *f* Europe

européen, enne [uhro-payAN(-payen)] *adj* European

eux [uh] *pron* they; them

évanouir [ayvan-weer] ◆ **s'évanouir** *v* to faint

évident, e [ayvee-dON(-dONt)] *adj* obvious ▸ c'est évident ! obviously!

éviter [ayvee-tay] *v* to avoid

excédent [eksay-dON] *m* (of luggage) excess ▸ j'avais un excédent de bagages de quinze kilos my luggage was 15 kilos over weight

exceptionnel, elle [eksep-syonel] *adj* exceptional ▸ ça n'a rien d'exceptionnel it's nothing special

excursion [ekskUr-syON] *f* trip ▸ faire une excursion to go on a trip

excuse [ekskUz] *f* excuse

excuser [ekskU-zay] ◆ **s'excuser** *v* to apologize, to say sorry ▸ excusez-moi I'm sorry

exemple [egzONpl] *m* example ▸ par exemple for example

expéditeur, trice [ekspay-deetuhr (-deetrees)] *m,f* sender

expliquer [eksplee-kay] *v* to explain

exposition [ekspo-zeesyON] *f* exhibition

exprès [ekspreh, ekspres] *adv* on purpose ▸ je ne l'ai pas fait exprès I didn't do it on purpose ▸ en exprès by special delivery

express [ekspres] *m* (train) express; (coffee) espresso

expresso [eks-presoh] *m* espresso

exprimer [ekspree-may] ◆ **s'exprimer** *v* to express oneself

extérieur, e [ekstayr-yuhr] *m* & *adj* outside ▸ à l'extérieur outside, outdoors

fac [fak] *f (informal)* college ▸ aller à la fac to go to/to be in college

face [fas] *f* face ▸ en face (de) opposite

fâché, e [fashay] *adj* angry

facile [faseel] *adj* easy ▸ facile (à) easy (to)

façon [fasON] *f* way ▸ de toute façon anyway

facteur, trice [faktuhr(faktrees)] *m,f* mailman, mailwoman

facture [faktUr] *f* bill

faible [febl] *adj* weak

faim [fAN] *f* ▸ avoir faim to be hungry

faire [fehr] *v* to do, to make ▸ que fais-tu dimanche ? what are you doing on Sunday? ▸ ça fait deux ans que je n'ai pas pris de vacances I haven't taken a vacation for 2 years ▸ ça ne fait rien it doesn't matter ▸ faire le ménage/la vaisselle to do the housework/the dishes

fait, e [feh(fet)] *adj* made ◆ **fait** *m* fact ▸ fait main hand-made ▸ en fait in fact ▸ au fait by the way

falaise [falez] *f* cliff

falloir [falwar] *v* ▸ il faut faire attention you/we/etc. must be careful ▸ il faut se dépêcher we have to hurry ▸ il me faut de nouvelles chaussures I need new shoes ▸ il faut que j'y aille I must go ▸ il faut que vous le voyiez you have to see it

famille [fameey] *f* family

fast-food [fast-food] *m* fast-food restaurant

fatigant, e [fatee-gON(-gONt)] *adj* tiring

fatigué, e [fatee-gay] *adj* tired

faute [foht] *f* mistake

fauteuil [foh-toy] *m* armchair ▸ fauteuil roulant wheelchair

faux, fausse [foh(fohs)] *adj (incorrect)* wrong; *(not true)* false

favori, ite [favo-ree(-reet)] *m,f* & *adj* favorite

fax [faks] *m* fax

félicitations ! [fayleesee-tasyON] *excl* congratulations!

femme [fam] *f* woman; wife

fenêtre [fuhnetr] *f* window

fer [fehr] *m* iron ▸ fer à repasser *(for ironing)* iron

férié, e [fayr-yay] *adj* ▸ jour férié public holiday ▸ lundi est férié Monday is a public holiday

fermé, e [fermay] *adj* closed, shut

fermer [fermay] *v* to close, to shut ▸ fermer la porte à clé to lock the door

festival d'Avignon

This month-long festival of theatre, dance, music and film, founded by Jean Vilar in 1947, is held every summer in Avignon. As well as the official festival, there is a thriving 'fringe' festival.

fermeture [fermuh-tUr] *f* closing ▸ fermeture Éclair® zipper

ferry [feree] *m* ferry

fesses [fes] *fpl* bottom, buttocks

festival [festee-val] *m* festival

fête [fet] *f* party ▸ faire la fête to party ▸ fête foraine amusement park ▸ fête nationale national holiday

feu [fuh] *m* fire ▸ tu as du feu ? do you have a light? ▸ feu rouge red light ▸ feux d'artifice fireworks

février [fayv-reeyay] *m* February

fiancé, e [fyONsay] *m,f* fiancé ▸ être fiancé to be engaged

fichu, e [feeshU] *adj* ▸ mon appareil photo est fichu *(informal)* my camera has had it ▸ c'est fichu pour ce soir *(informal)* we can forget tonight

fier [fyehr] *adj* proud

fièvre [fyevr] *f* fever ▸ avoir de la fièvre to have a fever

fille [feey] *f* girl; daughter

film [feelm] *m* movie

fils [fees] *m* son

fin, e [fAN(feen)] *adj* fine ◆ **fin** *f* end ▸ en fin de, à la fin de at the end of

finalement [feenal-mON] *adv* finally

finir [feeneer] *v* to finish

flan [flON] *m* baked custard dessert ▸ une part de flan a piece of baked custard dessert

flash [flash] *m* flash

fleur [fluhr] *f* flower

fleuve [fluhv] *m* river

foie [fwah] *m* liver

foire [fwar] *f* fair

fois [fwah] *f* time ▸ à la fois at the same time ▸ combien de fois… ? how many times…? ▸ une fois once ▸ deux fois twice ▸ trois/quatre fois three/four times

festival de Cannes

The Cannes Film Festival, held annually in May, is one of the most important in the world. Films, actors, and film-makers compete for awards, the most prestigious being the *Palme d'Or* for best film. A jury composed of cinema professionals chooses the winners.

la fête de la musique

On June 21st each year, free concerts and performances of all types of music by both professional and amateur musicians are given in streets and squares throughout France. Founded in 1982, the festival rapidly gained in popularity and is now held in a large number of other countries.

folklorique [folklo-reek] *adj* traditional

foncé, e [fONsay] *adj* dark ▸ bleu foncé dark blue

fond [fON] *m (of container)* bottom; *(of room)* back ▸ au fond de at the bottom of; at the back of

forêt [foreh] *f* forest

forfait [forfeh] *m (for transportation, skiing)* pass

formidable [formee-dabl] *adj* great ▸ c'est formidable! that's great/wonderful!

formulaire [formU-lehr] *m* form ▸ remplir un formulaire to fill in a form

formule [formUl] *f* menu ▸ formule à six euros *six-euro meal deal* ▸ formule entrée-plat *two-course menu consisting of an appetizer and a main course* ▸ formule entrée-plat-dessert *three-course menu*

fort, e [for(fort)] *adj* strong; loud ▸ parler plus fort to speak more loudly

foulard [foolar] *m* scarf

fouler [foolay] *v* ▸ se fouler la cheville to sprain one's ankle

four [foor] *m* oven

fourchette [foorshet] *f* fork

fourmi [foormee] *f* ant ▸ avoir des fourmis to have pins and needles

fourrière [fooryehr] *f (for cars)* impound lot ▸ mettre à la fourrière to tow away

fracture [fraktUr] *f* fracture

fragile [frazheel] *adj* fragile

frais, fraîche [freh(fresh)] *adj (weather)* chilly; *(food)* fresh; *(drink)* cold

français, e [frONsay(frONsez)] *adj* French ♦ **français** *m (language)* French

Français, e [frONsay(frONsez)] *m,f* French person

France [frONs] *f* France

frein [frAN] *m* brake ▸ frein à main handbrake

freiner [fraynay] *v* to brake

frère [frehr] *m* brother

Frigidaire® [freezhee-dehr] *m* refrigerator

frigo [freego] *m (informal)* refrigerator

froid, e [frwah(frwad)] *m & adj* cold ▸ il fait froid it's cold ▸ avoir froid to be cold ▸ prendre froid to catch cold

fromage [fromazh] *m* cheese ▸ fro-

le fromage

Brie, Camembert, Roquefort – these are just three of the more than 400 different types of cheese that France produces. Cheeses made from unpasteurized milk using traditional methods account for 15% of those produced. Pasteurized milk is used in all industrially produced cheeses.

mage blanc fromage frais ▸ fromage de chèvre goat's cheese

front [frON] *m* forehead

frontière [frONtyehr] *f* border

fruit [frwee] *m* fruit ▸ fruit sec dried fruit ▸ fruits de mer seafood

fuite [fweet] *f* escape ▸ prendre la fuite to run away

fumée [fUmay] *f* smoke

fumer [fUmay] *v* to smoke

fumeur, euse [fUmuhr(fUmuhz)] *m,f* smoker ▸ non-fumeur/non-fumeuse non-smoker ▸ fumeurs *(room, compartment)* smoking

fusible [fUzeebl] *adj* fuze

g

gâcher [gashay] *v* to waste

gagner [ganyay] *v* to win; *(money)* to earn; *(money, time)* to save

galerie [galree] *f* gallery

galette [galet] *f* pancake

gant [gON] *m* glove ▸ gant de toilette washcloth

garage [garazh] *m* garage

garagiste [gara-zheest] *m* mechanic

garantie [garON-tee] *f* guarantee

garçon [garsON] *m* boy; waiter

garder [garday] *v* to keep

gare [gar] *f* station ▸ gare routière bus station

garer [garay] ◆ **se garer** *v* to park

gâteau [gatoh] *m* cake ▸ gâteau sec cookie

gauche [gohsh] *f* left ▸ à gauche (de) to the left (of)

gaufre [gohfr] *f* waffle ▸ gaufre nature

la galette des rois

This puff pastry and almond paste 'Kings' Cake,' named after the Three Kings in the Bible story, is traditionally eaten in France on Twelfth Night. Each cake contains a *fève*, a porcelain lucky charm, and the person whose slice contains it is crowned king or queen.

gîte rural ⭕

These are rural vacation cottages that provide facilities allowing guests and residents to prepare their own meals. They are regulated, and categorized by the awarding of 1 to 5 *épis* (ears of corn), by an organization called *Gîtes de France*, which is officially recognized by the French Ministry of Tourism. They are extremely popular, especially with families with children or people with pets, so you need to book well in advance!

plain waffle ▸ gaufre à la chantilly waffle with Chantilly whipped cream

gaz [gaz] *m* gas

gaze [gaz] *f (bandage)* gauze

gazeux, euse [gazuh(gazuhz)] *adj (drink)* fizzy

gel [zhel] *m* frost; *(for hair)* gel ▸ gel douche shower gel

généraliste [zhaynay-raleest] *mf* general practitioner

génial, e [zhayn-yal] *adj* brilliant

genou [zhuhnoo] *m* knee

genre [zhONr] *m* ▸ quel genre de... ? what kind of...?

gens [zhON] *mpl* ▸ les gens people

gentil, ille [zhONtee(zhONteey)] *adj* nice

gilet [zheeleh] *m* cardigan; *(sleeveless)* vest ▸ gilet de sauvetage lifejacket

gîte [zheet] *m* guesthouse

glace [glas] *f* ice; ice cream; mirror

glacé, e [glasay] *adj (covered in ice)* frozen; *(weather)* freezing cold

glaçon [glasON] *m* ice cube

golf [golf] *m* golf

gorge [gorzh] *f* throat

gourde [goord] *f* flask

goût [goo] *m* taste

goûter [gootay] *v* to taste ▸ *m (afternoon)* snack

gouttes [goot] *fpl (for eyes, ears)* drops

grâce [gras] *f* grace ▸ grâce à thanks to

gramme [gram] *m* gram

grand, e [grON(grONd)] *adj* big; tall

Grande-Bretagne [grONd-bruhtan-yuh] *f (Great)* Britain

grandir [grONdeer] *v* to grow ▸ j'ai grandi en France I grew up in France

grand-mère [grON-mehr] *f* grandmother

grand-père [grON-pehr] *m* grandfather

grands-parents [grON-parON] *mpl* grandparents

gras, grasse [grah] *adj* fat

gratuit, e [gratwee(gratweet)] *adj* free

grave [grav] *adj* serious ▸ ce n'est pas grave it doesn't matter

grippe [greep] *f* flu ▸ avoir la grippe to have the flu ▸ grippe aviaire bird flu ▸ grippe intestinale gastric flu

gris [gree] *m & adj* gray

gros, grosse [groh(grohs)] *adj* big, large; fat

groupe [groop] *m* group

guêpe [gep] *f* wasp

guérir [gayreer] *v* to get better; *(wound)* to heal

gueule [guhl] *f* ▸ gueule de bois *(informal)* hangover

guichet [geesheh] *m (in station, post office)* ticket window ▸ guichet automatique (de banque) ATM

guide [geed] *m* guide(book); *(person)* guide ▸ guide des spectacles listings magazine

gynécologue [zheenay-kolog] *mf* gynecologist

h

habiller [abee-yay] ✦ **s'habiller** *v* to get dressed

habiter [abee-tay] *v* to live

habitude [abee-tUd] *f* habit ▸ d'habitude usually ▸ j'ai l'habitude I'm used to it ▸ je n'ai pas l'habitude de manger aussi tôt I'm not used to eating so early

hanche [ONsh] *f* hip

handicapé, e [ONdee-kapay] *adj* handicapped, disabled

hasard [azar] *m* ▸ au hasard at random ▸ par hasard by chance

haschich [asheesh] *m* hashish

haut, e [oh(oht)] *adj* high ✦ **haut** *m* top; upstairs ▸ en haut at the top ▸ dix mètres de haut ten meters tall

héberger [ayber-zhay] *v* to put up

hémorroïdes [ay-moro-eed] *fpl* hemorrhoids

herbe [erb] *f* grass ▸ fines herbes herbs

hésiter [ayzee-tay] *v* to hesitate

heure [uhr] *f* hour ▸ à quelle heure... ? what time...? ▸ quelle heure est-il ? what time is it? ▸ à cinq heures at five o'clock ▸ à l'heure on time ▸ à tout à l'heure see you later ▸ heure locale local time

heureux, euse [uhruh(uhruhz)] *adj* happy

hier [yehr] *adv* yesterday ▸ hier soir last night

histoire [eestwar] *f* history; story

hiver [eevehr] *m* winter

homéopathie [homay-opatee] *f* homeopathy

homme [om] *m* man

homosexuel, elle [omo-seksUel] *m,f & adj* homosexual

honnête [onet] *adj* honest

honte [ONt] *f* shame ▸ c'est une honte! that's outrageous!

hôpital [opee-tal] *m* hospital

horaire [orehr] *m* timetable

horloge [orlozh] *m* clock

hors [or] *prep* ‣ hors service out of order

hôtel [otel] *m* hotel ‣ hôtel de ville city hall

huile [weel] *f* oil

huit [weet] *num* eight

huitième [weetyem] *adj* eighth

humide [Umeed] *adj* damp; *(weather)* humid

hygiénique [eezh-yayneek] *adj* hygienic ‣ serviette hygiénique sanitary napkin

hypertension [eeper-tONsyON] *f* high blood pressure

hypotension [eepo-tONsyON] *f* low blood pressure

ici [eesee] *adv* here ‣ d'ici from around here ‣ d'ici un quart d'heure in a quarter of an hour ‣ par ici this way

idée [eeday] *f* idea

il [eel] *pron* he ‣ il y a there is ‣ il y a un château there is a castle ‣ il y a deux musées there are 2 museums ‣ il y a deux ans 2 years ago

île [eel] *f* island ‣ presqu'île peninsula

ils [eel] *pron* they

immeuble [eemuhbl] *m* building; apartment building

imperméable [ANpehr-mayabl] *m* raincoat ♦ *adj* waterproof

important, e [ANpor-tON(-tONt)] *adj* important

impossible [ANpo-seebl] *adj* impossible

imprimer [ANpree-may] *v* to print

incendie [ANsON-dee] *m* fire ‣ incendie de forêt forest fire

indépendant, e [ANday-pONdON (-pONdONt)] *adj* independent

indicatif [ANdee-kateef] *m (telephone)* area code

infection [ANfek-syON] *f* infection

infirmier, ère [ANfeer-myay(-myehr)] *m,f* nurse

informations [ANfor-masyON] *fpl* information; *(TV or radio broadcast)* news

infusion [ANfUz-yON] *f* herbal tea

inquiéter [ANkyay-tay] ♦ **s'inquiéter** *v* to worry

inscrire [ANskreer] ♦ **s'inscrire** *v* to sign up

insecte [ANsekt] *m* insect

insecticide [ANsek-teeseed] *m* insecticide

insolation [ANso-lasyON] *f* sunstroke

insomnie [ANsom-nee] *f* insomnia

instant [ANstON] *m* ‣ un instant, s'il vous plaît one moment, please

intention [ANtON-syON] *f* ‣ avoir

l'intention de… to intend to…

interdit, e [ANter-dee(-deet)] *adj* forbidden ▸ 'entrée interdite' 'no entry'

intéressant, e [ANtay-resON] *adj* interesting

intérieur [ANtayr-yuhr] *m* ▸ à l'intérieur inside

international, e [ANter-nasyo-nal] *adj* international

Internet [ANter-net] *m* ▸ l'Internet the Internet

intoxication [ANtok-seeka-syON] *f* ▸ intoxication alimentaire food poisoning

invité, e [ANvee-tay] *m,f* guest

inviter [ANvee-tay] *v* to invite

ivre [eevr] *adj* drunk

j

jamais [zhamay] *adv* never ▸ ne… jamais never ▸ si jamais if ever ▸ le meilleur spectacle que j'aie jamais vu the best show I've ever seen

jambe [zhONb] *f* leg

jambon [zhONbON] *m* ham ▸ jambon blanc boiled, cured and ready-to-serve ham ▸ jambon cru raw ham ▸ jambon-beurre ham sandwich

janvier [zhONv-yay] *m* January

jardin [zhardAN] *m* garden

jaune [zhohn] *m & adj* yellow ▸ jaune d'œuf egg yoke

je [zhuh] *pron* I

jean [jeen] *m* jeans

jetable [zhuhtabl] *adj* disposable

jeter [zhuhtay] *v* to throw; *(trash)* to throw out

jeu [zhuh] *m* game

jeudi [zhuhdee] *m* Thursday

jeune [zhuhn] *mf* young person ◆ *adj* young ▸ les jeunes young people ▸ jeune homme/femme young man/woman ▸ jeune fille girl

jogging [jogeeng] *m* jogging; jogging suit

joli, e [zholee] *adj* pretty

jouer [zhway] *v* to play ▸ jouer au foot to play soccer ▸ ça joue à… it's on at…

jouet [zhweh] *m* toy

jour [zhoor] *m* day ▸ de nos jours nowadays ▸ l'autre jour the other day

journal [zhoornal] *m* newspaper

journée [zhoornay] *f* day ▸ à la journée per day

juillet [zhwee-yeh] *m* July

juin [zhwAN] *m* June

jumeaux [zhUmoh] *mpl* twins

jumelles [zhUmel] *fpl* female twins; binoculars

le 14 juillet

This French national holiday commemorates the most famous act of the French Revolution, the storming of the Bastille, the royal prison, by the people of Paris on July 14th, 1789. It is celebrated with a military parade in Paris, and dances and firework displays throughout the country.

jupe [zhUp] *f* skirt

jus [zhU] *m* juice ▸ jus de fruit fruit juice

jusqu'à [zhUska] *prep* until

juste [zhUst] *adj* fair ◆ *adv* just ▸ juste avant/un peu just before/a little ▸ c'est trop juste *(clothes)* it's too tight

k

kayak [ka-yak] *m* kayak

kilo [keelo] *m* kilo

kilométrage [keelo-maytrazh] *m* ≃ mileage

kilomètre [keelo-metr] *m* kilometer

kiosque [kyosk] *m* ▸ kiosque à journaux newsstand

Kleenex® [kleeneks] *m* Kleenex®

K-way® [kaweh] *m* raincoat

la [la] *art* the ◆ *pron* her ▸ la fenêtre the window ▸ je la connais bien I know her well

là [la] *adv* there

là-bas [la-bah] *adv* over there

lac [lak] *m* lake

là-haut [la-oh] *adv* up there; upstairs

laine [len] *f* wool ▸ laine vierge new wool

laisser [laysay] *v (allow)* to let ▸ laissez-moi tranquille leave me alone ▸ laisser tomber to drop

lait [lay] *m* milk ▸ lait demi-écrémé 2% milk ▸ lait entier whole milk ▸ lait après-soleil after-sun moisturizer ▸ lait hydratant moisturizing lotion

laitue [laytU] *f* lettuce

lame [lam] *f* ▸ lame de rasoir razor blade

lampe [lONp] *f* lamp ▸ lampe de poche flashlight

langue [lONg] *f* tongue; language ▸ tirer la langue to stick one's tongue out ▸ parler deux langues to speak two languages

large [larzh] *adj* wide

lavable [lavabl] *adj* washable

lavabo [lava-boh] *m* bathroom sink

laver [lavay] *v* to wash ◆ **se laver** *v* to wash oneself ▸ se laver les dents to brush one's teeth ▸ se laver les cheveux to wash one's hair

laverie [lavree] *f* Laundromat®

lave-vaisselle [lav-vesel] *m* dishwasher

le [luh] *art* the ◆ *pron* him; it ▸ le chien the dog ▸ l'amour love ▸ les enfants the children ▸ je les connais bien I know them well ▸ donne-le moi give it to me

leçon [luhsON] *f* lesson

léger, ère [layzhay(layzhehr)] *adj* light

légume [laygUm] *m* vegetable

lent, e [lON(lONt)] *adj* slow

lentement [lONtmON] *adv* slowly

lentilles [lONteey] *fpl* lentils; contact lenses

lequel, laquelle [luhkel(lakel)] *pron* whom; which ▸ lequel ? which one?

les [lay] *art* the ◆ *pron* them

lessive [leseev] *f* laundry detergent ▸ faire la lessive to do the laundry

lettre [letr] *f* letter

leur [luhr] *pron* them, to them ◆ *adj* their ▸ je leur ai donné la lettre I gave them the letter ▸ c'est leur tour it's their turn ▸ leurs enfants their children ▸ les leurs theirs

levée [luhvay] *f (mail)* collection

lever [luhvay] ◆ **se lever** *v* to get up ▸ lever du soleil sunrise

lèvre [levr] *f* lip

librairie [leebray-ree] *f* bookstore

libre [leebr] *adj (room)* available; *(seat, person)* free

lieu [lyuh] *m* place ▸ au lieu de instead of ▸ avoir lieu to take place

ligne [leen-yuh] *f* line ▸ ligne de métro subway line ▸ ligne de bus bus route

linge [lANzh] *m (dirty clothes)* laundry ▸ linge sale dirty laundry

liquide [leekeed] *m* liquid; cash ▸ payer en liquide to pay cash ▸ liquide vaisselle dishwashing liquid

lire [leer] *v* to read

lit [lee] *m* bed ▸ lit de camp camp bed

litre [leetr] *m* liter

livraison [leevreh-zON] *f* delivery ▸ 'livraison' 'deliveries'

livre [leevr] *m* book ◆ *f* half a kilo

location [loka-syON] *f (of car, bike, apartment)* rental, renting

loge [lozh] *f* box ▸ 'loges' 'boxes'

logement [lozhmON] *m* accommodations

loger [lozhay] *v (friends, guests)* to put up; to live

loin [lwAN] *adv* far ▸ loin de far from ▸ au loin in the distance

long, longue [lON(lONg)] *adj* long ▸ chaise longue deckchair

loto

The French national lottery, run by the company *Française des Jeux*, is played by between sixteen and twenty million people a week. The *Loto Sportif* is a version of the *Loto* that involves betting on the results of soccer matches. At Christmas and other festivals there's also the *Super Loto*.

longtemps [lONtON] *adv* a long time

lorsque [lorsk] *conj* when

loto [loto] *m* national lottery

louer [lway] *v* to rent

lourd, e [loor(loord)] *adj* heavy; *(weather)* muggy

Louvre [loovr] *m* ▸ le Louvre the Louvre (museum)

loyer [lwa-yay] *m* rent

lui [lwee] *pron* (to) him; (to) her; (to)

it ▸ je lui ai parlé I've spoken to him

lumière [lUmyehr] *f* light

lundi [lANdee] *m* Monday

lune [lUn] *f* moon ▸ lune de miel honeymoon

lunettes [lUnet] *fpl* glasses ▸ lunettes de soleil sunglasses ▸ lunettes de ski ski goggles

luxe [lUks] *m* ▸ de luxe luxury

le Louvre

This former royal palace houses one of the greatest collections of paintings, sculptures, and antiquities in the world. A national museum since 1793, it was expanded to become the *Grand Louvre* in 1999. You enter it through the famous glass pyramid in the center of its courtyard.

ma [ma] *adj* my

machine [masheen] *f* machine ▸ machine à laver washing machine

madame, Madame [madam] *f (title)* Mrs., Ms.; *(form of address)* madam, m'am ▸ mesdames! ladies! ▸ bonjour madame ! good morning madam!

mademoiselle, Mademoiselle [madmwa-zel] *f* Miss ▸ pardon mademoiselle excuse me, Miss

magasin [maga-zAN] *m* store ▸ grand magasin department store

magazine [maga-zeen] *m* magazine

magnifique [man-yeefeek] *adj* magnificent

mai [may] *m* May

maigre [mehgr] *adj* thin

maillot [ma-yoh] *m* ▸ maillot de bain *(for women)* swimsuit; *(for men)* swimming trunks

main [mAN] *f* hand

maintenant [mANtnON] *adv* now

mairie [mehree] *f* city hall

mais [may] *conj* but ▸ mais non ! of course not!

maison [mayzON] *f* house ▸ à la maison at home ▸ maison de campagne house in the country

mal [mal] *m* pain ◆ *adv* badly ◆ *adj* bad ▸ ça fait mal it hurts ▸ avoir mal au cœur to feel sick to one's stomach ▸ avoir mal à la tête/à la gorge/au ventre to have a headache/a sore throat/a stomachache ▸ avoir le mal de mer to be seasick ▸ avoir du mal à faire quelque chose to have trouble doing something ▸ se sentir mal to not feel well ▸ pas mal de quite a lot of ▸ c'est pas mal it's not bad

malade [malad] *adj* ill

maladie [mala-dee] *f* illness

malentendu [malON-tONdU] *m* misunderstanding

maman [mamON] *f* mommy

manche [mONsh] *f* sleeve ▸ la Manche the Channel

mandat [mONdah] *m* ▸ mandat international international money order

manger [mONzhay] *v* to eat

manière [manyehr] *f* way ▸ de toute manière in any case

manifestation [manee-festas-yON] *f* demonstration; *(cultural)* event

manquer [mONkay] *v* to miss ▸ il manque deux valises there are two suitcases missing ▸ il me manque deux euros I'm 2 euros short ▸ tu me manques I miss you

manteau [mONtoh] *m* coat

marchand [marshON] *m* storekeeper ▸ marchand de journaux newsdealer

marchandises [marshON-deez] *fpl* goods

marche [marsh] *f* step ▸ faire de la marche to go walking ▸ marche avant/arrière forward/reverse gear ▸ mettre en marche to put in gear

marché [marshay] *m* market ▸ faire le marché to go shopping

marcher [marshay] *v* to walk; *(machine)* to work

mardi [mardee] *m* Tuesday

marée [maray] *f* tide ▸ marée basse/haute low/high tide

mari [maree] *m* husband

mariage [mar-yazh] *m* marriage; wedding

marié, e [mar-yay] *adj* married

marre [mar] *adv* ▸ en avoir marre (de) to be fed up (with) ▸ j'en ai marre ! I've had enough!

marron [marON] *m & adj (color)* brown; *(nut)* chestnut

mars [mars] *m* March

match [match] *m* match

matelas [matlah] *m* mattress ▸ matelas pneumatique air mattress

matériel [matayr-yel] *m* equipment

matin [matAN] *m* morning ▸ le matin in the morning ▸ de bon matin early in the morning

matinée [matee-nay] *f* morning; *(performance)* matinée ▸ faire la grasse matinée to sleep in

mauvais, e [mohveh(mohvehz)] *adj* bad ▸ il fait mauvais the weather's bad

maximum [maksee-mom] *m & adj* maximum

me [muh] *pron* me; to me; myself ▸ me voici here I am

mec [mek] *m (familiar)* guy

méchant, e [mayshON(mayshONt)] *adj* bad

médecin [mayd-sAN] *m* doctor ▸ médecin de famille family doctor ▸ médecin généraliste general practitioner

médicament [maydee-kamON] *m* medicine

meilleur, e [meyuhr] *adj* better ▸ le meilleur the best ▸ meilleur que... better than...

mélanger [maylON-zhay] *v* to mix

membre [mONbr] *m (of club)* member ▸ carte de membre des auberges de jeunesse youth hostel membership card

même [mem] *adj* same ◆ *adv* even ▸ même si even if ▸ moi-même myself ▸ lui-même himself

ménage [maynazh] *m* ▸ faire le ménage to do the housework

mentir [mONteer] *v* to lie

menton [mONtON] *m* chin

menu [muhnU] *m* menu; prix-fixe menu ▸ menu enfant children's menu

mer [mehr] *f* sea ▸ la mer Méditerranée the Mediterranean ▸ la mer du Nord the North Sea

merci [mersee] *excl* thank you!, thanks! ‣ merci beaucoup thank you very much ‣ non merci no, thank you

mercredi [merkruh-dee] *m* Wednesday

mère [mehr] *f* mother ‣ mère célibataire single mother ‣ belle-mère mother-in-law

mes [may] *pron* my

message [mesazh] *m* message

messe [mes] *f* mass

météo [maytay-oh] *f* ‣ (bulletin) météo weather forecast ‣ météo marine shipping forecast

métier [maytay] *m* occupation

mètre [metr] *m* meter

métro [maytro] *m* subway

mettre [metr] *v* to put ‣ mettre un vêtement *(clothes)* to put something on ‣ mettre du temps to take

micro-ondes [meekro-ONd] *m* microwave

midi [meedee] *m* midday, noon ‣ 'fermé le midi' 'closed at lunchtime'

mien, enne [myAN(myen)] *pron* ‣ le mien/la mienne mine ‣ les miens/miennes mine

mieux [myuh] *adv* better ‣ mieux que... better than... ‣ il va mieux he's doing better

milieu [meel-yuh] *m* middle ‣ au milieu (de) in the middle (of)

mille [meel] *m* a thousand

mince [mANs] *adj* thin

minimum [meenee-mom] *m & adj* minimum

minuit [meenwee] *m* midnight

minute [meenUt] *f* minute

Mobylette® [mobee-let] *f* moped

moderne [modern] *adj* modern

moi [mwa] *pron* me ‣ c'est pour moi it's for me ‣ moi aussi me too ‣ moi-même myself

moins [mwAN] *adv* less ‣ au moins at least ‣ moins que less than ‣ dix heures moins le quart a quarter to ten

mois [mwa] *m* month

moitié [mwatyay] *f* half ‣ la moitié de ce fromage half of that cheese

moment [momON] *m* moment ‣ un moment ! just a moment! ‣ en ce moment at the moment ‣ pour le moment for the moment ‣ à ce moment-là then ‣ au moment où... as...

mon [mON] *adj* my

monastère [monas-tehr] *m* monastery

monde [mONd] *m* world ‣ tout le monde everybody ‣ il y a du monde there are lots of people ‣ pas grand-monde not many people

monnaie [moneh] *f* currency; *(coins)* change

monsieur, Monsieur [muhsyuh] *m (title)* Mr.; *(form of address)* Sir ‣ messieurs gentlemen ‣ messieurs dames ladies and gentlemen ‣ pardon monsieur excuse me, Sir

montagne [mONtan-yuh] *f* mountain

le muguet

On May Day (May 1st) in France, people sell bunches of lily of the valley in the streets. You give someone a bunch to bring them good luck. Originally a symbol of the return of spring, the lily of the valley became associated with Labor Day in 1936.

monter [mONtay] *v (person)* to go/come up; *(road, plane)* to climb; *(train)* to get on; *(car)* to get in; *(price, temperature)* to rise; *(sound, heating)* to turn up

montre [mONtr] *f* watch

montrer [mONtray] *v* to show

monument [monU-mON] *m* monument

moquer [mokay] ◆ **se moquer** *v* ▸ se moquer de to laugh at, to make fun of

morceau [morsoh] *m* ▸ un morceau de a piece of ▸ manger un morceau to have a bite to eat

mort, e [mor(mort)] *adj* dead ◆ **morte** *f* death

mosquée [moskay] *f* mosque

mot [moh] *m* word; *(written)* note ▸ gros mot swear word ▸ mot à mot word for word

moteur [motuhr] *m* engine

moto [motoh] *f* motorcycle ▸ moto tout terrain all-terrain motorcycle

mouche [moosh] *f* fly

moucher [moosh-ay] ◆ **se moucher** *v* to blow one's nose

mouchoir [moosh-war] *m* handkerchief

mouillé, e [moo-yay] *adj* wet

mourir [mooreer] *v* to die

mousse [moos] *f* mousse ▸ mousse au chocolat chocolate mousse ▸ mousse à raser shaving cream

moustique [moosteek] *m* mosquito

moutarde [mootard] *f* mustard

mouton [mootON] *m* sheep; *(meat)* mutton

moyen, enne [mwa-yAN(-yen)] *adj* average ◆ **moyen** *m (method of doing)* way ▸ la classe moyenne the middle classes

muguet [mUgeh] *m* lily of the valley

mur [mUr] *m* wall

mûr, e [mUr] *adj* ripe

muscle [mUskl] *m* muscle

musée [mUzay] *m* museum ▸ musée d'art art gallery

musique [mUzeek] *f* music

n

nager [nazhay] *v* to swim ▸ est-ce que tu sais nager ? can you swim?

naître [nehtr] *v* ▸ je suis né le/en... I was born on the/in...

natation [natas-yON] *f* swimming

nationalité [nasyo-nalee-tay] *f* nationality

nature [natUr] *f* nature

nausée [nohzay] *f* ▸ avoir la nausée to feel sick

navette [navet] *f* shuttle

navré, e [navray] *adj* sorry ▸ être navré de quelque chose to be sorry about something

ne [nuh] *adv* ▸ elle ne vient pas she is not coming ▸ ne... plus no more ▸ ne... jamais never

nécessaire [naysay-sehr] *adj* necessary

négatif, ive [nayga-teef(-teev)] *m & adj* negative

neige [nezh] *f* snow

neiger [nezhay] *v* to snow

nerveux, euse [nervuh(nervuhz)] *adj* nervous

nettoyer [netwa-yay] *v* to clean

neuf, neuve [nuhf(nuhv)] *adj* new ◆ *num* nine

neuvième [nuhv-yem] *adj* ninth

neveu [nuhvuh] *m* nephew

nez [nay] *m* nose

nièce [nyes] *f* niece

ni [nee] *conj* ▸ ni... ni... neither... nor...

n'importe [nANport] *adv* ▸ n'importe où anywhere ▸ n'importe quand anytime ▸ n'importe quel/quelle any ▸ n'importe qui anyone ▸ n'importe quoi anything

niveau [neevoh] *m* level

Noël [no-el] *m* Christmas ▸ joyeux Noël ! Merry Christmas!

noir [nwar] *m & adj* black ▸ noir et blanc black and white

nom [nON] *m* name ▸ nom de famille last name ▸ nom de jeune fille maiden name

nombre [nONbr] *m* number

non [nON] *adv* no ▸ je ne fume pas – moi non plus I don't smoke – neither do I ▸ moi non not me ▸ c'est une bonne idée, non ? it's a good idea, isn't it?

non-fumeur, euse [nON-fUmuhr(-fU-muhz)] *m,f* nonsmoker

nord [nor] *m* north ▸ au nord in the north ▸ au nord de north of

normal, e [normal] *adj* normal

nos [noh] *pron* our

note [not] *f* bill; note; *(in a restaurant, hotel)* check

Noël

Many of our Christmas traditions are the same in France. There, however, Christmas Dinner is traditionally eaten on Christmas Eve before going to *Messe de Minuit* (Midnight Mass). It typically consists of *dinde aux marrons* (turkey with chestnuts), followed by a *bûche de Noël* (Yule log).

---

noter [notay] *v* to write down

notre [notr] *adj* our

nôtre [nohtr] *pron* ▸ le/la nôtre ours ▸ les nôtres ours

nourriture [nooree-tUr] *f* food

nous [noo] *pron* we; us

nouveau, elle [noovoh(noovel)] *adj* new ◆ **nouvelle** *f* short story; (piece of) news ▸ à/de nouveau again ▸ Nouvel An New Year ▸ bonne/mauvaise nouvelle good/bad news ▸ les nouvelles the news

novembre [novONbr] *m* November

noyer [nwa-yay] ◆ **se noyer** *v* to drown

nu, e [nU] *adj* naked

nuage [nUazh] *m* cloud

nuit [nwee] *f* night ▸ bonne nuit goodnight ▸ de nuit at night ▸ nuit blanche sleepless night

nul, nulle [nUl] *adj* useless ▸ nulle part nowhere

numéro [nUmay-roh] *m* number ▸ numéro d'immatriculation license number ▸ numéro de téléphone telephone number

objectif [obzhek-teef] *m* (of camera) lens

objet [obzheh] *m* object

obligatoire [oblee-gatwar] *adj* compulsory

obligé, e [oblee-zhay] *adj* ▸ être obligé de to be obliged to, to have to

occasion [okaz-yON] *f* opportunity ▸ d'occasion second-hand

occupé, e [okU-pay] *adj* (toilet) occupied; (person) busy; (telephone line) busy

occuper [okU-pay] ◆ **s'occuper** *v* ▸ s'occuper à quelque chose to be busy with something ▸ s'occuper de quelque chose to take care of something ▸ s'occuper de quelqu'un to look after someone

océan [osay-ON] *m* ocean ▸ l'océan Atlantique the Atlantic Ocean

octobre [oktobr] *m* October

odeur [oduhr] *f* smell

œil [oy] *m* eye ▸ les yeux eyes ▸ à l'œil *(informal)* (for) free

œuf [uhf] *m* egg ▸ œuf à la coque soft-boiled egg ▸ œuf dur hard-boiled egg ▸ œuf sur le plat fried egg ▸ œufs brouillés scrambled eggs

office [ofees] *m* office ▸ d'office automatically ▸ office du tourisme tourist office

offrir [ofreer] *v* to offer; *(present)* to give

oiseau [wazoh] *m* bird

ok [okeh] *excl* OK!

ombre [ONbr] *f* shade, shadow ▸ à l'ombre in the shade

on [ON] *pron* one; we ▸ on ne sait jamais you never know ▸ on m'a dit que... I've been told that... ▸ on s'en va we're going

oncle [ONkl] *m* uncle

onde [ONd] *f* wave

ongle [ONgl] *m* nail

onze [ONz] *num* eleven

onzième [ONz-yem] *adj* eleventh

opérer [opay-ray] *v* ▸ se faire opérer to have an operation

opticien, enne [optees-yAN(-yen)] *m,f* optician

orage [orazh] *m* storm

orange [orONzh] *m & adj (color, fruit)* orange

orchestre [orkestr] *m* orchestra

ordinateur [ordee-natuhr] *m* computer ▸ ordinateur individuel PC, personal computer ▸ ordinateur portable laptop

ordures [ordUr] *fpl* garbage

oreille [orey] *f* ear

oreiller [orey-yay] *m* pillow

organiser [orga-neezay] *v* to organize

origine [oree-zheen] *f* origin ▸ être d'origine irlandaise to be of Irish descent ▸ appellation d'origine contrôlée *government certification guaranteeing the origin and quality of French food and wine*

ou [oo] *conj* or ▸ ou... ou... either... or...

où [oo] *pron* where ▸ où est... ? where is...? ▸ où sont... ? where are...? ▸ où vas-tu ? where are you going? ▸ d'où viens-tu ? where are you from?

oublier [ooblee-yay] *v* to forget

ouest [west] *m* west ▸ à l'ouest in the west ▸ à l'ouest de west of

oui [wee] *adv* yes

ouvert, e [oovehr(oovert)] *adj* open

ouvre-boîtes [oovr-bwat] *m* can opener

ouvre-bouteilles [oovr-bootey] *m* bottle opener

ouvrir [oovreer] *v* to open

pack [pak] *m* pack ▸ un pack de bières a pack of beer

page [pazh] *f* page

pain [pAN] *m* bread ▸ un pain a loaf (of bread) ▸ pain de campagne country loaf ▸ pain au chocolat chocolate croissant ▸ pain complet whole-wheat bread ▸ pain d'épices ≃ gingerbread ▸ pain au lait sweet roll ▸ pain de mie sandwich bread ▸ pain aux raisins raisin Danish ▸ pain de seigle rye bread ▸ pain de son bran loaf

palais [palay] *m* palace; palate

pâle [pal] *adj* pale

panne [pan] *f* breakdown ▸ tomber en panne to break down ▸ être en panne d'essence to be out of gas

panneau [panoh] *m* sign; road sign

pansement [pONsmON] *m* (for wound) dressing; Band-Aid®

pantalon [pONta-lON] *m* pants

papa [papa] *m* dad, daddy

papier [pap-yay] *m* paper ▸ papier à cigarette cigarette paper ▸ papier alu aluminum foil ▸ papier cadeau gift wrap ▸ papier hygiénique toilet paper ▸ papiers d'identité identity papers ▸ papier à lettres writing paper ▸ papier toilette toilet paper

Pâques [pak] *fpl* Easter ▸ joyeuses Pâques ! Happy Easter!

paquet [pakeh] *m* packet, parcel; (of cigarettes) pack ▸ paquet cadeau gift-wrapped package

par [par] *prep* by ▸ par train by train ▸ par accident by accident; by chance ▸ une fois par jour/heure once a day/an hour ▸ par terre on the ground

paracétamol [para-sayta-mol] *m* acetaminophen

paraître [paretr] *v* ▸ il paraît que... it seems that...

parapluie [para-plwee] *m* umbrella

parasol [para-sol] *m* beach umbrella

parc [park] *m* park ▸ parc d'attractions theme park

parce que [pars kuh] *conj* because

parcmètre [park-mehtr] *m* parking meter ▸ vous devez prendre un ticket au parcmètre you have to get a parking ticket from the machine

pardon [pardON] *excl* (I'm) sorry; (to

---

pardon

These pilgrimages are made in Brittany, generally in honor of local saints who are patrons of particular groups of people, professions or trades. Pilgrims march to the tombs of the saints carrying banners and crosses. After confession and mass, they celebrate with a *fête* or carnival.

attract attention) excuse me ▸ pardon ? pardon me?

pare-brise [par-breez] *m* windshield

pare-chocs [par-shok] *m* bumper

pareil, eille [parey] *adj* same

parents [parON] *mpl* parents

parfois [parfwah] *adv* sometimes

parfum [parfAN] *m (substance)* perfume; *(of ice cream)* flavor; *(of flower)* scent

parking [parkeeng] *m* parking lot

parler [parlay] *v* to speak

parmi [parmee] *prep* among

part [par] *f* part ▸ autre part somewhere else ▸ d'autre part besides, moreover ▸ quelque part somewhere

partager [parta-zhay] *v* to share

partie [partee] *f* part ▸ faire partie de to be a part of ▸ une partie de tennis a tennis match

partir [parteer] *v* to leave ▸ à partir de... from...

partout [partoo] *adv* everywhere

pas [pa] *adv* ▸ ne... pas not ▸ pas du tout not at all ▸ elle ne vient pas she's not coming

passage [pasazh] *m* ▸ être de passage to be passing through ▸ 'céder le passage' *(on road)* 'give way'

passager, ère [pasa-zhay(-zhehr)] *m,f* passenger

passé, e [pasay] *adj* last, past ▸ la semaine passée last week

passeport [paspor] *m* passport

passer [pasay] *v (time)* to spend;

(place) to pass ▸ je suis passé ver six heures I came by around ' o'clock ▸ passer chercher quelqu'u to go and pick someone up ▸ passe un coup de téléphone to make phone call

patiner [patee-nay] *v (skater)* t skate; *(car)* to skid; *(wheel)* to spi

patinoire [pateen-war] *f* ice rink

patins [patAN] *mpl* skates ▸ patins roulettes roller skates ▸ patins glace ice skates

pâtisserie [patee-sree] *f* pastry; pas try shop, bakery

patron [patrON] *m* boss

pause [pohz] *f* break

pauvre [pohvr] *adj* poor

payant, e [pay-yON(-yONt)] *a* ▸ l'entrée est payante there's an admission fee

payer [pay-yay] *v* to pay

pays [pay-yee] *m* country

paysage [payzazh] *m* landscape scenery

PCV [paysay-vay] *m* collect call

péage [pay-azh] *m* toll

peau [poh] *f* skin

pêcher [payshay] *v* to fish

peigne [pen-yuh] *m* comb

peine [pen] *f* ▸ à peine hardly ▸ ça vaut la peine it's worth it

peler [puhlay] *v* to peel

pellicule [pelee-kUl] *f (for camera)* film

pendant [pONdON] *prep* during

pendant une heure for an hour ▸ pendant que while

pénicilline [paynee-seeleen] *f* penicillin

penser [pONsay] *v* to think ▸ penser à to think about

pension [pONsyON] *f (small hotel)* guesthouse ▸ demi-pension *hotel room with breakfast and one main meal included* ▸ pension complète *hotel room with all meals included*

perdre [perdr] *v* to lose ◆ se perdre to get lost ▸ être perdu to be lost ▸ perdre du temps to waste time

père [pehr] *m* father

périmé, e [payree-may] *adj* out of date

permettre [permetr] *v* to allow

permis [permee] *m* license ▸ permis de conduire driver's license ▸ permis de pêche fishing license

personne [person] *f* person, people ▸ *pron* nobody

perte [pert] *f* loss

petit, e [puhtee(puhteet)] *adj* small, little ▸ petit ami boyfriend ▸ petite amie girlfriend ▸ petit copain boyfriend ▸ petit copine girlfriend ▸ petit à petit little by little

petit-déjeuner [puhtee-dayzhuh-nay] *m* breakfast

petite-fille [puhteet-feey] *f* granddaughter

petit-fils [puhtee-fees] *m* grandson

petits-enfants [puhteez-ONfON] *mpl* grandchildren

peu [puh] *adv* not much, little; not very; few, not many ▸ il mange peu he doesn't eat much ▸ peu de few, not many ▸ peu de temps not long ▸ un peu a little ▸ un peu de vin a little wine ▸ à peu près almost, about

peur [puhr] *f* fear ▸ avoir peur (de) to be scared (of)

peut-être [puht-etr] *adv* maybe, perhaps

phare [far] *m* headlight; lighthouse

pharmacie [farma-see] *f* drugstore

photo [fotoh] *f* photo ▸ prendre quelqu'un en photo to take someone's picture ▸ prendre une photo to take a photo

photocopie [foto-kopee] *f* photocopy ▸ faire une photocopie to make a photocopy

pichet [peesheh] *m* jug ▸ un pichet de la cuvée du patron a carafe of house wine

pièce [pyes] *f* part; coin; room ▸ pièce de rechange spare part ▸ pièce de théâtre play ▸ pièce montée ornamental cake

pied [pyay] *m* foot ▸ aller à pied to walk, to go on foot

pierre [pyehr] *f* stone

piéton, onne [pyaytON(pyayton)] *m,f* pedestrian ▸ rue piétonne pedestrians-only street

pile [peel] *f* battery ▸ trois heures pile three o'clock on the dot

pilule [peelUl] *f* pill ▸ prendre la pilule

to be on the pill ▸ pilule du lendemain morning-after pill

pipe [peep] *f* pipe

pipi [peepee] *m* pee ▸ faire pipi to pee

pique-nique [peek-neek] *m* picnic

pique-niquer [peek-neekay] *v* to have a picnic

piquer [peekay] *v* to sting ▸ se faire piquer (par) to get stung (by)

piqûre [peekUr] *f* injection; *(of bee, mosquito)* sting

pire [peer] *adv* worse ▸ c'est pire (que) it's worse (than)

piscine [peeseen] *f* swimming pool

piste [peest] *f* track, trail; *(of circus)* (circus) ring; *(skiing)* run ▸ piste cyclable *(on road)* bicycle lane

place [plas] *f* seat; *(in town)* square ▸ il n'y a plus de place there's no more room ▸ sur place on the spot ▸ à la place (de) instead of ▸ place de parking parking space

plage [plazh] *f* beach ▸ plage arrière *(of car)* back shelf

plaie [pleh] *f* wound

plaindre [plANdr] ◆ **se plaindre** *v* to complain

plainte [plANt] *f* moan; complaint

plaire [plehr] *v* to please ▸ s'il te/vous plaît please ▸ ça me plaît I like it

plaisanterie [plezON-tree] *f* joke

plaisir [plezeer] *m* pleasure ▸ avec plaisir! with pleasure!

plan [plON] *m* plan; map

planche [plONsh] *f* ▸ planche à voile

windsurfing ▸ planche de surf surf board, snowboard

plante [plONt] *f* plant

plaque [plak] *f* ▸ plaque électriqu hotplate ▸ plaque de verglas *(o road)* icy patch

plastique [plasteek] *m* & *adj* plastic

plat, e [pla(plaht)] *adj* flat ◆ **plat** *n* dish ▸ plat de résistance main cours ▸ plat du jour today's special, dish o the day

plâtre [platr] *m* ▸ avoir un plâtre to b wearing a cast

plein, e [plAN(plen)] *adj* full ▸ plein d full of ▸ faire le plein to fill up wit gas

pleurer [pluhray] *v* to cry

pleuvoir [pluhv-war] *v* ▸ il pleut it' raining

plombage [plONbazh] *m (in tooth* filling

plombier [plONb-yay] *m* plumber

plongée [plONzhay] *f (scuba)* divin ▸ faire de la plongée to go diving

plonger [plONzhay] *v* to dive; t plunge

pluie [plwee] *f* rain

plupart [plUpar] *f* ▸ la plupart mos ▸ la plupart des gens most people

plus [plU] *adv* more ▸ il n'y a plus de. there are no more... ▸ il ne me rest plus que deux jours I have only days left ▸ ce que j'ai le plus aim what I liked most ▸ ne... plus n longer, no more ▸ moi non plus m

PMU

This is the abbreviation of *Pari Mutuel Urbain*, the French authority in charge of betting on horseracing. You can place bets at any of the 8,000 *Points PMU* or counters in bars, as well as by telephone, *Minitel*, or over the Internet.

neither ▸ plus ou moins more or less ▸ plus que more than

plusieurs [plUzyuhr] *adj & pron* several

plutôt [plUtoh] *adv* rather

pneu [pnuh] *m* tire

PMU *abbr of* Pari Mutuel Urbain *m system for betting on horses*

poêle [pwal] *f* frying pan

poignet [pwan-yay] *m* wrist

poil [pwal] *m* hair

point [pwAN] *m* point ▸ être sur le point de faire to be about to do ▸ à point *(steak)* medium ▸ mettre au point *(machine)* to adjust; *(idea)* to finalize ▸ point de départ starting point ▸ point mort *(of car)* neutral

pointure [pwANtUr] *f* (shoe) size

poisson [pwasON] *m* fish

poissonnerie [pwason-ree] *f* fish shop

poitrine [pwatreen] *f* chest ▸ poitrine de porc breast of pork

poivre [pwavr] *m* pepper

police [polees] *f* police

policier [polees-yay] *m* policeman, police officer

politesse [polee-tes] *f* politeness

politique [polee-teek] *f* policy

pommade [pomad] *f* ointment

pomme [pom] *f* apple; *(of shower)* head ▸ pomme de terre potato

pompe [pONp] *f* ▸ pompe à vélo bicycle pump

pompier [pONpyay] *m* firefighter ▸ les pompiers the fire department

pont [pON] *m* bridge ▸ faire le pont to have a long weekend

porc [por] *m (meat)* pork; *(animal)* pig

port [por] *m* port

portable [portabl] *m* cellphone; laptop

porte [port] *f* door; *(at airport)* gate

porte-bagages [port-bagazh] *m inv (on car, train)* luggage rack; *(on bike)* carrier

portefeuille [portuh-foy] *m* billfold, wallet

porte-monnaie [port-moneh] *m* change purse

porter [portay] *v* to carry; to wear

portion [porsyON] *f* portion

portrait [portreh] *m* portrait

possible [poseebl] *adj* possible ▸ le plus tôt possible as soon as possible

poste [post] *f* mail; post office ▸ poste restante general delivery

pot [poh] *m* pot; jar ▸ pot d'échappement tail pipe

potable [potabl] *adj* ▸ eau potable drinking water ▸ eau non potable non-potable water

poubelle [poobel] *f* garbage can ▸ mettre à la poubelle to throw out

poudre [poodr] *f* powder ▸ chocolat en poudre drinking chocolate

poulet [poolay] *m* chicken

poumon [poomON] *m* lung

pour [poor] *prep* for ▸ pour que so that ▸ pour faire quelque chose to do something ▸ pour cent percent ▸ une table pour quatre a table for four

pourboire [poorbwar] *m* tip

pourquoi [poorkwa] *adv* why

pousser [poosay] *v* to push

poussette [pooset] *f* stroller

pouvoir [poovwar] *v* to be able to ◆ *m* power ▸ je ne peux pas I can't ▸ on peut y aller demain we can go tomorrow

pratique [prateek] *adj* practical

précédent, e [praysay-dON(-dONt)] *adj* previous

préféré, e [prayfay-ray] *adj* favorite

préférer [prayfay-ray] *v* to prefer

premier, ère [pruhm-yay(-yehr)] *adj* first; *(floor)* second

prendre [prONdr] *v* to take ▸ ça prend deux heures it takes 2 hours

prénom [praynON] *m* first name

préparer [praypa-ray] *v* to prepare

près [preh] *adv* near ▸ (tout) près de (right) beside

présentation [prayzON-tasyON] *f* presentation

présenter [prayzON-tay] *v* to introduce ▸ je te présente... this is...

préservatif [prayzer-vateef] *m* condom

presque [presk] *adv* almost

pressé, e [presay] *adj* ▸ être pressé to be in a hurry ▸ citron pressé freshly-squeezed lemon juice

pressing [preseeng] *m* dry cleaner's

pression [presyON] *f* (draft) beer; *(of tire)* pressure

prêt, e [preh(pret)] *adj* ready ▸ être prêt à to be ready to

prêter [pretay] *v* to lend

prévenir [prayvuh-neer] *v* to warn

prévision [prayvee-zyON] *f* ▸ prévisions météo weather forecast

prévoir [prayvwar] *v (activity)* to plan; *(weather)* to forecast

prier [pree-ay] *v* ▸ je t'en prie /je vous en prie you're welcome

principal, e [prANsee-pal] *adj* main

printemps [prANtON] *m* spring

priorité [pree-oree-tay] *f* priority; right of way ▸ laisser la priorité to yield

prise [preez] *f (for electricity)* outlet; plug

privé, e [preevay] *adj* private

prix [pree] *m* price

probablement [probab-luhmON] *adv* probably

problème [problem] *m* problem

prochain, e [proshAN(proshen)] *adj* next ▸ à une prochaine ...! see you (soon)!

proche [prosh] *adv* near ▸ le plus proche the nearest

produit [prodwee] *m* product

professeur [profe-suhr] *m* teacher

profession [profes-yON] *f* profession

profiter [profee-tay] *v* ▸ profiter de to make the most of

profond, e [profON(profONd)] *adj* deep

programme [program] *m* program

promenade [promnad] *f (on foot)* walk; *(on bike)* ride; *(in car)* drive ▸ faire une promenade to go for a walk/ride/drive

promener [promnay] ◆ **se promener** *v* to go for a walk

promettre [prometr] *v* to promise

proposer [propo-zay] *v* to propose, to suggest

propre [propr] *adj* clean; tidy; *(personal)* own

propriétaire [propree-aytehr] *mf* owner ▸ 'le propriétaire de la voiture immatriculée 8710–BG–76 est prié de venir changer son véhicule de place' 'the owner of vehicle number 8710–BG–76 is requested to move the vehicle'

protection [protek-syON] *f* protection

protéger [protay-zhay] ◆ **se protéger** *v* to protect oneself

provenance [provnОns] *f* origin ▸ 'le train en provenance de Paris va entrer en gare dans quelques instants' 'the train from Paris will be arriving shortly'

prudent, e [prUdON] *adj* careful

public, ique [pUbleek] *m* & *adj* public

puisque [pweesk] *conj* since

pull [pUl] *m* sweater

pyjama [peezha-ma] *m* pyjamas

q

quai [keh] *m (at station)* platform; *(at port)* quay

qualité [kalee-tay] *f* quality ▸ de bonne qualité good-quality

quand [kON] *conj* when ▸ quand même all the same

quarante [karONt] *num* forty

quart [kar] *m* quarter ▸ un quart d'heure a quarter of an hour ▸ et quart quarter after ▸ moins le quart quarter of, quarter to

quartier [kartyay] *m* neighborhood

quatorze [katorz] *num* fourteen

quatorzième [katorz-yem] *adj* fourteenth

quatre [katr] *num* four ▸ quatre-quarts pound cake ▸ quatre-quatre four-wheel vehicle

quatre-vingt-dix [katr-vAN-dees] *num* ninety

quatre-vingts [katr-vAN] *num* eighty

quatrième [katr-yem] *adj* fourth

que [kuh] *conj* that ▸ ne... que only ▸ que veux-tu ? what do you want?

▸ qu'est-ce... ? what...? ▸ qui est-ce... ? who...? ▸ plus petit que smaller than ▸ je pense que... I think (that)...

quel [kel] *adj* what, which

quelque [kelkuh] *adj* some

quelque chose [kelkuh shohz] *pron* something

quelquefois [kelkuh-fwah] *adv* sometimes

quelque part [kelkuh par] *adv* somewhere

quelqu'un [kelkAN] *pron* someone, somebody

quelques-uns [kelkuhz-AN] *pron* some, a few

question [kestyON] *f* question

queue [kuh] *f* line ▸ faire la queue to stand in line

qui [kee] *pron* who

quinze [kANz] *num* fifteen

quinzième [kANzyem] *adj* fifteenth

quitter [keetay] *v* to leave ▸ ne quittez pas *(on phone)* please hold

---

le Quartier Latin

This area of Paris on the Left Bank of the Seine is traditionally associated with students and artists. It contains many important historical buildings such as the Sorbonne university. It is also famous for being at the center of the student protests of May 1968.

quoi [kwa] *pron* what ▸ il n'y a pas de quoi you're welcome

quoique [qwakuh] *conj* although

quotidien, enne [koteed-yAN(-yen)] *adj* daily ◆ **quotidien** *m* daily newspaper

r

rabais [rabeh] *m* discount ▸ faire un rabais à quelqu'un to give someone a discount

raccrocher [rakro-shay] *v* to hang up ▸ 'raccrochez (le combiné)' 'hang up (the receiver)' ▸ ça a raccroché they hung up

raccourci [rakoor-see] *m* short cut

raconter [rakON-tay] *v* to tell

radiateur [radya-tuhr] *m* radiator

radio [radyoh] *f* radio; X-ray

rage [razh] *f* ▸ rage de dents severe toothache

raison [rehzON] *f* reason ▸ avoir raison to be right

randonnée [rOndo-nay] *f* hiking ▸ faire de la randonnée to go hiking

rang [rON] *m* row ▸ 'rang pair' 'even-numbered row' ▸ 'rang impair' 'odd-numbered row'

ranger [rONzhay] *v* to tidy

rapide [rapeed] *adj* quick

rappeler [raplay] *v* (on telephone) to call back ◆ **se rappeler** *v* to remember ▸ ça me rappelle... it reminds me of...

rapporter [rapor-tay] *v* to bring back

raquette [raket] *f* racket ▸ raquette de ping-pong table tennis bat

rare [rar] *adj* rare

rarement [rarmON] *adv* rarely

raser [razay] ◆ **se raser** *v* to shave

rasoir [razwar] *m* razor ▸ rasoir électrique electric shaver

rater [ratay] *v* (train, airplane) to miss

ravi, e [ravee] *adj* delighted, pleased ▸ ravi de faire votre connaissance pleased to meet you

rayon [ray-yON] *m* (of store) department ▸ rayons X X-rays

réception [raysep-syON] *f* (in hotel) reception desk; (of cellphone) signal ▸ à la réception at the front desk

réceptionniste [raysep-syoneest] *mf* receptionist

recette [ruhset] *f* recipe

recevoir [ruhsuh-vwar] *v* to receive, to get ▸ je te reçois très mal (on cellphone) the signal's very bad ▸ recevoir quelqu'un à dîner to have somebody to dinner

rechange [ruhshONzh] *m* ▸ ... de rechange spare...

recharger [ruhshar-zhay] *v* to recharge

les régions

France is made up of twenty-two *régions*, subdivided into 96 *départements*. Each region is run by a regional council. The administrative power they were given under decentralization legislation was intended to create a better balance between Paris and the rest of France, *la province*.

---

réclamation [raykla-masyON] *f* complaint

recommandé, e [ruhko-mONday] *adj* ▸ en recommandé registered

recommander [ruhko-mONday] *v* to recommend

reconnaître [ruhko-netr] *v* to recognize

reçu [ruhsU] *m* receipt

reculer [ruhkU-lay] *v (car)* to back up

réduction [raydUk-syON] *f* reduction

refaire [ruhfehr] *v* to do again

réfléchir [rayflay-sheer] *v* to think

réfrigérateur [rayfree-zhayra-tuhr] *m* refrigerator

refuge [ruhfUzh] *m* ▸ refuge de montagne mountain hut

refuser [ruhfU-zay] *v* to refuse

regarder [ruhgar-day] *v* to look at, to watch

régime [rayzheem] *m* diet ▸ être au régime to be on a diet

région [rayzh-yON] *f* area ▸ dans la région in the area

régler [rayglay] *v* to adjust; *(check)* to pay; *(problem)* to sort out

règles [regl] *fpl (menstruation)* period ▸ avoir ses règles to be having one's period

regretter [ruh-gretay] *v (decision)* to regret; *(person)* to miss

rein [rAN] *m* kidney

rejoindre [ruhzhwANdr] *v* to meet

religieuse [ruhleezh-yuhz] *f* choux pastry ▸ une religieuse au café coffee-flavored choux pastry

remarquer [ruhmar-kay] *v* to notice

rembourser [rONboor-say] *v* to refund ▸ se faire rembourser to get a refund

remercier [ruhmers-yay] *v* to thank

remontée [ruhmON-tay] *f* ▸ remontée mécanique ski lift

remplacer [rONpla-say] *v* to replace; to take over from

remplir [rONpleer] *v* to fill; *(form)* to fill in, to fill out

rencontrer [rONkON-tray] *v* to meet ◆ se rencontrer *v* to meet (each other)

rendez-vous [rONday-voo] *m (professional, medical)* appointment; *(romantic)* date ▸ prendre un rendez-vous to make an appointment ▸ se donner rendez-vous to arrange to meet ▸ avoir rendez-vous avec *(with friend)* to meet; *(with client, doctor)* to have an appointment

la rentrée

The *rentrée scolaire* or start of the new school year is usually at the beginning of September. Universities go back a month later. The term *la rentrée* is also used for the general return to work in September after the long vacation months of July and August.

with; *(romantic)* to have a date with

rendre [rONdr] *v* to give back

renseignement [rOnsen-yuhmON] *m* piece of information ▸ les renseignements information

renseigner [rONsayn-yay] ◆ **se renseigner** *v* to find out

rentrée [rONtray] *f* return

rentrer [rONtray] *v* to go home

renverser [rONver-say] *v* to knock over ▸ se faire renverser to get knocked over

réparer [raypa-ray] *v* to repair ▸ faire réparer to get repaired

repas [ruhpah] *m* meal

repasser [ruhpa-say] *v* to iron

repère [ruhpehr] *m* ▸ point de repère landmark

répéter [raypay-tay] *v* to repeat

répondeur [raypON-duhr] *m* answering machine

répondre [raypONdr] *v* to answer ▸ ça ne répond pas there's no answer

réponse [raypONs] *f* answer

reposer [ruhpoh-zay] ◆ **se reposer** *v* to rest

réseau [rayzoh] *m* network ▸ il n'y a

pas de réseau there's no reception

réservation [rayzer-vasyON] *f* reservation, booking

réservé, e [rayzer-vay] *adj* reserved

réserver [rayzer-vay] *v* to reserve, to book

respirer [respee-ray] *v* to breathe

responsable [respON-sabl] *mf* person in charge ◆ *adj* responsible

ressembler [ruhsON-blay] ◆ **se ressembler** *v* to look like each other ▸ ressembler à to look like

restaurant [resto-rON] *m* restaurant

reste [rest] *m* rest ▸ le reste the rest

rester [restay] *v* to stay ▸ est-ce qu'il reste des places ? are there any tickets left?

retard [ruhtar] *m* delay ▸ en retard late

retardé, e [ruhtar-day] *adj* delayed

retirer [ruhtee-ray] *v* *(money)* to withdraw

retour [ruhtoor] *m* return ▸ être de retour to be back

retourner [ruhtoor-nay] *v* to return ▸ retourner chez soi to go home

retrait [ruhtreh] *m* ▸ faire un retrait *(at bank)* to withdraw money

‣ **retrait des bagages** baggage claim

retraite [ruhtret] *f* retirement ‣ prendre sa retraite to retire

retrouver [ruhtroo-vay] *v* to find ◆ **se retrouver** *v* to meet

rêve [rev] *m* dream ‣ faire un rêve to have a dream

réveil [rayvey] *m* alarm clock

réveiller [ray-veyay] *v* to wake up ◆ **se réveiller** *v* to wake up

revenir [ruhvneer] *v* to come back

rêver [revay] *v* to dream

revoir [ruhvwar] *v* ‣ au revoir goodbye ◆ **se revoir** *v* to see each other again

revue [ruhvU] *f* magazine

rez-de-chaussée [ray-duh-shohsay] *m* first floor

rhumatismes [rUma-teesm] *mpl* rheumatism

rhume [rUm] *m* cold ‣ rhume des foins hay fever

riche [reesh] *adj* rich

rien [ryAN] *pron* nothing ‣ ne... rien nothing, not... anything ‣ de rien not at all ‣ rien du tout nothing at all ‣ rien d'autre nothing else

rigoler [reego-lay] *v* to laugh; to have a laugh; to joke

rire [reer] *v* to laugh

risque [reesk] *m* risk

risquer [reeskay] *v* ‣ il risque de pleuvoir it might rain

rivière [reevyehr] *f* river

robe [rob] *f* dress ‣ robe de chambre (bath)robe ‣ robe de soirée evening dress

robinet [robee-neh] *m* faucet ‣ robinet d'arrêt stopcock

rocher [roshay] *m (stone)* rock

rollers [rolehr] *mpl* Rollerblades®

roman [romON] *m* novel

rond-point [rONpwAN] *m* traffic circle

rose [rohz] *m* & *adj* pink ◆ *f* rose

rosé [rohzay] *m (wine)* rosé

roue [roo] *f* wheel ‣ roue avant front wheel ‣ roue de secours spare wheel, spare tire ‣ grande roue Ferris wheel

rouge [roozh] *m* & *adj* red

rouler [roolay] *v* to go ‣ 'rouler au pas' 'slow'

route [root] *f* road

rouvrir [roovreer] *v* to reopen

Royaume-Uni [rwa-yohm-Unee] *m* United Kingdom

rue [rU] *f* street

ruines [rween] *fpl* ruins ‣ en ruines in ruins

S

sa [sa] *adj* his; her

sable [sabl] *m* sand

sac [sak] *m* bag ‣ sac de couchage sleeping bag ‣ sac à dos backpack sac à main purse ‣ sac plastique plastic bag ‣ sac poubelle garbage bag

saignant, e [sen-yON(-yONt)] *adj (meat)* rare

saigner [sen-yay] *v* to bleed

saison [sezON] *f* season ‣ la haute/basse saison the high/low season

salade [salad] *f* lettuce; *(with dressing)* salad ‣ salade mixte/composée mixed salad

sale [sal] *adj* dirty

salé, e [salay] *adj* salted; salty; savory

salir [saleer] *v* to (get) dirty ♦ **se salir** *v* to get dirty

salle [sal] *f* room ‣ salle de bains bathroom ‣ salle de cinéma auditorium ‣ salle de concert concert hall ‣ salle d'embarquement departure lounge ‣ salle à manger dining room ‣ salle de séjour living room

salon [salON] *m* living room

salut ! [salU] *excl* hi!; bye!

samedi [samdee] *m* Saturday

sandales [sONdal] *fpl* sandals

sang [sON] *m* blood

sans [sON] *prep* without

santé [sONtay] *f* health ‣ être en bonne santé to be in good health ‣ santé ! cheers!

sardine [sardeen] *f* sardine; tent peg

saucisse [sohsees] *f* sausage

sauf [sohf] *prep* except

sauvage [sohvazh] *adj* wild

sauvegarder [sohvgar-day] *v* to save

savoir [savwar] *v* to know ‣ sais-tu nager ? can you swim?

savon [savON] *m* soap

scooter [skootuhr] *m* scooter

scotch [skoch] *m (drink)* scotch

Scotch® [skoch] *m* Scotch tape®

se [suh] *pron* oneself; himself; themselves; itself; each other ‣ se laver les mains to wash one's hands ‣ elles se sont parlé they spoke to each other

sec, sèche [sek(sesh)] *adj* dry

sèche-cheveux [sesh-shuhvuh] *m* hairdryer

sécher [sayshay] *v* to dry ‣ faire sécher *(laundry)* to dry

séchoir [sayshwar] *m* ‣ séchoir (à linge) tumble-dryer

second, e [suhgON(suhgONd)] *adj* second ♦ **seconde** *f (time)* second; second class ‣ voyager en seconde to travel second class

secours [suhkoor] *m* help ▸ au secours ! help! ▸ appeler au secours to call for help ▸ les secours the emergency services

sécurité [saykU-reetay] *f* security, safety ▸ en sécurité secure, safe

sein [sAN] *m* breast ▸ donner le sein à to breastfeed

seize [sez] *num* sixteen

seizième [sezyem] *adj* sixteenth

séjour [sayzhoor] *m* stay

sel [sel] *m* salt

self-service [self-servees] *m* self-service

selon [suhlON] *prep* according to; depending on ▸ selon moi, ... in my opinion, ...

semaine [suhmen] *f* week ▸ en semaine during the week ▸ toute la semaine all week

sens [sons] *m* direction; *(meaning)* sense ▸ dans le sens des aiguilles d'une montre in a clockwise direction ▸ en sens inverse in the opposite direction ▸ avoir le sens de l'orientation to have a good sense of direction ▸ avoir le sens de l'humour to have a good sense of humor ▸ avoir le sens de l'hospitalité to be very hospitable

sensible [sONseebl] *adj* sensitive

sentier [sONtyay] *m* path

sentir [sONteer] *v* to smell; to feel ▸ sentir bon/mauvais to smell good/bad ▸ se sentir bien/mal to feel good/bad

séparer [saypa-ray] *v* to separate ◆ **se séparer** *v* to split up

septembre [septONbr] *m* September

septième [setyem] *adj* seventh

sérieux, euse [sayr-yuh(-yuhz)] *adj* serious

serré, e [seray] *adj* tight

serrure [serUr] *f* lock

serveur, euse [servuhr(servuhz)] *m,f (in a bar)* bartender; *(in a restaurant)* waiter, waitress

service [servees] *m (in restaurant)* tip ▸ rendre (un) service à quelqu'un to do someone a favor ▸ service après-vente maintenance and repair service

serviette [serv-yet] *f* towel; napkin ▸ serviette en papier paper napkin ▸ serviette hygiénique sanitary napkin, pad

servir [serveer] *v* to serve ▸ servir à to be used for ◆ **se servir (de)** *v* to help oneself (to)

ses [say] *adj* his; her

seul, e [suhl] *adj* only; alone ▸ un seul just one ▸ voyager seul to travel alone

seulement [suhlmON] *adv* only

sexe [seks] *m* sex

shampooing [shONpwAN] *m* shampoo

shopping [shopeeng] *m* shopping ▸ aller faire du shopping to go shopping

short [short] *m* (pair of) shorts

si [see] *adv (really)* so; *(for emphasis)* yes; if

siècle [syekl] *m* century ▸ au XIXe siècle in the 19th century

sien, sienne [syAN(syen)] *pron* ▸ le sien/la sienne his, hers ▸ les siens/siennes his, hers

sieste [syest] *f* nap ▸ faire la sieste to take a nap

signer [seenyay] *v* to sign

signifier [seenyee-fyay] *v* to mean

simple [sANpl] *adj* simple

sinon [seenON] *conj* otherwise

sirop [seeroh] *m* syrup

site [seet] *m* site; *(countryside)* beauty spot ▸ site touristique tourist spot ▸ site Internet website

six [sees] *num* six

sixième [seezyem] *adj* sixth

ski [skee] *m* ski; skiing ▸ faire du ski to go skiing ▸ ski de fond cross-country skiing ▸ ski nautique waterskiing

slip [sleep] *m (male undergarment)* boxer shorts; *(female undergarment)* panties ▸ slip de bain swimming trunks

société [sosyay-tay] *f (business)* company; *(community)* society

sœur [suhr] *f* sister

soif [swaf] *f* ▸ avoir soif to be thirsty

soir [swar] *m* evening ▸ ce soir this evening, tonight ▸ le soir in the evenings

soirée [swaray] *f* evening; party ▸ dans la soirée in the evening

soixante [swasONt] *num* sixty

soixante-dix [swasONt-dees] *num* seventy

sol [sol] *m* ground; floor

soldes [sold] *mpl* sales ▸ en solde on sale

soleil [soley] *m* sun ▸ au soleil in the sun

sommeil [somey] *m* sleep ▸ avoir sommeil to be sleepy

sommet [someh] *m* summit

somnifère [somnee-fehr] *m* sleeping pill

son [sON] *m* sound ◆ *adj* his; her

sonner [sonay] *v* to ring

sorte [sort] *f* sort, kind

sortie [sortee] *f* exit, way out; *(on freeway)* exit ▸ sortie de secours emergency exit

sortir [sorteer] *v* to go out; *(film)* to come out ▸ sortir avec quelqu'un to go out with someone ▸ sortir les poubelles to take the garbage out

souci [soosee] *m* worry ▸ se faire du souci (pour) to worry (about)

souffrir [soofreer] *v* to suffer

souhait [sweh] *m* wish ▸ à tes/vos souhaits! bless you!

soûl, e [soo(sool)] *adj* drunk

sourd, e [soor(soord)] *adj* deaf

sourire [sooreer] *v* to smile ◆ *m* smile

souris [sooree] *f* mouse

sous [soo] *prep* under

sous-titré [soo-teetray] *adj* subtitled

sous-vêtements [soo-vetmON] *mpl* underwear

soutien-gorge [sootyAN-gorzh] *m* bra

souvenir [soovneer] *m* memory; souvenir ▸ en souvenir de in memory of
♦ **se souvenir** *v* ▸ se souvenir (de) to remember

souvent [soovON] *adv* often ▸ pas souvent seldom

sparadrap [spara-drah] *m* adhesive tape

spécial, e [spaysyal] *adj* special

spécialité [spaysya-leetay] *f* specialty

spectacle [spektakl] *m* show

sport [spor] *m* sport

sportif, ive [sporteef(sporteev)] *adj* sporty

stade [stad] *m* stadium

stage [stazh] *m* ▸ stage de voile/ d'anglais sailing/English classes

standardiste [stONdar-deest] *mf* (switchboard) operator

station [stasyON] *f* station ▸ station balnéaire seaside resort ▸ station de métro subway station ▸ station de radio radio station ▸ station de ski ski resort ▸ station de taxis taxi stand ▸ station thermale spa

stationnement [stasyon-mON] *m* parking ▸ 'stationnement gênant' 'no parking' ▸ 'stationnement payant' 'metered parking'

stationner [stasyo-nay] *v* to park ▸ 'interdiction de stationner (jour et nuit)' 'no parking (at any time)'

station-service [stasyON-servees] *f* gas station

steak [stek] *m* steak ▸ steak frites steak and fries

stérilet [stayree-leh] *m* IUD

stop [stop] *m* hitchhiking; stop sign ▸ faire du stop to hitchhike

store [stor] *m* (on window) blind

studio [stUdyoh] *m* studio

stylo [steeloh] *m* pen

sucre [sUkr] *m* sugar

sucré, e [sUkray] *adj* sweet

sud [sUd] *m* south ▸ au sud in the south ▸ au sud de south of

suffire [sUfeer] *v* to be enough ▸ ça suffit that's enough ▸ il suffit d'appuyer sur ce bouton you just have to press this button

suivant, e [sweevON(sweevONt)] *adj* next

suivre [sweevr] *v* to follow ▸ faire suivre to forward

super [sUpehr] *m* premium gas ♦ *adj* great

supérette [sUpay-ret] *f* mini-market

supermarché [sUpehr-marshay] *m* supermarket

supplément [sUplay-mON] *m* supplement

supplémentaire [sUplay-mONtehr] *adj* extra

supporter [sUpor-tay] *v* to put up with

sur [sUr] *prep* on ▸ sur la table on the table

sûr, e [sUr] *adj* sure ▸ bien sûr of course

surf [suhrf] *m* surfing ▸ faire du surf to go surfing

surprise [sUrpreez] *f* surprise ▸ par surprise by surprise

surveiller [sUrvey-yay] *v* to look after, to keep an eye on

sympa [sANpa] *adj* nice

synagogue [seena-gog] *f* synagogue

syncope [sANkop] *f* blackout

syndicat [sANdee-kah] *m* (trade) union ▸ syndicat d'initiative tourist office

ta [ta] *adj* your

tabac [tabah] *m* tobacco; tobacconist

table [tabl] *f* table ▸ à table! let's eat!, lunch/dinner etc. is ready!

tableau [tabloh] *m (art)* painting

tache [tash] *f* stain

taie [teh] *f* ▸ taie (d'oreiller) pillowcase

taille [ta-yuh] *f* size; waist

talon [talON] *m* heel

tampon [tONpON] *m* tampon

tant [tON] *adv* so much ▸ tant mieux all the better ▸ tant pis too bad

tante [tONt] *f* aunt

taper [tapay] *v (on computer)* to type

tapis [tapee] *m* rug ▸ tapis de bain bath mat ▸ tapis de sol ground cloth ▸ tapis de souris mousemat

tard [tar] *adv* late ▸ à plus tard ! see you later! ▸ au plus tard at the latest ▸ trop tard too late

tarif [tareef] *m* price; *(public transportation)* fare ▸ plein tarif full price; full fare ▸ tarif réduit discount (fare)

tarte [tarte] *f* pie ▸ tarte aux pommes/au citron apple/lemon pie

tasse [tas] *f* cup

taux [toh] *m* ▸ taux de change exchange rate

taxe [taks] *f* tax ▸ hors taxes tax-free ▸ taxe d'aéroport airport tax

taxi [taksee] *m* taxi

te [tuh] *pron* you; yourself

tee-shirt [teeshuhrt] *m* T-shirt

télé [taylay] *f* TV ▸ télé réalité reality TV

télécommande [taylay-komONd] *f* remote control

téléphone [taylay-fon] *m* telephone ▸ téléphone portable cellphone

téléphoner [taylay-fonay] *v* to telephone

télésiège [taylay-syezh] *m* chairlift

télévision [taylay-veezyON] *f* tele-

vision ▸ télévision câblée/par satellite cable/satellite television

tellement [telmON] *adv* so much; so ▸ pas tellement not particularly

température [tONpay-ratUr] *f* temperature ▸ prendre sa température to take one's temperature

tempête [tONpet] *f* storm

temple [tONpl] *m* temple; *(Protestant)* church

temporaire [tONpo-rehr] *adj* temporary

temps [tON] *m* weather; time ▸ de temps en temps from time to time ▸ tout le temps all the time ▸ ces derniers temps lately ▸ avoir le temps de... to have (the) time to

tenir [tuhneer] *v* to hold

tennis [tenees] *m* tennis ◆ *f* tennis shoe

tension [tONsyON] *f* blood pressure; voltage ▸ 'haute tension, danger de mort' 'danger: high voltage'

tente [tONt] *f* tent

terminal, e [termee-nal] *adj* terminal

terminus [termee-nUs] *m* terminus ▸ 'terminus : tous les voyageurs sont invités à descendre' 'end of the line: please leave the train'

terrain [terA] *m* ▸ terrain de camping campground ▸ terrain de golf golf course ▸ terrain de tennis tennis court

terrasse [teras] *f (balcony)* terrace; *(of café, restaurant)* outdoor dining area ▸ en terrasse outside

terre [tehr] *f* earth, soil; ground ▸ par terre on the ground ▸ la Terre Earth

terrible [teribl] *adj* terrible

tes [tay] *adj* your

tête [tet] *f* head ▸ tête-à-queue spin

TGV *abbr of* **train à grande vitesse** [tayzhay-vay] *m* high-speed train ▸ le TGV numéro 8785 pour Marseille partira de la voie six TGV number 8785 for Marseilles will leave from platform six

thé [tay] *m* tea ▸ thé nature tea without milk ▸ thé au lait tea with milk

théâtre [tay-atr] *m* theater

thermomètre [termo-metr] *m* thermometer

Thermos® [termos] *m* Thermos®

ticket [teekeh] *m* ticket ▸ ticket de caisse receipt ▸ ticket jumelé *museum ticket admitting holder to two or more exhibits*

tiède [tyed] *adj* lukewarm

tien, tienne [tyAN(tyen)] *pron* ▸ le tien/la tienne yours ▸ les tiens, tiennes yours ▸ à la tienne ! cheers!

timbre [tANbr] *m* stamp

timide [teemeed] *adj* shy

tire-bouchon [teer-booshON] *m* corkscrew

tire-fesses [teer-fes] *m* T-bar

tirer [teeray] *v* to pull

tisane [teezan] *f* herbal tea

tissu [teesU] *m* fabric

toi [twa] *pron* you ▸ toi-même yourself

le Tour de France

First run in 1903, the gruelling 3,000 km cycle race is held annually in July, ending amid cheering crowds on the *Champs-Élysées* in Paris. Each stage is timed separately and the winner with the fastest time overall is given the famous yellow jersey, the *maillot jaune*.

toilettes [twalet] *fpl* rest room ▸ toilettes pour femmes ladies' room ▸ toilettes pour hommes men's room

tomate [tomat] *f* tomato

tomber [tONbay] *v* to fall ▸ tomber amoureux to fall in love ▸ tomber malade to fall ill

ton [tON] *adj* your

tongs [tONg] *fpl* flip-flops

torchon [torshON] *m* dish towel

tôt [toh] *adv* early

toucher [tooshay] *v* to touch

toujours [toozhoor] *adv* always; still

tour [toor] *m* turn ♦ *f* tower ▸ faire un tour to go for a walk ▸ faire le tour du monde to travel around the world

touriste [tooreest] *mf* tourist

touristique [toorees-teek] *adj* tourist

tournée [toornay] *f* ▸ c'est ma tournée this round's on me

tourner [toornay] *v* to turn

tous, toutes [too(toot)] *adj* all ▸ tous les deux both ▸ tous les jours every day

Toussaint [toosAN] *f* ▸ la Toussaint All Saints' day

tousser [toosay] *v* to cough

tout, e [too(toot)] *adj* all, everything ▸ c'est tout that's all ▸ tout à coup suddenly ▸ tout à fait quite; exactly ▸ tout le temps all the time ▸ tout le monde everybody ▸ toute la journée all day ▸ tout de suite right away ▸ tout droit straight ahead

toux [too] *f* cough ▸ avoir de la toux to have a cough

traditionnel, e [tradees-yonel] *adj* traditional

traduire [tradweer] *v* to translate

train [trAN] *m* train ▸ train corail express regional train ▸ être en train de faire quelque chose to be doing something

traiteur [traytuhr] *m* deli

tramway [tramway] *m* tramway

la Toussaint

All Saints' Day on November 1st, is a public holiday in France. People traditionally visit cemeteries to lay flowers, usually chrysanthemums, on the graves of their loved ones.

tranche [trONsh] *f* slice

tranquille [trONkeel] *adj* quiet

transpirer [trONspee-ray] *v* to sweat

transport [trONspor] *m* transportation ▸ 'conservez votre titre de transport' 'retain your ticket until the end of your journey'

travail [travay] *m* work, job

travailler [trava-yay] *v* to work ▸ travailler dans to work in

travaux [travoh] *mpl* construction

traveller [travluhr] *m* traveler's check

travers [travehr] ▸ à travers across

traverser [traver-say] *v* to cross

treize [trez] *num* thirteen

treizième [trezyem] *adj* thirteenth

trente [trONt] *num* thirty

très [treh] *adv* very ▸ très bien very well

triste [treest] *adj* sad

trois [trwah] *num* three

troisième [trwazyem] *adj* third

tromper [trONpay] ◆ **se tromper** *v* to be mistaken, to make a mistake

trop [troh] *adv (very)* too; too much; too many ▸ trop de too much, too many ▸ trop loin too far

trottoir [trotwar] *m* sidewalk

trou [troo] *m* hole

trousse [troos] *f* ▸ trousse de toilette shaving kit, cosmetic bag

trouver [troovay] *v* to find ▸ trouver quelque chose difficile to find something difficult ◆ **se trouver** *v* ▸ où se trouve la gare ? where is the station? ▸ si ça se trouve maybe

truc [trUk] *m (informal)* thing

tu [tU] *pron* you

tuer [tUay] *v* to kill

tunnel [tUnel] *m* tunnel ▸ le tunnel sous la Manche the Channel Tunnel

Tupperware® [tUper-wehr] *m* Tupperware®

TVA [tayvay-ah] *f* sales tax

type [teep] *m* type; *(informal)* guy

U

un, une [AN(Un)] *art* a, an; *(number)* one ‣ *pron* & *m* one ‣ un homme/une femme a man/a woman

union [UnyON] *f* ‣ Union européenne European Union

université [Unee-versee-tay] *f* university

urgence [UrzhONs] *f* emergency ‣ en cas d'urgence in an emergency

‣ appeler les urgences to call 9-1-1
‣ urgences emergency room

urgent, e [UrzhON(UrzhONt)] *adj* urgent

utile [Uteel] *adj* useful

utiliser [Utee-leezay] *v* to use ‣ 'merci de ne pas utiliser de téléphone portable' 'cellphones must not be used'

V

vacances [vakONs] *fpl* vacation ‣ en vacances on vacation ‣ les grandes vacances the summer vacation

vacciner [vaksee-nay] *v* ‣ être vacciné contre to be vaccinated against

vague [vag] *f* wave

vaisselle [vesel] *f* ‣ faire la vaisselle to do the dishes

valable [valabl] *adj* valid ‣ valable pour valid for

validité [valee-deetay] *f* ‣ en cours de validité valid

valise [valeez] *f* suitcase ‣ faire ses valises to pack one's bags

vallée [valay] *f* valley

valoir [valwar] *v* to be worth ‣ ça vaut... *(money)* it's worth... ‣ il vaut

mieux... it's better to...

veau [voh] *m* veal

végétarien, enne [vayzhay-taryAN (-taryen)] *mf* & *adj* vegetarian

veille [vey] *f* day before ‣ en veille *(computer)* in sleep mode

vélo [vayloh] *m* bike

vendeur, euse [vONduhr(vONduhz)] *m, f* (sales)clerk

vendre [vONdr] *v* to sell ‣ à vendre for sale

vendredi [vONdruh-dee] *m* Friday

venir [vuhneer] *v* to come ‣ je viens de Paris I come from Paris ‣ je viens d'arriver I've just arrived

vent [vON] *m* wind

vente [vONt] *f* sale

Versailles

This former royal palace, situated to the southwest of Paris, was transformed by Louis XIV from a hunting lodge into one of the grandest and most magnificent royal residences in the world. It is set within a vast park containing elegant formal gardens with ornamental fountains and statues.

ventilateur [vONtee-latuhr] *m* fan

ventre [vONtr] *m* stomach

verglas [verglah] *m* (black) ice

vérifier [vayreef-yay] *v* to check

verre [vehr] *m* glass ▸ verre d'eau/de vin glass of water/wine ▸ prendre un verre to have a drink

verrou [veroo] *m* bolt

vers [vehr] *prep* toward; around

Versailles [vehrsa-yuh] *m* Versailles

version [versyON] *f* ▸ en version originale in the original language

vert [vehr] *m* & *adj* green

veste [vest] *f* jacket

vestiaire [vestyehr] *m* coat check

vêtement [vetmON] *m* piece of clothing ▸ des vêtements clothes

veuf, veuve [vuhf(vuhv)] *m,f* widower, widow ◆ *adj* widowed

viande [vyONd] *f* meat

vide [veed] *m* vacuum ◆ *adj* empty ▸ sous vide vacuum-packed

vie [vee] *f* life

vieux, vieille [vyuh(vyey)] *adj* old ▸ les vieux old people ▸ se faire vieux to get old

villa [veela] *f* villa

village [veelazh] *m* village

ville [veel] *f* town; city ▸ en ville downtown ▸ vieille ville old town

vin [vAN] *m* wine ▸ vin blanc/rouge/rosé white/red/rosé wine ▸ vins de qualité supérieure superior-quality wines ▸ vins de pays local wines ▸ vins de table table wines

vingt [vAN] *num* twenty

vingtaine [vANten] *f* ▸ une vingtaine de... about twenty...

viol [vyol] *m* rape

violet [vyoleh] *m* & *adj* purple

le vin

French wines are officially divided into four categories: wines labelled *Appellation d'Origine Contrôlée* (AOC) are of the highest quality; next in quality come those classed as *Vins De Qualité Supérieure* (VDQS); then *vins de pays*, local wines from an identifiable region; and lastly *vins de table*, generic table wines.

virement [veermON] *m* (bank) transfer

virus [veerUs] *m* virus

visa [veeza] *m* visa

visage [veezazh] *m* face

visite [veezeet] *f* visit ▸ rendre visite à to visit ▸ visite guidée guided tour

visiter [veezee-tay] *v* to visit

vite [veet] *adv* fast, quickly

vitesse [veetes] *f* speed

vitrail [veetray] *mpl* stained-glass window

vitre [veetr] *f* window

vitrine [veetreen] *f* ▸ en vitrine in the window

vivant, e [veevON(veevONt)] *adj* living, alive

vivre [veevr] *v* to live

vœux [vuh] *mpl* ▸ meilleurs vœux best wishes

voici [vwasee] *prep* here is; here are ▸ le voici here he is/here it is

voie [vwa] *f* (on road) lane; (at train station) platform ▸ voie ferrée railway ▸ voie sans issue dead end

voilà [vwala] *prep* there is; there are ▸ les voilà there they are

voile [vwal] *f* (of boat) sail; (activity) sailing ▸ faire de la voile to go sailing

voir [vwar] *v* to see

voisin, e [vwazAN(vwazeen)] *m,f* neighbor

voiture [vwatUr] *f* car; (of train) car ▸ en voiture by car

voix [vwah] *f* voice ▸ à voix haute aloud ▸ à voix basse in a low voice

vol [vol] *m* theft; flight

volant [volON] *m* (of car) steering wheel; (of skirt) flounce; (badminton) shuttlecock

voler [volay] *v* to steal; to fly

volet [voleh] *m* (of window) shutter

voleur, euse [voluhr(voluhz)] *m,f* thief

volley-ball [voleh-bol] *m* volleyball

volontiers [volONt-yay] *adv* willingly

vomir [vomeer] *v* to vomit ▸ avoir envie de vomir to feel sick

vos [voh] *adj* your

votre [votr] *adj* your

vôtre [vohtr] *pron* yours ▸ le/la vôtre yours ▸ les vôtres yours ▸ à la vôtre to your good health!

vouloir [voolwar] *v* to want ▸ vouloir dire to mean ▸ je voudrais... I'd like...

vous [voo] *pron* you ▸ vous-même yourself ▸ vous-mêmes yourselves

voyage [vwa-yazh] *m* journey, trip ▸ bon voyage ! have a good trip! ▸ voyage d'affaires business trip ▸ voyage de noces honeymoon ▸ voyage organisé package vacation

voyager [vwa-yazhay] *v* to travel

voyageur, euse [vwa-yazhuhr(yaz-huhz)] *m,f* passenger ▸ 'ce train ne prend pas de voyageurs' 'not in service'

voyelle [vwa-yel] *f* vowel

vrai, e [vreh] *adj* true; real

vraiment [vrehmON] *adv* really

VTT [vaytay-tay] *m* mountain bike

vue [vU] *f* view ▸ vue sur mer ocean view

W, y, z

wagon-restaurant [vagON-resto-rON] *m (on train)* café car

Walkman® [wokman] *m* personal stereo, Walkman®

WC [vaysay] *m* toilet

week-end [weekend] *m* weekend ▸ bon week-end ! have a good weekend! ▸ partir en week-end to go away for the weekend

y [ee] *adv* there

yaourt [ya-oort] *m* yogurt ▸ yaourt nature natural yogurt

yeux [yuh] *mpl* eyes

zéro [zayroh] *num* zero

zone [zon] *f* area ▸ zone euro euro zone ▸ zone fumeur smoking area ▸ zone piétonne pedestrian zone ▸ zones un et deux *(Paris and the inner suburbs)* zones 1 and 2 ▸ 'zone de stationnement alterné' *zone in which vehicles park on one side of the road for the first half of the month and on the other for the second*

zoo [zoh] *m* zoo

zoom [zoom] *m* zoom (lens)